Illegal Procedure

Illegal Procedure

A Sports Agent Comes Clean
on the Dirty Business
of College Football

Josh Luchs
and James Dale

B L O O M S B U R Y
NEW YORK · LONDON · NEW DELHI · SYDNEY

From Josh Luchs:

To my father, Dr. Saul M. Luchs, M.D., graduate attorney, and eternal scholar—my inspiration—for setting an example of high goals and overcoming all obstacles, for having confidence in me even as I traveled an "unconventional path." And to my mother, Barbara Luchs, for giving me your unconditional love, passing on your sense of humor that makes challenges surmountable and good times better; your warmth and compassion live on in me and my children.

From James Dale:

To my wife, Ellen, who recognizes a great project when it comes along (like this one), who is supportive through all the hours of writing and rewriting, who tells me I'm crazy (in a loving way) when I get discouraged, and who reads the final manuscript and turns out to be right in the first place—it was a great project.

CONTENTS

FOREWORD

I first met Josh Luchs in the summer of 2010, and I learned his name only a few days before we gathered at his home in Southern California, but it would not be inaccurate to say I had been searching for him for a decade.

Anyone who has covered or worked in sports understands the integral role that agents play at almost every level. They occupy the space between the players and the professional teams, and it is in this gray area where so many of the great stories begin. When I joined *Sports Illustrated* in 2000, as an investigative reporter, one of my goals was to find an agent willing to disclose how the business *really* worked. This was no small task; there is no incentive for agents to talk. Disclosing the inner workings of that world would anger the athletes, fellow agents, and raise the ire of coaches and league officials. An agent who was honest about how he rose up in the profession and how he succeeded would be blacklisted—out of the profession forever.

It was no wonder then that I failed many times in my efforts to find an agent willing to blow the lid on the profession. But then, ten years after I started searching, happenstance led me to Josh and to one of the most important stories of my career.

In Josh, I found an agent who had seen the business from

all angles. He started at the bottom, the youngest agent ever to be registered by the NFL Players Association, with few clients and little understanding of how the business worked. Year by year he moved up the ladder, eventually representing All-Pro players and conducting business from the swank offices of a Hollywood talent agency. The triumphs and setbacks he experienced along the way make his story a universal one: A young man who succeeds but pays a price for his success.

The *Sports Illustrated* article I wrote with Josh—his first-person account of his career—was over seven thousand words, one of the longest narratives to run in the magazine in several years. Yet even at that length it felt like a thin outline of his incredible journey. During the editing process, anecdotes ranging from funny to poignant to heartbreaking were chopped. I knew a book publisher would be eager to bring Josh's full story to light, and so with each painful trim I offered a consoling mantra:

"Save it for the book."

The complexity and significance of Josh's story will become apparent as you read *Illegal Procedure*. As an avid consumer of sports titles, I find that too many are propaganda, tools used to burnish the image of an athlete or coach. In *Sports Illustrated* and now with this book, Josh has offered something different: an uncompromised examination. Rare is the insider willing to give an unvarnished account of themselves and their profession, for whom getting the truth out supersedes self-interest.

Some have branded Josh a whistle-blower, but that descriptor has never been a perfect fit. He exposed wrongdoing,

pulled back the curtain on some of football's shadiest dealings, but his wild odyssey through a cutthroat business is
about far more than the rules that were broken.

Simply put: It is a heck of a story, an important story, and
one well worth the wait.

—George Dohrmann
2011

Why Should You Believe Me?

My name is Joshua Morrison Luchs. I was an NFL agent for eighteen years. And I broke the rules, over and over. Not minor technicalities but brazen flaunting of the rules. I learned how to do it from other agents: paying players while they were in college, slipping cash to players' friends or families, doctoring data on past players' draft grades or contracts to convince new ones to sign on as clients, feeding Wonderlic IQ tests and answers to players, getting coaches to funnel prospects our way, buying trips, tickets, dinners, and favors and more. Much more. It's rampant. It's flagrant. It's the norm. Some agents did it—and do it—more than I; some do it less. Some former agents will admit what they did and some former players will, too. And some may claim they've never broken the rules. They're lying. After all, it's just one more offense.

If we all know it's wrong, how does it happen? The same way most wrongs happen. A little at a time. Almost unnoticeably. Five miles over the speed limit, "borrowing" someone's Internet signal, bootleg DVDs, cheating—just a little—on your income tax or on your spouse, fake IDs, too many groceries in the fifteen items or less line . . . Small sins, white lies, and gray areas. Is it okay to admit an athlete to a college he couldn't get into on his grades? Is it all right to give him a scholarship? And tutors? And professors who go easy on jocks? What if coaches "find" playbooks from opposing teams? Is it pass interference if the referee doesn't see it? Can't a player sell his own jersey since the school does? Is it wrong to buy a steak dinner for a hungry nineteen-year-old offensive tackle? How about a plane ticket home to see his mom? Extra money for rent or gas? How about an American Express card billed to someone else? How about a Cadillac Escalade?

Where along that list did you say, whoa, that's going too far? At the beginning, it's not so obvious. By the time you get to the end, you know it's wrong. And somewhere in the middle it crosses a line. But it's gray, it's vague, it slides by. And pretty soon you're deep in the muck. Climbing out of the muck is a lot harder than slipping into it.

So now I'm coming clean, confessing my sins. Why should you believe me? Why am I suddenly telling the truth now? Once a scoundrel, always a scoundrel, right? Well, sometimes a scoundrel can't live with himself anymore. I got sick and tired of being me. I looked around at my colleagues and didn't like them. I looked in the mirror and didn't like what I'd become. All those reasons. But the biggest reason was vanity. I have two little girls who think their daddy is a really nice, kind, good guy. I want to be that guy. I don't want to be the other guy anymore, the one who pays players and fixes stats and slips into and out of the gray areas. I think there's something wrong with a system that makes that kind of be-havior acceptable, widespread, and almost okay. I don't want to pass that legacy on to my two little girls. I want them to be proud of me. And I don't think it's too late.

I can't make you believe me. I can only tell my story. You be the judge.

CHAPTER 1

Congratulations Mrs. Luchs, it's a 7-pound 9-ounce sports agent . . .

I was born in Brooklyn on September 8, 1969. In 1989, as a nineteen-year-old NFL agent, I handed an envelope full of cash to a college player.

Contract Advisors (agents) are prohibited from: Providing or offering money or any other thing of value to any player or prospective player to induce or encourage that player to utilize his/her services.

SECTION B (2), NATIONAL FOOTBALL LEAGUE

PLAYERS ASSOCIATION REGULATIONS

Agents pay college players every day. A few hundred dollars or several thousand. Players and their families take money every day. As much as they can get. The agents are investing in the players' futures, to represent them when they turn pro. The players need cash, want cash, figure they've earned it by playing for free in college, or just feel everybody does it—so why not them? The National Football League Players Association (NFLPA), which makes the rules for agents, doesn't want to know about it. The National Collegiate Athletic Association (NCAA), the body that enforces the rules for college players, doesn't want to know about it. And of course, the fans don't want to know about it. Everyone just wants the best football money can buy. And that's what they get. Agents make sure.

No one is born a sports agent. You don't come out of the womb clutching a BlackBerry preloaded with the private number of the maître d' at The Palm. Some time after breast-feeding and potty-training, circumstances collide to make you an agent. It can start with a primal love of sports, jumping off furniture, tackling the dog, or thinking the "Star-Spangled Banner" means "game time!" It can be wanting to rub shoulders with heroes—the neighborhood kid who can hit the ball over the fence or the proverbial captain of the football team who's shtuping the prom queen. It can be impressing your friends that you know and hang out with the guys in ESPN highlight films. It can be trying to win the most elusive prize, parental approval, especially when, like me, your father is an academic professional, your mother holds you to high standards, and your siblings outshine you in the classroom and out. It's finding your own niche; instead of SATs, Law Boards, and CPA exams, it's people-skills, networking, persuasion, and deal-making. You're the puppeteer behind the scenes who helps stars who are good at what they do but not so good at looking out for themselves. And you're the guy everyone wants to talk to at the cocktail party. *What's Ryan Leaf really like? Who's better, Manning or Brady? How intimi-*

dating is Al Davis? What's the biggest deal you ever made? No doubt, all agents share one trait: the need to be liked and trusted by the most popular guy on campus. If you can't be the star, you can be the star's confidant, advisor, and shrink.

That was me. And, in one way or another, it's most agents. A combination of love of sports, being in the right place at the right time, and a large dose of chutzpah makes us who we are. Tank Black, one of the first powerful African-American agents, was an assistant coach at the University of South Carolina who set up his business with one marquee client: the Gamecocks' star receiver, Sterling Sharpe. Tom Condon, who played for the Kansas City Chiefs, was described as ". . . a very mediocre player on a very bad football team," but he thought he was smart enough to make deals for other players. He went to law school in the off-season, joined sports management giant IMG, later went to CAA to form the premier Hollywood sports agency, and was named by *Sporting News* the most powerful agent in football. Drew Rosenhaus, the first agent to be featured on the cover of *Sports Illustrated*, self-described as "a ruthless warrior" and "hit man," grew up worshipping the Miami Dolphins and the Miami Hurricanes. To bluff his way into Dolphins' practice in his teens, he told the security guard that he and his brother were punter Reggie Roby's nephews. Roby is black; Rosenhaus is white, but he and his brother got in anyway. And he's been "persuading" people ever since. Jimmy Sexton, one of today's elite agents, especially renowned for representing marquee coaches, began his "career" in 1984 by being the college roommate of Tennessee star defensive end Reggie White. According to at least one sports blogger and numerous chat sites, the USFL paid Sexton's way to the Hula Bowl to keep an eye on White to assure one of their teams signed him. When he did sign with the USFL Memphis Showboats for more than $1 million a year for five years, White said twenty-year-old Sexton was his agent, so from then on (after certification), he was one. Don Yee, who now represents, among others, four-time Super Bowl quarterback Tom Brady, was a first-generation Chinese-American whose mother never spoke a word of English. At age thirteen Yee applied to be a batboy for a Triple A baseball team and fell in love with American sports. Leigh Steinberg, who was one of the inspirations for the movie *Jerry Maguire* and its eponymous lead character, was originally going to be a public defender after UC Berkeley Law School but met Cal's star quarterback Steve Bartkowski along the way, and helped make him the number-one overall pick of the 1975 NFL draft, which helped create Steinberg's reputation as *the* quarterback agent.

Why do we want to be agents? Because it's fun. It's that simple. Every day is a contest, a game, a showdown. Who's ahead; who's behind? I win; you lose. Next game. Next match. Gladiators and lions, glory and agony, Hail Mary passes and goal-line interceptions. Overtime is even called "sudden death." It's all adrenaline and testosterone. It's a lot more exciting than being a dentist.

And don't forget the money. Sports make fortunes. Especially at big-time colleges, where they make headlines and wow alums. College sports revenue builds arenas and domes and complexes and monuments—the Big House in Ann Arbor, the Rose Bowl in Pasadena, and Cameron Indoor Arena at Duke. It's March Madness and the Bowl Championship

Series. It's season tickets, network TV ratings, thirty-second ad sales, Nike shoes, UnderArmour sweats, and $200 official jerseys. It's the glamorous, glitzy, glittery, greedy world of I-want-it-now. Everyone sees the big life and everyone lusts after a piece.

You may read about how most college programs don't show a profit, but profits are what's left after expenses; and when it comes to sports, colleges have lots of expenses. They put the money to work on their entire sports programs, with profitable sports—football and basketball—underwriting unprofitable sports such as lacrosse, swimming, track, and, right or wrong, many women's sports. And remember, many colleges, including the massive state schools that seem to win conference titles every year, tend to be nonprofit institutions. They're not supposed to make money. Suffice it to say, their sports programs generate sizable revenues and priceless publicity that often results in staggering alumni donations and powerful school brands. Profitable or not, college sports is a multi-billion-dollar enterprise. It's an economy bigger than most nations.

Sports agents like me find that a very attractive business.

From Brooklyn to Beverly Hills

My parents met during my father's medical training, and soon married; he adopted my mom's young son, Gary, from her first marriage, and then they had two more kids, my sister, Stacy, and me. Gary is sixteen years older, and I didn't know he had a different father until my bar mitzvah. My sister was serious, strict, rigid, disciplined, uptight, and well-behaved. I wasn't.

She could never figure out how I got through life. She still can't.

We lived on Ditmas Avenue and East Nineteenth Street, in this big old house that used to be the French consulate, with twenty-one rooms, inlaid marble hearths, frescoes on the walls, statues and antiques my parents bought around the world, at auctions. With a kid's imagination, I thought I was a prince—not a little Jewish American Prince, but a real royalty-type prince, living in a castle that was different from my friends' houses.

My father, who was a urologist, practiced out of a wing of our house, and he worked nonstop. My mother was a classic, dedicated mom. When my father did take time off, he took me to Shea Stadium to see the Mets, Madison Square Garden to see the Knicks, and the Meadowlands for Jets' games. I was five when I saw my first pro football game, featuring "Broadway" Joe Namath. It was freezing and even though we had great seats, close to the field, my father had passes to go upstairs to the skybox area, where it was warm. He said, "Come on, let's get some hot chocolate," but I wouldn't leave my seat. My father always told that story, as if it explained how fanatical I was. Spencer Haywood and Earl the Pearl Monroe, the Knicks stars, came to our house for acupuncture treatments from my father, who'd been one of the first to go to the Orient and learn about it. I'd be shooting hoops in front of the house and Earl or Spencer would show up. These superstars were just people to me, but the fact that they dropped by our house made other kids on the block want to be my friend.

I loved sports from an early age but they were asphalt sports—football in the street, running between cars, no grassy fields or bleachers. We'd play wrestlers and, being bigger than some of the kids, I'd be Andre the Giant and we'd beat the snot out of each other, pretending we were jumping off the ropes. Except we were a bunch of Jewish kids who'd never grow up to be wrestlers. Our mothers wouldn't let us.

My sister and I were sent to the neighborhood preschool . . . until the Christmas pageant. When my parents saw that my sister had been picked to play the baby Jesus in the manger, they pulled us out and put us into the yeshiva, East Midwood Jewish Center on Ocean Avenue. I wasn't good at school, I got in trouble, I didn't want to go to class. I was running a kind of baseball card flipping ring in the boys' bathroom. I suspect I had ADD before it was labeled. My parents came to see the principal-rabbi and he said, "Look at his punum" (Yiddish for "face"). "Look how handsome he is. He'll be fine." I learned at a young age that a winning smile could get me a long way. An early agent lesson? Maybe.

To get away from the city, my parents bought a fifty-acre farm in upstate New York—near Peekskill—with horses and cows and sheep. And they sent me to summer camp in Pennsylvania. At five, the youngest kid at the camp, I got locked in a trunk, but I thought, hey, at least they're paying attention to me. I always craved that. Then the family decided to really get away from the city when I was about ten, and we moved to Beverly Hills, California, a greater culture-shock than the Christmas pageant.

What I knew about Beverly Hills was the TV show, *The Beverly Hillbillies*. Cool, we're going where the Clampetts live . . . swimming pools, movie stars. But we actually went from the huge castle to a little townhouse on the fringe of

Beverly Hills, the slums if they had any, where people moved to get their kids into the school district. My father drove across country, back and forth, for quite a while until we got settled and he had his new practice set up. Meanwhile, I was loving my new freedom—swimming pools, and sunshine, two things we'd never had before. In Brooklyn I couldn't go more than a block by myself. Here I had free rein—*Go play and be back by dinnertime.* But I did get mugged and somebody stole my bike, which had never happened in New York. At La Cienega Park, I played Little League, a big, wild-throwing pitcher. I wasn't very good, other than at hitting batters, but I loved the camaraderie. I'd always felt like I didn't fit in anywhere. It was one of my oldest memories, feeling out of place, that other people were more popular, or better behaved, or smarter than me. When I played sports, I felt like I fit in.

It was in the fifth grade at Horace Mann Elementary that they had me tested and determined I was dyslexic. So, on top of my New York accent, being bigger than a lot of kids, and having trouble sitting still, now they had a name for my learning problems. It wasn't something my charming smile could overcome. Again, I didn't fit in. Eventually they sent me to another school in the district. I liked the new school better, we moved closer to it, and I had my first girlfriend there. It was around that time that my dad got season tickets to the Raiders games. The team had moved to L.A., to the Coliseum, from Oakland (before they moved back) and I fell totally in love with them. When I felt bad about life or school or fighting with my sister and got depressed, I would imagine what it would be like to not be here, and then I'd realize I wouldn't be around for the Raiders' games, or to see a new draft choice play, and I couldn't miss out on that.

Then I became a man . . . or the thirteen-year-old version. I had my bar mitzvah. Like everything else to do with studying, I had trouble learning Hebrew. Reading English from left to right and then Hebrew from right to left was torture to a dyslexic kid. But I was a performer, and in the end, I rose to the occasion. It was important to my father that I not just read the minimum Torah portion that coincided with the time of my bar mitzvah, but that I lead the entire service—the *musaf, maftir,* and the complete *haftorah,* the full text of my Torah section—the whole megillah, so to speak. My rabbi, Rabbi Pressman, in classic L.A. style, was the identical twin brother of Monty Hall, the host of *Let's Make A Deal.* What better pedigree as the spiritual guide for a future sports agent? *"Josh, do you want to keep that check your uncle just stuffed in your pocket or trade it for what's behind door number one, two, or three?"* Afterward, my mother put on a big blowout party with a western ranch theme, my "Barn Mitzvah," with hay, and stunt men, sets from 20th Century Fox, steaks branded with my initials, and a cake in the shape of a cowboy hat, just like the one I was wearing. And I had my pockets stuffed with checks, over $5,000, a lot of money for a kid. Like a good boy, or now young man, I put it all in the bank, saved for something important. Little did I suspect what that would be.

When I got to Beverly Hills High School, I played football, defensive lineman and tight end. And of course, I was still struggling in class, especially in math. I could do the problems in my head faster than most of the other kids but I couldn't show how I got there. Again, a good skill for an agent, it turns out, figuring stats, contracts, percentages in your head, but it won't get you through tenth-grade algebra. I was passing each year, by the grace of God and the school wanting to push the problems out the door. I was just getting interested in broadcasting, working at the school radio and TV stations, K-BEV. Rhoda Sharp, the woman who headed up the internship programs at school, told me about a one-day visit to KABC radio to sit in on the broadcast of Bud Furillo, "The Steamer," a legend who used to be the sports editor of the *Herald Examiner*, with ties to every team in town. I jumped at the chance, and I took along a copy of a funny sports report I'd written. I read it to Bud and his producer.

> Merchants on Rodeo Drive were stunned yesterday as the Beverly Hills High School girls' varsity shopping team, the Plastiques, were upset by the Credit Card Cuties of Inglewood in overtime in the first round of the Southern California Invitational Shop-off. When asked why they lost, Plastiques team captain Stacy Schwartz was quoted as saying, "Someone left home without it." This makes the chances of getting new Gucci uniforms for next season very slim unless the Shopsters can come back victorious and outspend Encino at their home court, the Galleria.

Bud loved it and let me read it on-air. People called in, laughed, loved it, and I was flying high.

So I had the chutzpah to just show up at the station the next day and they let me in. That's all the encouragement I needed. I went every day after that. The producer, Michael Setsuda, sort of made a job for me—an unpaid job—in the booth, editing, splicing, researching, anything. I had gotten this little electronic Casio Wizard, back before BlackBerrys, that would store information and I collected every name and phone number of everyone who came through or called the station, and everybody I ever met. Nobody had a cell phone so these were the office numbers and home numbers, for people like Magic Johnson and Tommy Lasorda, some of the biggest sports personalities in town, who were remarkably willing to give them to me. At the time, I didn't know why I was collecting all these numbers, but it turned out to be like a super-Rolodex. Maybe I was an agent-prodigy without knowing it.

I kept at the job, unpaid year after year. One day, as a reward, Bud invited me to go with him on a road trip to Dallas for a Monday-night game, flying on the Raiders' plane. I thought I was dreaming and didn't want to wake up. My parents were ecstatic just to see that I was interested in something. My dad said, "If you learned your schoolwork the way you learn the bios and stats of every player on every roster, you'd be a straight-A student." I went on the trip and Bud took me to the media lunch before the game, up into the press box, down into the locker room. I met Marcus Allen, the running back. (Actually, I'd met him a year earlier, through a family friend, a pretty girl in her twenties who knew Marcus, knew I worshipped him, called him, got invited over, and took me along—which was not what Marcus had in mind with what he thought was a booty call. But I got to meet him and see his Heisman Trophy and hang out while he played the piano.) When I saw him after the Raiders game, he remembered me and said, "Man, what you doing here? I remember you from my living room." On the plane, on the way back, I talked to James Davis, defensive back, Mike Davis, safety, Greg Townsend, defensive end, and Sean Jones, who had to fold down the seats in front of him because his legs were so long. I was just sixteen! They talked to me like friends. I fit in. Without exaggeration, it was the single greatest experience of my life to that point.

Raiders Ball Boy: Does life get any better than this?

After a year of working with Bud Furillo, he told me he couldn't pay me, but asked what he could do for me. I didn't even have to think. "Can you get me a job as a ball boy with the Raiders for the summer?" He made a couple of calls, ostensibly to Al Davis, the team owner, and then announced on his show, "Josh, guess what? You're going to training camp at Oxnard. You're going to be a ball boy for the Raiders this summer." I went berserk. Instead of going to sleep-away camp, I was going to the Raiders training camp! I got there and checked in with the security guard, who pointed me past the Radisson bungalow suites where everybody lived for the summer, to the locker room and Dick Romanski, aka Oscar the Grouch, the equipment manager. The only problem was, Oscar/Dick had never heard of me. "I was told Mr. Davis had arranged for me to come here today," I explained. Within seconds, he'd handed me a mesh bag and a room key and said, "If Mr. Davis sent you, it's okay." He gave me Raiders T-shirts, Raiders shorts, Raiders socks and shoes, and a little hat and pointed me to where lunch was served. They weren't expecting me (or Bud had never confirmed the job) but they were all so intimidated by the mention of Mr. Davis's name, the wheels started spinning into motion. I was officially a Raiders ball boy, one of about six, being paid $50 a week. Right away, I wasn't like the other guys. The first day of camp, there was a wide receiver named Christopher Woods, who'd come from the Canadian Football League, and he was stretching on the field. He asked me to push down on his back to do a hurdler's stretch. Instead of just pushing, I sat on his back. There was a herd of photographers looking for anything out of the ordinary and there I was sitting on Chris, relaxing, hat tilted, on this guy's back, like I was getting a tan. The cameras started clicking and the next day, there were Chris Woods and I on the front of the sports section. The other ball boys told me that Oscar the Grouch Romanski was pissed because he'd been there since before cameras were invented and nobody had ever taken his picture.

And he took it out on me with extra "dick watch" duty. We were all supposed to rotate through "dick watch," scooping soggy bandages off the shower-room floor with a snow shovel while players were showering and our point of view was dick level. Let's just say, I saw more than my share that summer. It wasn't the only disgusting job, either. We wheeled a plastic garbage can through the locker room picking up towels. I remember one day seeing Bruce Wilkerson, an offensive lineman, stark naked with a towel that looked like a wash cloth in his hands, wiping the crack of his ass with the towel and then dropping it on the floor, where I was supposed to reach down and pick it up. No way. Where was that snow shovel when I needed it?

It was that first summer that I got to know Greg Townsend,

the defensive end. I'd met him on the trip with Bud Furillo, so I could hardly wait for him to get to camp. He pulled up in his black Mercedes, license plate GET 93, his jersey number, and I was like a puppy, opening the door, grabbing his bags: "Greg, how are you?" But he didn't remember me, so I reintroduced myself, carrying his stuff to his room, reminding him we had met on the Raiders' plane to Dallas. Then he asked me where I was from but I didn't want to tell him and sound like a spoiled little brat. So I tried to avoid answering.

"Man," he said, referring to himself in the third person, "Greg's from Compton. So where you from can't be that bad. Just tell Greg where you're from." I mumbled, "Beverly Hills" but I followed with, "but not the rich part, the rougher part, south of Wilshire." He got hysterical. "Man, you're a funny motherfucker." That was the beginning of our bond. It was no doubt more from my end than his; that is, I thought he was pretty cool and so did he so we had something in common. I'd check in on him to see what he needed, or just to talk, me trying to be around him. I was sixteen and he was maybe twenty-six but we'd hang out together and he started to trust me. That turned out to be one of my intangible agent talents—winning people's trust—and it's not something you learn in school. Either you have it or you don't.

It was clear to me very early that I wasn't going to be asked back as a ball boy for another season. Romanski probably thought I didn't deserve to be there, I'd come from too much privilege and was connected to Mr. Davis instead of him. I knew I'd have to find another way to stay on.

I grabbed the job of holding up a white board during practice that had each play on it so the team could review it on the films. I had a big smile on my face, so happy that I was the guy holding the white board for the Raiders. Finally they had to tell me to stop grinning and hamming it up, that it was too distracting. But they remembered me.

And I remembered something I heard from one of the players, Todd Christensen. An interviewer asked him how he made these incredible acrobatic catches, one-handed juggling, falling backward—how did he get open all the time? Todd said, "They don't suspect me. They never pay attention to the slow white guy up the middle." I heard that and I thought, he's not the fastest or the biggest or strongest but he outsmarts everybody. That's what I'm going to do. I listened to everything he said, between plays, on the sidelines, as if he were my tutor. And I was determined to make myself something more than a ball boy.

There was a guy named Don DeBaca in the front office and I went to him and said I wanted to answer phones and was willing to work all night, when the other ball boys were finished for the day, after practice, before dinner, or even later. I'd take calls from the press, from vendors, from wives and girlfriends (plenty of players had both). And as always I had my Wizard with me, taking down any information that might ever be valuable—players' home numbers, coaches, agents, girlfriends, anything. I had the direct lines for Bill Parcells, then head coach of the Giants; Georgia Frontiere, then majority owner of the Rams; and plenty of other big shots. I'd sort mail, work the phones, whatever they asked. I became an asset to George Karas, team executive and Al Davis's right-hand man. He taught me the value of information and also to shred everything.

Future Agent Lessons: "Josh, can
Greg trust your piss?"

Every day was a learning experience, like a series of case-book studies for an MBA, real-life encounters—some crazy, some humiliating, some challenging, some profound—in what turned out to be my advanced degree.

One time, a six-foot-three, 250-pound linebacker named Jamie Kimmel ripped into me because somebody—I had no idea who—had been rude to his wife on the phone. He seemed as if he was 'roided out of his mind, ready to kill me, and not open to my protests that it hadn't been me, so I just waited for the rage to recede and escaped with all my limbs. Mostly, I was distraught that a Raider player would be mad at me. I never wanted to do anything to upset any of them.

I learned the value of silence. Like when Zeph Lee, a running back, showed me and another ball boy a documentary video about rock music and the devil (featuring AC/DC's no-doubt satanically inspired "Back in Black"), the message being that if we didn't accept Jesus Christ as our Lord and Savior, we were going straight to hell. I didn't think it was a good idea to tell him I'd been a yeshiva boy so I did a lot of nodding and waited for it to be over.

I learned to play along. I was surrounded by Howie Long, Lyle Alzado, Lester Hayes, Mike Haynes, all kinds of stars I was in awe of. One day Marcus Allen was sitting in his Ferrari in the parking lot between the bungalows and said, "Josh, come here." I trotted over thinking, *How cool, Marcus Allen wants to talk to me.* He asked me, "Yo man, you a virgin?" I wanted to be cool so I said, "I get my share." But I had no idea why he was asking. He explained, "There's these girls in the hotel room over there and they been blowing up the phone all night [calling him]. There's two of them. I need you to go up the steps to that room up in the corner, and I'll pull my car around, and you get them to come out so I can see what they look like. If they're good-looking, I'll come up, one for me, one for you. But I want to judge for myself." I was thinking this was great. I was wearing my ball-boy shirt and my ball-boy shorts and socks and my Raider cap—a total Raider geek. And I was jazzed. At that age, if the wind blew, I was sporting wood—this was my lucky day. Not only was I going to get laid—I was going to get laid with Marcus Allen! So I ran up the stairs, doing the Heisman pose on the landing halfway up, looking down at Marcus in the parking lot. I knocked on the door and said, "Raiders Welcoming Committee." I heard giggling and laughing and the door opened to reveal two of the most enormous Samoan women I've ever seen. Huge. Beyond huge. One of them said, "Hey ball boy, how would you like to be a ball *man*?" I looked down at the parking lot and Marcus was pulling away, laughing hysterically. I made an excuse—"Sorry, I thought this was one of the players' rooms"—and backpedaled as fast as I could. I'm sure Marcus got a kick out of messing with me. I was there to make the stars happy, after all.

I learned it helps to be liked or lucky or both. Like in the Mike Shanahan incident. He was the head coach, and I was a lowly ball boy. I didn't want to piss him off. I took my job seriously; but I was seventeen, so I horsed around with the players. One day Stefon Adams, the cornerback, had a bucket of water and it was a hot day and he was throwing it on people, including me, and I wanted to get back at him. So I went up-stairs in the two-level bungalow where there was a landing, and I had a big cup of cold water I was ready to pour down onto Stefon from one story up. I dumped the water on Ste-fon's head, laughing hysterically—until I realized it was not him at all, but Mike Shanahan. When I saw my mistake, I panicked. I was screwed, done. My life was over. I said, "Coach, I'm so sorry. I thought you were Stefon. I didn't mean to . . ." He was soaking wet but he's a very low-key guy and he just looked up at me, shook his head, and kept walking. It's kind of the story of my life. I get in trouble, doing things a little bit wrong, and I'm lucky enough to get away with it. People shrug a lot. Or they kind of like me. It turns out to be another qualification for the agent business.

I learned to be there. One night, at two A.M., I was asleep in my room at training camp. The phone rang and this voice said, "Josh? It's Greg . . . Greg Townsend." He told me he wanted me to go over to his room right then. "It's important," he said. "I need to talk to you." I asked if it could wait until morning and he said, "It's important, motherfucker." I didn't know it at the time, but this was another preview of being an agent—dropping whatever you're doing to take care of who-knows-what. So I threw on a pair of jeans and a T-shirt and I walked past the seven or eight bungalow buildings to his room.

He opened the door wearing black silk pajamas and a red smoking jacket with black satin collar, Grand Marnier in one hand and a Salem hanging off his lip. I didn't have any idea what I was getting into but I was there, sitting on the sofa, and he just stared at me in total silence. Finally he said, "Can Greg trust you? Are you there for Greg?" again talking about himself in the third person because he must have thought it sounded more important, or he'd heard Ricky Henderson do it. I said, "Sure Greg, you can trust me with anything," hoping it wasn't something too crazy. "Josh, do you do drugs?" I declined, thinking it was an offer. "No, motherfucker, I ain't offering you drugs. I'm asking if you does drugs."

I was relieved to be able to tell him what he wanted to hear. "No, I don't touch the stuff, never have, never tried it, never . . ." But he interrupted me. "Don't be bullshitting Greg. You Beverly Hills kids, you get the good shit. Don't lie to Greg." I told him, "I swear, I don't do drugs." Evidently he believed me because he reached down next to his chair, picked up this glass jug, put it on the table, and looked at me like I was supposed to understand. After a pause he explained, as if he was talking to a little kid. "Josh, Greg needs some piss. Can Greg trust your piss? Is your piss trustworthy?" I was slowly beginning to get it. He went on. "I was with this fine lady and we smoked a little weed. Now I got a drug test tomorrow and Greg needs some clean piss. Can Greg trust your piss, Josh? Are you gonna step up for Greg?" "You want me to pee in the jar right now?" He nodded. I thought for a second, and decided I wanted to do anything to help. I didn't want him to get suspended. I didn't want to hurt the team and as far as I knew, my pee had always been trustworthy. I said okay. I knew it was kind of wrong, but it wasn't *that* wrong—he seemed like a good guy, and he trusted me. And it was for the Raiders and Greg. It was another preview of the agent world, where the gray areas get darker and darker, a little bit wrong at a time. But I didn't care about the gray at the time, just about my duty to help. Or try. The problem was, I had trouble peeing in the living room with an audience. He said, "Don't worry, Greg is a patient man. We'll wait." He got me some water; I relaxed and filled up half the jar. He said, "Thanks, that's why we're tight," and sent me back to my room.

I didn't hear anything about it for several days. Greg didn't say anything. Then one day, one of the other ball boys came into the office and said, "Josh, they nailed your boy, Greg." When I asked what he was talking about, he said that Greg was leaving camp because he'd tested positive on the drug test. I turned white. How could this happen? I didn't do drugs. He used my piss. And now he was going to kill me. He was from Compton, not Beverly Hills, even the rough part. The team was going on a road trip for a preseason game and left me, along with some other office staff, back at training camp in Oxnard. I drove from Oxnard as fast as I could, to see my father. Who better to talk to about my situation than a urologist? I told him everything, while he sat in the backyard Jacuzzi, his cigar in his mouth, insisting I didn't do drugs but had peed for Greg, and now somehow he had tested positive. My dad asked, "Is there anything else you want to tell me?" as in, "Josh, if you do drugs, say so." I swore to him I didn't. He asked again. I swore again. Finally he believed me and said there had to be some other explanation.

I had to confront Greg. I went to his apartment and knocked on the door, and he answered in his full lounging uniform. He didn't look upset; he was very cool, like a bald, black Hugh Hefner. I blurted out, "Greg, I'm so sorry. I don't know what to say, I don't do drugs. I don't know how it happened." He burst out laughing. "They wouldn't take your piss, man. They said, 'Greg, you can't hand us piss. You need to piss in front of us.'" He wasn't mad at me or my pee. It was his that had failed the test. Thank god.

From there, our relationship grew. I guess he figured if I'd do that for him, and come to his house to see what had happened, I must be okay. I looked out for him and he came to trust me. A couple different times he asked me if I'd ever considered repping athletes, just because I cared, because I was willing to do things to help.

But at the time, I wasn't really thinking about becoming a sports agent. I had my heart set on sports broadcasting. I'd been doing it at school and working at the radio station. I could hear myself on ESPN or doing Raiders play-by-play. But Greg said his deal would be up in a year or two and by then, he might need someone new. He didn't make promises but it was out there. He said, "You're a smart Jewish guy and you have to deal with Al Davis. He's a smart Jewish guy. You like to look out for players. You could do this." That was my qualification—a smart Jewish guy. I was only seventeen, going into my senior year of high school, but the fact was, Greg wasn't much older. When you're both naive about the world, this kind of talk doesn't sound so crazy.

Future Agent Lessons Continued

End of the summer, I go back to high school. I'm doing the play-by-play for Beverly Hills High and I'm still working at KABC. I stayed in contact with Don DeBaca, not wanting him to forget me, as if he had a chance. I told him I wanted to come back, to work in the office, to work with him. Finally, he took me out for a sandwich and said he was going to have me back. It was as if I'd just become an executive in the Raiders front office. Me, Don DeBaca, and Al Davis. Only a slight exaggeration in my mind . . . or a fantasy . . . but close enough for me. I worked two more summers for the Raiders, one more in high school, and another after graduation.

One of my jobs, one that I liked a lot, was bringing lunch to Raiders' owner Al Davis. I'd already gotten to know him, or gotten him to know me, the summer before when I was still a ball boy. We always had a towel hanging from our shorts and one day he called me over to wipe his glasses with my towel, and asked my name. I said, "Joshua," and went on, "Mr. Davis, I'm originally from New York, and my mother went to Erasmus Hall High School when you were coaching there." I knew he'd been a coach there and I wanted to make a connection with him, to differentiate myself. He smiled and said, "Oh, really? Erasmus." And right there I felt like this guy, Al Davis, would remember me. And he did.

So, later I'd bring lunch or game films or whatever to his room. His was the only one that had a black toilet, an odd thing to remember but it must have been on purpose for the owner. I took him his typical lunch, the same almost every day, tuna on dry white toast and water with a little bit of lemon. One day I brought it to him and he was lying on the bed in his undershirt and underpants, hair disheveled. He told me to come in, and asked me a question. "Josh, do you think my players like me?" I didn't know what to say. I'd been there for the summer and by then I knew he was an intimidating guy, unforgettable. In fact, he wore this strong cologne that I could smell for a half hour after he left a room. You literally knew when Al Davis was there, or had been there. (In fact, his employees would say that aroma kept people from talking about him because as long as you could smell it, you were never quite sure he'd left.) So, I put his lunch down on the side of the bed, trying to figure out how to answer him on his players liking him. I answered him quickly but with what turned out, in hindsight, to be a pretty wise response. "I don't really know, Mr. Davis, but I know that they respect you."

I remember he seemed to think about it and made a little clicking noise with his mouth, as if to say my answer was okay. Over time, I had more interactions with him, driving him from Oxnard to his apartment in Marina del Rey. When we got there, he'd take out these Famous Amos cookies that looked like they'd been sitting around for five years, but he offered them to me to be gracious, in his own odd way. He was respectful of people but they all seemed afraid of him. I wasn't. Maybe I just didn't know better but I was comfortable with him and he seemed to be comfortable with me. More lessons.

By this time, Art Shell was the head coach. Al Davis had set some kind of record with three coaches in my three years there—Tom Flores, Mike Shanahan, and then Art Shell, who was only the second black head coach in professional football. And as with Shanahan, I had an Art Shell incident. He's an enormous man, an eight-time Pro Bowl and Hall of Fame offensive tackle. And that day, he was doing a publicity shot in which the photographers had him lying on his side on the field, his head propped up on one elbow, wearing jeans, in almost a fashion pose. I walked by and said, "Nothing comes between me and my Calvins," quoting the Calvin Klein ad slogan of the time. And he laughed. It could have backfired.

He could have thought, "Who's this wise-ass making cracks about the head coach?" But he didn't. He thought it was funny and he remembered me because of it. It differentiated me. I wasn't a great student in school but I was a pretty good student of human nature.

Meanwhile, back at school, I was working at the radio and TV station, K-BEV, not playing football anymore. There's no chance of somebody stepping on your hand, or of helmet-to-helmet contact, when you're broadcasting. By this time, Bud Furillo, my mentor at KABC, had left there to start a show on a small station in Redondo Beach, KFOX. So I went there to produce his show.

In the fall I was heading off to Santa Monica, a two-year junior college. Education was like a religion at my house, so community college wasn't exactly what they dreamed of for their kids. My brother had gone to Marquette and my sister was a very good student. My parents' attitude was I needed to go somewhere and get serious and then transfer to a "real" four-year school. That was the plan, though I kind of doubted it from day one. I was taking basic education courses, just the requirements. My heart wasn't in it. To me, college was high school with ashtrays. I did a marketing report for one class with a product and a slogan and I felt pretty good about it but the professor gave me a laughable grade, and I didn't think it was funny. I wasn't getting any feedback that told me I was any good the way I did around sports.

Meanwhile, I had my friendship with Greg Townsend and he was telling me about how his agent might be going to jail and may be "unavailable" to represent him anymore. He said, "You know, my deal will be up next year and Mr. Davis seems to like you," and again, "You're a Jewish guy from New York like Al Davis"—the ultimate qualification, two guys with circumcisions. I was eighteen years old; I had no idea what it meant to be an agent.

CHAPTER 2

I'm an agent; now all I need is a client.

At a young age, I became a networker; I just didn't know there was a name for it. Bud Furillo had a friend named Frazier Smith, a classic rock disk jockey, and I started booking guests for him on his Saturday morning show on KSLX. And he was friendly with the Goossen brothers, all of whom were involved in sports: Mike, an attorney; Joe, a trainer; and Dan, the boss. I got to know Mike, asked him what it took to become an agent, and he got the forms for me and walked me through the process. "Send in the paperwork and a check for three hundred dollars and you're licensed with the Players Association." That's it. They don't care if you have a college degree, a graduate degree, experience, nothing. Just have the check and no criminal record. By those standards, I qualified. Two months later, I got a certificate in the mail saying I was an NFLPA licensed agent. I was nineteen. Cool. Plus they sent me a little card that had the NFLPA logo on it.

The State of the Business 1989

It was well into the modern era of pro and college football—big TV contracts, big Bowl games, big revenue. The AFL and NFL had long since merged. It was Super Bowl XXIII and Joe Montana's 49ers were winning their third championship of the '80s. The University of Miami Hurricanes were voted number one in the nation by sportswriters and coaches, the third time in the decade. The NCAA had adopted the "Sanity Code" after World War II to curb abuses in recruitment and financial aid, and became a full-time organization by the 1950s, "to protect young people from the dangerous and exploitive athletics practices of the time." The NFLPA, established in 1956 to look out for the players, by 1970 had gotten the NFL owners to agree to a player's right to representation by an agent, and in the Collective Bargaining Agreement of 1982, to NFLPA certification of agents. The qualifications to be certified: 1) a completed application form, 2) a signed statement that the applicant was not a convicted criminal, and 3) a check for $300. No specified level of education. No exam. No hard guidelines for conduct. No formal investigative mechanism for alleged violations. And there was building pressure to lower agent commissions from a *maximum* of 5 percent of a player's contract. (In the '90s, the NFLPA dropped the maximum to 4 percent, then 3 percent, and almost got to 2 percent.) The lower the commission, the more brutal the competition for players, especially the stars who would be most lucrative.

The stakes were rising in the battle for young college players, and at the same time, a door was left wide open. If the NFLPA wasn't policing agent-recruitment practices, who was watching college players? The NCAA? The conferences? The individual schools? The states? Or had college sports become wholesome and innocent, with no significant problems?

Agent-turned-attorney Mike Trope, in his book *Necessary Roughness*, published in 1987, tells how after getting friendly with some athletes, he became an agent in 1972 and stumbled across the underground economics of college sports. Boosters paid players and families, coaches steered players to agents, and players took money from agents on the promise of signing with them. Trope says he was literally competing with the team coaches, having to dive into "a cesspool" in order to succeed. And for a while it worked. In one draft, Trope represented four of six top selections. One of the stories is of Eric Dickerson, who was wooed by a University of Texas coach with a promise/threat that if Dickerson didn't go to UT, he'd never get a job in the state of Texas. Ironically, Dickerson went to Southern Methodist University, another Texas school that, in 1985, received the NCAA's famous "death penalty"— loss of a full season—for booster-payment violations. When Trope finally decided he couldn't do it anymore, he took the bar exam, became an attorney, and wrote his book.

In *The Business of Sports Agents*, written twenty years later, authors Kenneth Shropshire and Timothy Davis claim that in 1979 Trope paid former University of Maryland player Steve Atkins $1,000. Atkins told *Sports Illustrated*, "I knew I did something wrong. I didn't want the NCAA to do something to Maryland . . . I didn't want to sign with him [Trope], but I just needed some money to pay some bills."

In 1986, then-agent Mel Levine (and mentor to agent Drew Rosenhaus) said in his book, *Life in the Trash Lane*, that he won over future clients with similar tokens of appreciation, a practice he says was commonplace. "These kids come to your door, their hands are out. They said if I didn't give them money, they could get it from other agents." Levine handed the keys to a used silver Corvette to University of Miami running back Cleveland Gary, then gave a new black Corvette to Miami defensive tackle Jerome Brown, at which point Gary objected: Why had he been stuck with a used car? He demanded a new one.

Levine ultimately lost more than $80,000 in money advanced to players but never repaid. Was he punished by the NFLPA? Were the players penalized by the NCAA? No. In fact, it was only when the state of Florida made paying college-eligible athletes a felony that he got out. Mel Levine did go to prison, but it was for crimes unrelated to football: tax and bank fraud.

In 1987, Norby Walters, a show-business booking agent, had begun to pay promising college players to buy their allegiance when they entered the NFL draft. He claimed to have given money to at least five first-round picks in one year, plus many others, all prior to their

eligibility, "investing" as much as $800,000. The prob-
lem was, some of the players decided to sign with other
agents and Norby Walters thought he was entitled to get
his money back. Walters's associate, Lloyd Bloom, was
accused of passing the word along to those who owed,
saying, "Players who don't pay their debts can have their
hands broken." It led to an FBI and grand jury investigation, as well as NCAA and NFLPA reviews. Never convicted, Walters said paying players was nothing new.
In 1989, they were convicted but the convictions were
overturned. In 1993, in an unrelated incident, Bloom
was found murdered in a Malibu home.

How widespread was paying players at this time? According to a *Dallas Morning News* story in November
1985, a former University of Texas All-American defensive lineman said well over half the players were "being
taken care of." Agent Leigh Steinberg estimated 40 percent of seniors were receiving money, but he insisted,
not his clients. In fact, he stipulated that players he
represented set up foundations to give back to their
hometowns and high schools. Moral stance, marketing
tactic, or both?

By the time I was certified in 1989, the NCAA already had no shortage of questionable behavior.

So, just like that, I became a sports agent. The only thing I
didn't have was a client. I had a "maybe" from Greg Townsend.
Before I tried to officially sign him up, I went through my
self-styled "Rolodex," every name and number I'd collected

in my Casio Wizard since I was sixteen years old, searching for the one and only agent I'd ever met, an African-American guy named Neil Allen, who represented Stefon Adams. Allen was a powerful presence, handsome, well dressed, well spoken; he looked like Denzel Washington and sounded like Barack Obama. I called and ask if he remembered me from Raiders camp and he said he did. In hindsight, he may have been bluffing, but he was smooth enough to sell it. I told him about my opportunity to become Greg Townsend's agent, which got his attention. I explained that I needed some guidance and was hoping he'd help. He offered to buy me lunch in Beverly Hills and I walked from my house to meet him, I was certainly the only sports agent who lived with his parents.

As we talked, he came around to his angle: "Maybe we could work on Greg together, cut a deal together," which sounded good for me since I had no idea what I was doing; and maybe it would lead to more deals. All I knew about Neil was that he had a couple of Raiders he repped and he was charming and charismatic. We agreed to go see Greg together and be co-agents if he signed.

When we arrived at Greg's house and told him our plan he thought I'd gone insane. Be his agent? What? He'd just been talking. He hadn't promised me anything. I was blown away. I was a naive—okay, maybe dumb—kid who'd bought what he had said. *Your deal was up in a year. Your agent might be going to jail. You needed me. I went to the NFLPLA. I sent them $300. I got licensed. I hooked up with an experienced agent. I did it all because Greg Townsend, LA Raiders defensive end, told me I was a smart Jewish guy who could talk to Al Davis, who could be Greg Townsend's agent. This was my plan, my dream. And* even though Greg was resistant at first, I just kept at it. And somehow, eventually, I got through to him and he agreed. It was a miracle, that seems obvious now, but I didn't know it at the time. That's the advantage of being dumb. You don't know what's impossible or a miracle. You just try to do it.

Then Neil introduced me to Mike Trope, an agent-turned-attorney in Century City. He'd been a pretty prominent agent but had had enough, especially of the recruiting part, the players' bad behavior from alcohol to weed to Quaaludes to girls to cars to money, what you had to do to win, and he had turned to practicing law. He had no interest in chasing players anymore but he was willing to advise us on negotiating. So I'd turned to Neil for counsel and now he was turning to Mike.

Mike is a story in and of himself. He started young, when he was in college or law school, and became an early superagent, before the era of Leigh Steinberg. His office was crammed full of pictures of him with some star athlete or another in glossy magazine spreads—Johnny Rodgers, the Heisman Trophy winner from Nebraska; Chuck Muncie, the running back from Cal who played for the Saints and the Chargers; Anthony Munoz, the USC offensive tackle who played for the Bengals. Trope was big-time, or had been at one point. Now, he told me, he just wanted to be a lawyer, leaning back in his big chair, in blue jeans, with shoes that had holes worn through, being comfortable and not killing himself in the crazy world of athletes anymore. Mostly, he had developed a cynicism about the business, and about life.

I should've learned something from that but I was young and intoxicated with the thrill. So now there were three of us—Neil, me, and Mike—but Mike didn't want to be the agent, just the advisor. Besides, he hated the NFLPA, hated the industry. He'd burned out. He shared stories now and then about what had happened to this player or that or a deal gone bad or someone in the union you couldn't trust; and how he was divorced and had two daughters now and didn't want to be in that kind of business. (That's a little ominous to look back on too, having two daughters of my own, not wanting them to see me in that business today.) He became my first mentor, even more so than Neil.

One day, I was in his office and he let me in on an odd secret. He was about to get married for the second time, to a beautiful blonde woman, and he said, "I want to show you something." He reached in a drawer and pulled out a big legal document and said, "These are my divorce papers, already filled out." I was thinking, "You have divorce papers for a marriage that hasn't even happened yet?" I was young and sheltered and thought of marriage as a permanent bond, not something disposable (and even now, older and wiser, I still do). I remember when the Raiders would have Family Day and all the players' families would come—the wives and kids—and take pictures and have a big day. I thought it was great. Of course, when it was over and the families went home, then the players' girlfriends would reappear. So I knew it wasn't the ideal picture it seemed to be. But I still thought marriage mattered and here was Mike Trope, who hadn't yet said "I do" and he'd already drafted the papers to get out. That's how jaded he'd become. And, of course, he wound up needing them when he got divorced again a few years later.

But I worked with him and learned from him, and he fronted me the money to travel and recruit players. That also had an odd twist to it years later. After all the trips he paid for, one day after I'd been in the business awhile, he asked to borrow $10,000 from my share of commissions we'd collected. He said he'd pay me 20 percent interest so it would be a good deal for me. And I felt like I owed him anyway. But why was this successful lawyer coming to me, still a kid, for that kind of money? I never asked. And he didn't pay me back for years. I'd almost given up on getting it but right before my own wedding, when I needed the money to buy an engagement ring, he made good. (Although not before taking me to a pawnshop and trying to convince me to buy a ring that I thought he must have had there on consignment.) He paid me back the money, though without interest. There were lots of lessons from Mike—some good, some not so good.

Here's how we were operating: Before Greg Townsend's deal came up for negotiating, I was doing some recruiting with Neil, and Mike was staying strictly in the background as backer/advisor, never the agent of record. I'd go to Mike's house, pick up a plane ticket and cash in an envelope, and take off to some campus. I was so young, I couldn't rent a car most places. I'd use Mike's name and track record to give me credibility with the players, get their attention, because otherwise why would they pay attention to me, a guy their age with nothing to sell of my own? I went to the University of Illinois at Urbana-Champaign to recruit defensive back Henry Jones, defensive tackle Moe Gardner, and defensive end Mel Agee, and then on to Fresno State, then to Boulder, Colorado, for linebacker Kanavis McGhee, in what turned out to be a fateful trip.

CHAPTER 3

Paying a player is like losing your virginity. You can never get it back.

Kanavis McGhee was the first player I ever paid. But not the last. (I would later learn, you don't "pay" players; you "loan" them money, a big difference but not one I knew at the time.) Kanavis was a big pass-rusher, touted to be a high draft pick in 1991. Somehow I convinced myself, and Mike Trope, that Josh Luchs, the boy-agent, could connect with him. I parked my somehow-rented SUV outside Kanavis's apartment, waited half a day, and practically followed him in the door, reeling off my pitch, barely taking a breath. "Kanavis, I'm Josh Luchs, a sports agent, and I flew in from L.A. and then drove here just to talk to you because you're a great football player and I can really help you, and I'll tell you how if you'll give me a few minutes, okay?" He said, "Okay, sure, come in," and I was already in the door, sitting on the couch. I proceeded to say anything and everything to create a bond. After a while, he asked if he could talk to me about something personal. I was thinking, *Great sign. He trusts me.* "Sure,

Kanavis, anything." He said, "My mom is not well and she just lost her job and she can't pay her rent. She's going to get evicted from her apartment . . .," dramatic pause, ". . . unless I can find twenty-five hundred dollars for her." And he looked to see if maybe the money had somehow appeared on the table across from him. Since I don't carry rolls of hundred-dollar bills and since I didn't know what to do, I said, "Let me think about it tonight. I'll come see you tomorrow and let you know." I was thinking that, no matter what, this would give me another chance to meet with him. But I had no idea what I was going to do. I went to my hotel room and made a list of why to do it and why not. I knew it was breaking NCAA rules to give money to a player before he'd played his last college game. But I also knew it would help a young guy and his mother. What if my mom was sick and needed money? What if I couldn't help her? But what if someone found out? And where would I get that kind of money? I called Mike Trope to ask for the money but he told me that whatever I did was up to me; he wanted no part of it, and didn't even want to know about it. I had to decide on my own. I had some money in a bank account, from my bar mitzvah. My parents had said to save it for something really important. Maybe this was it—an investment in my career. But it was wrong. Or was it? I went back and forth all night.

The next morning I went to the local bank, pulled the money from my account, went to Kanavis, and handed him $2,500 in cash. He shook my hand, put his arm around me, and said, "Thank you, Josh. Thank you so much. You're my boy. You really came through for me." I felt good, as if I'd helped somebody in need and created a relationship with a future client.

I went back to my hotel room and the phone rang. It was a teammate of Kanavis. "Kanavis told me you're cool, a good man, and I need some help 'cause my pop is sick and losing his home and I need twenty-five hundred dollars . . ." And—boom—I felt sick to my stomach. I was the sucker. One player tells another that there's a chump who's passing out money. How could I be so dumb? I beat myself up all the way home. And I didn't tell anybody about it for a long time—not Mike, not Neil, and definitely not my father—no one, until I did the *Sports Illustrated* story on my career as an agent. When contacted by the magazine for corroboration, Kanavis initially asked to be called back the next day, then did not return calls or e-mails, but some time after the article came out denied having taken the money.

Who Paid the First Player?

I was hardly the first to pay a player to win him over. The first time somebody tried to buy a college player with money? If Adam had played football in the Garden of Eden, an agent would have beaten Eve to giving him an apple . . . and some spending money. Here's an excerpt from an ESPN.com Commentary article by Patrick Hruby.

THURSDAY, OCTOBER 21, 2010

COLLEGE FOOTBALL, AGENTS GO WAY BACK
The Heisman Trophy winner checked into a Philadelphia hotel under a false name, the better to keep things

hush-hush. The agent handed him a contract, along with two bonus checks totaling $10,500. The young man signed.

Roughly a month later, the same Heisman Trophy winner placed a call with another agent, this one promising a more lucrative contract, along with a $20,000 bonus, ownership of five gas stations, half-interest in an as-yet-unformed eponymous oil company and, just because, a Cadillac for his father. The young man eagerly agreed.

Oh, and two days after that, he played his final college game.

The Heisman Trophy winner in question was LSU's Billy Cannon. (The alias in question? Peter Gunn.) The first "agent" was Los Angeles Rams general manager Pete Rozelle, who later became commissioner of the NFL. The second "agent" was Houston Oilers (now Titans) owner Bud Adams, who tells the story in his own words in "Going Long," an oral history of the AFL. (The whole case ended up in court, and Adams won.)

The year this all went down? 1959.

I did finally recruit a player, Latin Berry, an Oregon running back who became a defensive back in the pros. I had originally been after him, and a couple of other guys from Oregon, but didn't land any of them. Latin signed on with another agent, Bradley Peter in northern California, and then got drafted by the Rams in the third round. He was right in our backyard so I went after him again. There's a rule that you can't solicit clients once they're under contract to another agent, but that didn't stop me, or Neil, or most agents. It's one of the most flagrantly ignored rules in the business. *Thou shalt not steal thy neighbor's players . . . unless you want to and can.* If you lose a player to another agent and you think he was poached, you can file a grievance with the union. But guess who'll be the star witness in that case. Right—the player you just lost. And that new player isn't about to turn against his new agent, or he wouldn't have switched. He's going to swear he got to you on his own, not that you solicited him. That's why agents are able to raid competitors' client lists with little fear of NFLPA discipline.

Neil and I were out to win Latin over, after the draft but before it was time to negotiate his deal, through mini-camps, in April and in May, until July or early August, up to training camp. We told him we were local, we could do more for him in L.A., and we would be there when he needed us. He was young and I was young, and we could relate; I'd go to his hotel, take him out on the town, and have him over to my parents' house in Beverly Hills. Neil could be charming and persuasive, suggesting to Latin that he'd made his initial agent choice without all the information needed—what city he'd be playing and living in . . . and partying in. And since I was dating a Rams cheerleader, she and her girlfriends made his head spin to help make our case.

Latin jumped to us, a big score for me, my first negotiation. Neil did the negotiating and I watched and learned, and tried not to giggle out loud with excitement. Because I was sitting in the Rams office on Pico Boulevard with Jay Zygmunt, second only to the general manager (and later president himself). I was making a deal for an NFL player with the VP of the Rams! Un-fucking-real!

Okay, I wasn't making the deal personally. But I was there.

I signed the player. I got the call from the agent he fired, Bradley Peter, screaming and swearing and threatening to break my fingers. I got the next call from Mark Levin of the NFLPA, the first of many I'd get over the years, this one to scold me for behavior that was "not becoming" of an agent. I had a pretty arrogant attitude, almost dismissive. He didn't understand the reality of winning over a player. He sat in an office in Washington, D.C., and pushed paper around. We were in the trenches. And I wasn't too shaken by a finger-wagging from NFLPA since it was decertified at the time anyway— part of an ongoing labor dispute with the NFL during which it was legally advantageous for the Players Association to dissolve itself as a "union" (not unlike the one that happened in 2011). Once the disagreement was settled, the organization re-formed as a union for collective bargaining. But in the interim, ironically, more power with the league meant less power over agents. If you wanted to be a member, you had to follow their rules, but the penalty was more like a parking ticket than a moving violation. I appeased the union rep a little and got off the phone. I had players to pursue. I was an agent.

Kind of. Was I more of a runner than an agent? A recruiter more than a player rep? And what was the difference? I tracked down the players, made friends with their friends, or girlfriends, or found their home addresses or sat by their cars, or knew where they hung out. I was a runner on my way to being an agent. A lot of agents start that way. Like Gary Wichard, one of the biggest agents in the business, who was the other inspiration, along with Leigh Steinberg, for Jerry Maguire, and who I later worked for. According to Tom Friend of ESPN, "He entered the agent business at the urging of

NBA star Julius Erving, a friend from Long Island, who introduced him to his own agent, Irwin Weiner. Wichard recruited players for Weiner, bringing in Colts running back Don McCauley and hockey player Jean Potvin from the New York Islanders. He eventually branched off to start his own agency . . ." Running, recruiting, bird-dogging, whatever you want to call it, can be an apprenticeship. I was in Agent School, learning about contracts, deal points, bonus structures, endorsement deals. And I was an equal partner with Neil Allen, getting an equal share of whatever we earned. So it was like a scholarship to Agent School.

It's a Lot Easier to Pay Players than Get Paid by Them

In fact, getting paid was one of my early lessons. Get the money when you can. Agent commission was still 5 percent at the time and as soon as we consummated the Latin Berry–Rams deal, Neil got in the car with our new NFL player, went to a bank, opened an account for him, and deposited his signing bonus. The rule is the player has to pay you. You can't get your commission straight from the team. Neil said, "Once you do these deals, it's hard to get paid. When you have the opportunity to get paid, take it." He took our cut that day in cash and handed me a stack of one-hundred-dollar bills. I went home, to my bedroom, and threw the money all over my bed and rolled around in it—$6,500 in hundreds. My sister walked in and looked at me like I was nuts. She was on her way to USC, to be a double-major in political science and communications, and all I could think was, "Go ahead and kill yourself in school. I'm gonna make some real money in football." I was probably the only NFL agent rolling around in money in his bedroom in his parents' house.

Find the Fat Chick

Next, I was off to Knoxville to go after Chuck Webb, the Tennessee running back. He was a Red Shirt sophomore starting to get a name for himself. I had my plane ticket and some cash and I got there, went to the locker room, and couldn't find Webb. Then I remember something Neil had told me: "Find the fat chick." He said on every college campus there's a big girl with a big ass who hangs around the football building and knows every player on the team, everything about them, and is in love with them, and follows them like a stalker. It's a pretty crude observation but it served me well. There was an overweight girl wearing a Tennessee Vols T-shirt and warm-up pants hanging around the facility, just like Neil said she'd be. I'd dressed in jeans and a T-shirt so I looked like a student, and I struck up a conversation with her. "Do you know Chuck Webb?"

She proceeded to tell me every detail of his life, when his classes were, when he went to practice; she almost knew when he went to the bathroom. I waited outside the weight room when she told me to, and even though I had no idea what Chuck Webb looked like, the school made my job easier by plastering its players' jersey numbers on their school-issue backpacks, sweatshirts, hats, whatever—so I literally had Chuck Webb's number. *Hello 44, I'm Josh Luchs.* I told him I had flown all the way from Los Angeles to see him and wanted a couple minutes with him. He said he had to go in and lift but gave me his phone number and we met for dinner.

I was staying at the University Inn; every campus in the United States seems to have one. And they're all pretty crappy and overpriced. At this one, there was a big picture of the head coach, Johnny Majors, at the front desk, and it made me paranoid, as if he were looking right into the guest register, following my every move. Over dinner and the next day or so, Chuck and I talked, and he let me know he could use some money. At this point, I knew Kanavis McGhee had spread the word about my having given him money and made me look like an easy mark, but I didn't yet know that Kanavis was not going to sign with me. So I wasn't afraid to put up a little more. Just a little this time: $300 to $500. I made it clear to Chuck that if he chose to turn pro after his sophomore year, I wanted him to come to L.A. to meet with me and Mike Trope after the season. And I gave him a full dose of Mike's credentials—six Heisman Trophy winners, star running backs like Tony Dorsett, Earl Campbell, Johnny Rogers, and Mike Rozier—a legend in the business. I gave Chuck a few hundred bucks with the understanding he'd come see us, no agreement, no loan, nothing formal. And Mike didn't know I was doing it, just as he still didn't know anything about Kanavis. If I paid, it was my decision. I was just getting players for him, like a runner, but a runner who's a certified agent. I didn't know if Kanavis was going to sign and I didn't know if Chuck was turning pro and coming to L.A. But I had bet on it—an investment of sorts.

And I kept on recruiting. I went to Champaign, Illinois, for Henry Jones, the safety, and for defensive tackles Moe Gardner and Mel Agee. It's cornfield country, about as far from Beverly Hills as you can get, and of course, I was staying at the University Inn. I found the fat chick again, this time wearing a Fighting Illini T-shirt, and again, she delivered every detail on every player. I went to Henry Jones's apartment complex, got him to meet me later at a Burger King across from the hotel. He didn't ask for money and I didn't offer. The whole meeting cost me a Whopper (still enough to violate NCAA rules, by the way). Then I camped outside Mel Agee's apartment for three hours, sitting on the steps, smoking a cigar. He finally showed up and wasn't exactly cordial but I talked my way into his apartment. He kept asking, "Why do I even need an agent? What for? I'll give you three minutes to convince me I need an agent." I had to come up with something fast. I remembered a little word-play riddle I'd learned from a guy in high school. I told him to get a paper and pencil and said, "Now draw me a square with three lines." He wanted to know what that had to do with anything but I told him to just try it. He stared at the paper and after a while said it couldn't be done. I kept saying it could. He thought more and got more annoyed. Finally, I took the pencil and drew, first, a square and next to it, three lines. I said, "That's why you need an agent. Because it's all in the details. One word can change the meaning of anything. Like in your contract." And, amazingly, it worked.

I sold him on Mike Trope and he promised to come see us. All together, I had Kanavis McGhee, Chuck Webb, Mel Agee, and Leonard Russell, a running back from Arizona State, all promising to come see us in L.A. Or I had nothing—it all depended on whether they came. I had given money to Kanavis and Chuck (and a hamburger to Henry Jones). Once they were past their eligibility and announced they weren't returning to school, if they flew out to see us, we could pay for the plane tickets.

In the end, Chuck Webb and Mel Agee both flew out and Leonard Russell lived nearby. We met with all of them. Agee came to Mike's office in Century City. He said he'd sign with us but he needed money for an engagement ring for his girlfriend, which, according to the NFLPA rules, would be an "inducement to sign" and therefore was not allowed. Even though it was past his eligibility, Trope wouldn't go for it and sent him home. I couldn't help feeling frustrated: for the price of a ring, we could've had him. Agents were buying stuff for players all the time, especially after they announced they were coming out. But Mike wouldn't do it.

Then Chuck came to see us. And he signed a contract for representation. We met at a Hamburger Hamlet, and Leonard Russell was there too, an arrangement I would never have tried once I knew a little more about players and egos. The plan was, Chuck was going to go home to Ohio, get his stuff, then come back to Los Angeles for his training. I didn't want anyone coming between us—as I had done with Latin Berry and his agent. So I flew back home with him. Like a good babysitter, I took along a toy, a brand-new Game Boy, with a football game cartridge, probably the hottest toy around, and Chuck played the game all the way across the country. We landed in Toledo, Ohio, in the middle of a snowstorm, I rented an Avis car, went to his house, met his mom, and before I left for my hotel, he asked if he could keep the Game Boy to play overnight. Sure, no problem. The next day, I went by to get him and his mom said he wasn't there and she had no idea where he was.

I drove around, hung out at the hotel for a while, and went back—still no sign of Chuck. On about my fifth trip back to the house, his mother finally said he had gone to visit his uncle Ray. I asked her how to get to this guy Ray's house and she told me he didn't live in Ohio. (It turned out "Uncle Ray" was Ray Anderson, one of the most successful agents of all time, and now NFL Executive VP for Football Operations.) So not only did Chuck Webb strand me in the middle of Toledo, he stole my Game Boy. I went to the hotel and fell asleep, and when I got up the next day to drive to the airport, I stepped outside into forty-mile-an-hour wind, sideways snow, a full Midwestern blizzard—and discovered my rental car was gone.

I walked around the lot to make sure I hadn't parked it somewhere else. But right where I was sure I had parked was a little piece of window glass with the Avis logo on it. Fucked, fucked, and re-fucked. I ended up in a year-long battle of letters with Avis over who owed what to whom. Fucked some more. And, needless to say, I never heard from Chuck Webb again. He had signed with us, but what could we do? Say, hey, we gave you money and you signed? A player could fire an agent at any time, without reason, no questions asked. No, Chuck Webb was gone. He was drafted in the third round by the Packers and played one season. And for all I know, he still has my Game Boy. Ray Anderson was not his uncle, in case you were still wondering.

Out of my big recruits, that left Leonard Russell, another guy we thought we had in the bag but who I never talked to again. When I went to see him in Long Beach, there was this guy, Chuckie Miller, out of UCLA, a one-year defensive back with the Colts, who was training Leonard, but mostly acting as his gatekeeper thanks to Steve Feldman, who would end up his agent. And Miller kept the gate closed. (Later, when I went to work with Feldman, we ended up using Miller to train some of our players. It's a small world and all's fair. You go after whoever you can, you get them any way you can, and may the best, most aggressive, man win.) Chuckie made sure that Leonard signed with Feldman and I was kept at bay. Leonard Russell went on to be a first-round pick of the Patriots and was named Rookie of the Year.

Another strikeout. And it was pretty clear by then that I wasn't going to hear from Kanavis McGhee again. I called him over and over but you had to be careful what you left on a message. I couldn't say, "I'm the agent who gave you the money . . ." We had signed Latin Berry and Greg Townsend, but I'd had a lot of near-misses. I figured I was going after the right guys. I was getting in the door. These guys were big NFL prospects, and they were talking to me. I'd had some bad luck, but the glass was half-full. I was still a rookie at this, and still living in my parents' house, so I had, shall we say, low overhead. I was selling Mike Trope's history and Neil Allen's charm, and my mom was making tuna sandwiches for players who came over. It was a lot different than most agents' approach.

But it was also becoming clear that Mike Trope didn't have his heart in it and Neil Allen, well, that was an iffy situation, at best. I kept hearing rumors of Neil's reputation and conduct not being on the up and up but he'd just say it was all rumors. I should have known something. I finally got it when Neil convinced Greg to fire me (the first time). I don't know what he told Greg, maybe that I was a kid and didn't know what I was doing (sort of true) or that Neil would take better care of him (not true) or whatever. But I let the fox into the hen-house and he took the chicken—a big lesson lots of agents have learned, or should have learned, over the years. In the meantime, Greg was a holdout and hadn't signed with the Raiders yet. Neil had this lady friend for years who he had a tendency to cheat on regularly, and he was trying to salvage his relationship with her . . . again. So he took her to Hawaii, right in the middle of Greg's holdout from training camp. If you're holding out, you're not getting paid; you're not practic-ing; you're losing ground and you're anxious. And your agent is in Hawaii. But I was not in Hawaii. I was strategizing in my bedroom at my parents' house in Beverly Hills. This was my opportunity.

CHAPTER 4

Call the Doctor:
Harold "Doc" Daniels

I went to Mike Trope in need of some firepower to convince Greg I could get his deal done and get him back as a client. Mike didn't want to get back in the business, even for a few minutes, but he steered me to a guy he'd met while working on a case for him, an agent named Harold "Doc" Daniels. I had seen Doc before but had never met him. And seeing him was memorable. I was on a trip with Neil to the Atlanta Falcons training camp in Suwanee, Georgia, where Neil had a quarterback named Gilbert Renfroe whom he'd signed from the Canadian Football League. Doc Daniels had two Falcon players of his own, Darion Conner, a second-round line-backer, and first-round running back Steve Broussard. What I remember about Doc was how big he was, literally and figuratively. I remember seeing this guy driving up in this big, long car and I asked Neil, "Who the hell is that?" "Oh, that's Doc Daniels," he said, as if everybody knew him. And I asked, "How can he drive with his leg hanging out the window?" Neil answered, "That's not his leg. It's his arm."

That's how big Doc was. He sort of unfolded himself to get out of the car and there stood a massive character: six foot seven, four hundred pounds, gold-rimmed glasses, gold nugget jewelry, a one of a kind. He had played pro football for a few years, then had gone to become a professor at Harbor Community College, teaching phys ed and psychology, hence the nickname "Doc," which stuck when he began representing athletes.

He turned out to be my professor, too, tutoring me through the business. I went to see him in his little cubicle of an office, lined with pictures of him and the players he represented— Michael Cooper of the Lakers, Lions defensive back Bruce Alexander, Oilers wide receiver Drew Hill—and him behind his little desk, a stream of kids filing in and out, phone ringing with calls from every junior-college coach in the state; he was a full-time professor, part-time sports agent, helping everybody.

I explained the whole situation to him, what I was trying to do, and Doc found it pretty funny, how I'd brought Neil Allen in and then gotten shafted by him. He agreed that if I could get Greg back, he'd go with me to do the deal. He had a great relationship with Steve Ortmayer, who negotiated on behalf of the Raiders, so if we could nail down Greg, Doc would get us an audience. I then wrote a termination letter, copied word for word from the one I'd gotten from Greg firing me, just changing the name from Luchs to Allen. He'd be out and I'd be in. I printed it up on the dot matrix printer in my bedroom on Doc's company letterhead, Professional Stars, along with a two-page rep agreement (there was no standard form at the time), and I headed over to Greg's house.

Greg answered the door in his lounging outfit, as always. I started my pitch. "Greg, how much can this guy Neil care about you? He's off in Hawaii fucking around. I have a relationship with you. I'm here. I'm thinking about you. You're holding out of training camp. You're not part of the team. You're hurting yourself. Who's worrying about you? Me. While Neil's lounging on the beach." I could tell Greg was thinking about it. I kept going: "Neil isn't coming back for five days. Give me those five days." And I handed him the rep agreement that said that if I could negotiate a contract for him that he found acceptable before Neil returned to L.A., he would sign with us. I told him I'd do the deal with Doc, and Greg knew who Doc was. Just give us the five days, I said. If it was done, then he could sign the deal and simultaneously send Neil the termination letter. I said I'd hold on to the termination so that if we failed, it would be as if none of this had ever happened. No harm, no foul. I'd tear it up. You relax, enjoy your vacation, I told him. Doc and I will get your deal.

Greg was game for the idea. He was thinking he wasn't in camp, he was losing ground, and worrying, and his agent was on the beach in Hawaii. Plus Neil had made some statements in the press implying there was a race thing going on, that the Raiders had given big money to Howie Long, who's white, but had not given Greg what he was due. Knowing Mr. Davis, I knew he loved his players and would be offended by this. And since, at the time, there was no free agency, when a player's contract expired, he could only negotiate with his old team— meaning market value was whatever they said it was. Neil's position with the press wasn't very smart for Greg's future, nor for how Al Davis and the Raiders might view him. And

Greg knew it. He wanted a deal. He signed the rough agreement, giving us the small window to negotiate for him. I called Doc, who called Steve Ortmayer, and we went to the Raiders facility. We were very upfront with Steve that we had a short time frame. And he wasn't very happy with what Neil had said to the press, which only helped us. We put together a deal that made Greg the fourth-highest-paid defensive lineman in the NFL, not far behind Howie Long, who had already been a Pro-Bowler. (Greg would be, but hadn't been yet.)

We took the deal parameters to Greg and he liked them. We rushed him to the Raiders facility, and Greg signed the contract, with a day to spare. Twenty-four hours later, Neil Allen got off the plane from Hawaii, received his termination letter, and shit a brick. His little jaunt to Hawaii had just become the most expensive vacation he'd ever taken. He went wild and yelled and screamed to the press, tried to get Greg to fire me again, said he could make a better deal—but it was too late. The deal was good and the deal was done. Greg was happy, the team was happy, and man oh man, was I happy. I had made my first deal in the NFL. I really was an agent.

And I had a partner and mentor in Doc. Over the years, Greg fired me seven times and rehired me six times. And, in between, we had to chase him down for our commissions. One time he put me off, saying he was broke because of child support and alimony payments, but he was telling me this at the strip club he'd dragged me to, while throwing money at the stripper, making it rain twenties with what I considered to be our commissions. I had a flash fantasy of jumping onstage to wrestle my agent fee away from the girl on the pole, but I knew the scene would end with a bouncer drop-kicking me to the curb. Soon after that, I convinced Greg to get a vasectomy so he'd stop having kids and/or girlfriends claiming he was the father of their kids, to protect him and try to protect our commissions. I convinced my father, the urologist, to give him the vasectomy. And I kept refilling ice bags to put on his balls for the swelling after surgery. Ah, the glamour of life as an NFL agent.

College Student or Sports Agent: Hmm, four dull years or big-time football adrenaline 24/7?

Not long after signing Greg, I had to make a decision: College student or sports agent? It wasn't a tough choice since I hated one and loved the other. I'd finished a year of junior college, was going into my second year, and I'd learned a lot more in the real world than in the classroom. I kind of made the decision by not showing up for my second year at college. I was out recruiting ball players, not a good excuse for missing class. "Dear Professor, please excuse Josh from class yesterday. He was busy playing video games and chasing coeds with a UCLA defensive back in hopes of representing him in the NFL draft." And, at some point, I had to tell my parents. That was the hard part.

First I went to mom, hoping she'd be sympathetic and maybe help me figure out how to tell my dad. I had my whole pitch down pat: *I love sports, I've found my niche, done the radio producing, worked for the Raiders, and now an opportunity is here. I'm in with people who know what they're doing, Trope and Allen and now Doc, and I've landed a real client in Greg . . .*

I thought it all sounded pretty good. But my mom, my biggest fan, did not take it well. "It'll break your father's heart. You know how he feels about school, about academics. You need to stay in college." It was not what I had been hoping for. Now I had to have the talk with my father with no help from my mom, and I was panicking. He was intimidating and short-tempered. He was the one in the family everyone wanted to satisfy. And I was about to disappoint him. Somehow I got my story out. He listened thoughtfully, and eventually he said, "Josh, school isn't for everyone. I don't worry about you. I know you'll make your way."

He totally surprised me. He understood how I felt and what I wanted. And I knew how hard it was for him. I remember when I was a little kid in Brooklyn he put a stethoscope around my neck because he wanted me to be a doctor like him. Pretty early on, my grades made it clear that wasn't happening, but he still hoped I'd get a good education. But, over the years, he came to believe I'd get my education another way. He'd come to the Raiders camp; he'd met Greg; he'd seen me in my element and he believed in me. That made all the difference.

Agent 101: How to Pay Players in Eight Simple Steps, by Professor Harold Daniels

By this point, I was really learning the ins and outs of the business from an expert. My first course from Doc was: How to Pay Players . . . and How Not To. How not to was the way I had been doing it. When I told Doc what I'd done, he smiled and put his arm around my shoulder and said, "Son, that's not the way." Then he gave me step-by-step instructions on the right way to do the wrong things, and I began to employ them.

1. Establish that the player wants or needs money. Doc gave me the basics on this one but I was already pretty good at establishing rapport with players. I knew how to talk to them. I'd say to a player like Jamir Miller, "How are you getting by? Tell me about your scholarship and what it covers and what you really need to get by." And I'd ask, "Is anybody helping you from home? Is it putting a strain on your mom or dad or other relatives?" And the player would usually open up because I was showing sensitivity to his situation, and that gave me clues about what to do, when or whether to offer.

2. Determine the minimum amount that will be meaningful. Doc's approach was not to try to blow a player away with showy gifts of a thousand dollars here and two thousand there but instead with smaller, steady help. First, we'd find out the player's situation. He might say, "I get two hundred fifty dollars a month from my mother. That's all she can send me." And I'd say, "Whoa, is that enough to get by on?" And he'd say something like, "I scrape by. Of course, another hundred would help but she doesn't have it." Okay, I've got my first clue. Then I'd go a little farther, offering to help him and his mom. "So if you had an extra three or four hundred a month and you didn't have to take money from your mom, that would make your

life easier and hers, right?" At that point, if I'd read the player well, he'd say, "Yeah, dude, that would be incredible." And I could see the wheels turning in his head about telling his mom or uncle they didn't have to send money and about what he'd do with that money.

3. Go slow. Build a bond. We'd talk about it on and off over a few lunches or dinners, or hanging out playing Madden Football, not pressing too hard, waiting for the player to bring it up again. Then I'd say, "Hey, I know you're in a tough spot. Why don't I just do this for you? I did it for some other guys, guys you know. I'm open to it." I'd make it clear it was because we cared about him. We'd even turn him against the school, paying coaches so much, making a fortune from TV dollars, using the NCAA's oppressive rules, all on the backs of players like him. The player could trust us, maybe more than he could trust the school. It was a relationship. He would be part of our family.

4. Make it a loan, not a gift. When the player showed real interest, he'd ask how it worked. I'd say, "Hey, it's just a loan. A no-interest loan. Until you have the money to pay me back." They liked that. No interest was like free money. And because it was a loan, it felt legitimate, a loan to be repaid, not a gift that players weren't supposed to accept from schools or alums or boosters. It was just as much against the rules, but it didn't seem like it.

5. Make the relationship clear. We're doing this for you because we care about you and you'll work with us

because you trust us. I'd talk about our track record with players, our draft and contract results. I'd find out if there was a family member who had to be comfortable with us, or another agent he'd been talking to, or a family member who wanted to be the agent, any obligations that might get in the way of our working together. If there was resistance of any kind, I'd just wait, a week or a month, until they came up short on money and then I'd get a call.

6. Make it official. We had agreements printed up—our rep agreement on white paper and our loan agreement on pink paper. The player would sign both, but we'd tell the player we were not going to put a date on the rep agreement until after he'd played his last game as a college athlete—last game of the season or a Bowl game—to preserve his eligibility. So, at the end of the year, other agents would talk to these kids and tell them the contracts weren't enforceable, but once we put a date on them, they were . . . kind of. Of course, the player could fire us; but in fact, the loan agreement would still be in force—as long as we were willing to risk enforcing it, which was essentially a suicide mission.

Agent Norby Walters and partner Lloyd Bloom made loans to players only to have them defect to other agents when they turned pro. Then Walters tried to collect the loans, even filing lawsuits—a move that completely backfired. The contracts were ruled to be against public policy and thrown out of court, and Walters's agent status was destroyed.

Anyway, we weren't going to go that route for three reasons. One, if you sue a player, word spreads through the locker room; you're dead at that school for years, and no other player will talk to you. Two, it was a complicated path; you'd make a very different case to the NFLPA than you might make in a state court. The courts are governed by law: innocent until proven guilty. But the Players Association can judge you arbitrarily: guilty until proven innocent. Still, a loss in either one would be a killer. And three, because Doc Daniels was a badass and I never saw anyone cross him.

7. Do not pay in cash. Doc told me cash was a no-no, big mistake, bad, dumb, never. Cash had no record, which on the one hand was good because we didn't want it to be traced to us, but it also gave the players deniability. "What cash? I never took any money from you or anyone else." The answer was money orders. Growing up in Beverly Hills, I knew nothing about stores that cashed checks and sold money orders. If my family needed money, we went to banks, not the post office or bodegas or gas stations. A whole other world opened up. You could stop at the Exxon Station in Long Beach, fill up the car, buy a grape Slushee, and get $2,000 in money orders, all paid for in cash. Doc would buy stacks of money orders and we'd just fill in the To and From lines, usually From: the player's mother or girlfriend, and To: the player. From: Rhonda Miller, To: Jamir Miller, Amount: $300. When we filled them out, we pressed down hard and there was a carbon copy for us to keep.

8. Keep records. We kept our carbons of the money orders and our copies of the loan agreements, and I took it upon myself to keep a log of all transactions. On the rare occasions when I'd give a player a few bucks in cash, I'd initial my log and have him initial it too. Again, it's not as if we'd go to court with these records but just that we had a record and that it made everyone feel a real obligation to honor the contracts.

And that was it—a simple eight-step system that, if executed well, produced reliable results. I don't know if other agents followed the same steps, but I do know other agents were paying players. I know it because sometimes a player would tell us he didn't need money since he was already getting it from another agent. I know it because sometimes I got the feeling the players were shopping for the best deal. I know it because sometimes when a player signed with us, he'd have us pay back another agent. And I know it because it's common knowledge.

Arm-Wrestling for Players

Leigh Steinberg tells the story of sitting in the lobby of the hotel at the Senior Bowl one year and overhearing two agents across the room in a heated argument.

Agent 1: He's mine! I've been giving him money this whole year, five hundred a month.
Agent 2: No way, he's mine! I've been paying him since right after his red-shirt year.

Agent 1: I've paid him more than ten grand and he promised to go with me in the draft.

Agent 2: His dad said he's signing with us.

Agent 1: His dad said the same to me.

Agent 2: Maybe we should split him.

They were fighting over who had bought the player, who owned him, but this is a human being, not an object. They were going to divide him like Solomon splitting the baby. Exactly how could they split him? And who was in the wrong here, the agents, the player, or both?

Around the same time, Steinberg says, a story circulated about a USC running back who signed agreements, prior to his eligibility, with *six* agents. Was he more unscrupulous, or just better at gaming a system that was trying to game him too? Paying players, or lending them money, was commonplace; it was rampant and flagrant. If an agent didn't do it, he had to try to convince the players to hold off and that they'd get a plenty big enough payday by waiting, and not to jeopardize their futures. But it was a tough sell, some of them came from nothing, and money was being dangled in front of them and they simply hadn't had the chance to mature. We used to say, "Players get the agents they deserve." In hindsight, I'd say, "Players got the agent they were ready for"(meaning their level of maturity or understanding of the stakes and consequences).

Doc's Eight Steps worked. Jamir Miller was sort of a typical case; study that scenario and you understand how this stuff works, good and bad. You look for players who are good as juniors; with sophomores or freshmen you're taking too many chances on injury or being a hot prospect who flames out. And by the time they're seniors you're too late. You start by paying maybe $350 a month. Do the math and over a year and a half that's more than $6,000 for one player . . . who may or may not pan out in the draft. Still, I'd tell a guy, "If you need more sometimes, let me know and I'll see what I can do." And even if a player wasn't a star and dropped to a mid- or late-round pick, he might be a connection to another player. That's how I met Jamir. He looked like a star from the start. He was explosive, a great pass rusher, linebacker, defensive end—a hybrid. When I first met him, I'd go over to his place and hang out, just trying to establish a relationship. He found out I was a cigar smoker and he asked me to take him empty cigar boxes when I took his money. I was pretty naive so I just thought he was collecting cigar boxes or had something he kept in cigar boxes. Actually, I was right: he kept his weed in them. By the end of season, right before he was coming out, we were paying about $500 a month, and he looked like a first- round prospect. The stakes were getting higher to keep him as a client.

Doc made it clear that he had only so much money and was in no position to up the ante into the thousands or to buy the kid a car. So, he did something he did from time to time, and brought in a big money guy, an investor. In this case, it was a guy named Al, who had ties to the music business and lived in a huge house in Beverly Hills (not from the rougher part). He tried to impress players by bragging about his "in- volvement" producing disco hits, but they were more im- pressed with his house. We had to give away a third of our commission to him. The theory, though, was that the player would still pay back all the money once he signed with a team, even the cost of a car. But that theory was built on the premise the player would be drafted and drafted high.

Jamir wasn't working out as hard as he should have. We didn't have any formal structure to help him train like agents do now. It was up to the players to work out with the school's strength and conditioning coaches. Jamir didn't run well. His times in the forty-yard-dash weren't fast. A month or two before the draft, somebody from the Arizona Cardinals called and said if Jamir could run a 4.6 in the forty, they'd take him as their tenth pick in the first round. It was because of Doc pulling in favors, asking them to take another look at Jamir privately. We worked with him at a track away from UCLA so nobody would know about it. The Cardinals sent a scout and Jamir ran just well enough to satisfy them.

We threw a draft party, picked up the tab at a soul-food place called Creeque Alley on Melrose. Plenty of UCLA players came, including star wideout J. J. Stokes, who, like his teammates, was still college-eligible, and therefore not supposed to be there. But they were great contacts for us to make. Going forward, they would know us as the guys who had put on the big bash for Jamir Miller. The Cowboys even sent a scout to the party because they were thinking of trading up to get him, and if they decided to pull the trigger, the scout would get on a plane to Dallas with Jamir. When the tenth pick came, though, the Cardinals stuck to their plan and took him. And we celebrated. My parents were there. It was a big deal.

But, in fact, at that point, it was still no deal at all. The deals aren't made until training camp in late July or early August. I remember asking Doc why we and the teams weren't exchanging offers during that time and trying to get it done. He said, "If they have a choice of giving you a million dollars now or a million dollars later, which do you think they want to do?" I got it. And at this point in my career, I wasn't doing much negotiating, just learning. Doc did the deals. We finally agreed to terms with the Cardinals, through Bob Ackles, and Doc and I flew out to Phoenix. When we got there, the deal we thought we'd agreed to with Ackles was overruled and reduced by the head coach, Buddy Ryan. He wanted less on the signing bonus and a different contract structure, all at the eleventh hour. That led to us having Jamir hold out of training camp. He missed the first practice while we stayed in Arizona and negotiated. In the end, we had to "compromise," meaning we settled on a different deal than the one we'd agreed on, closer to Buddy Ryan's deal. We could either keep holding out, keeping Jamir off the practice field while Ryan ripped him in the press, or we could "compromise." There was no free agency so we had very little leverage. Even when a contract ran out, the team retained its exclusive rights to the player.

As soon as we made the deal, he got on the field. And a few days later we had our payday. We got our commission on the signing bonus and our loan money, but nothing was paid on the salary until the players started to get paychecks. And our investor got his piece.

Now jump ahead to year two with Jamir. In his second season with the Arizona Cardinals, he tested positive for drugs and got a four-game suspension. As a rule, agents are not informed of drug problems unless the player tells us. And according to league policy, a first-time offense means a rehab program, second-time offense a fine, and third-time, a fine and suspension. We didn't even know there was a problem until the third offense. Jamir was absolutely adamant that he had not done any drugs even though the NFL's tests were positive. So we arranged for another sample to be done, a "B Sample" of the same sealed and initialed specimen, and sent it off to an independent lab. It came back positive too. (I still have a copy of that report.) Jamir told his mom, still claiming to be clean, and she said, "If you say you didn't do drugs, then you didn't do drugs. And if you're going to get suspended anyway, then your agents must be no good. You need to fire them." So he did. He did pay off the loans, and the agent commissions owed from the signing bonus, and it was by far the biggest payday of my career to date.

And here's the big irony. He came back, played a long time, and even made a Pro Bowl. A few years ago, he was one of the candidates to succeed Gene Upshaw as NFLPA executive director (DeMaurice Smith eventually got the job). A guy who took money from agents when he was in college, a guy who tested positive for drugs, was up for the top job in setting and enforcing the rules. He'd already served as a member of CARD, the Players Association Committee on Agent Regulation and Discipline, passing judgment and suspension on agents. What's wrong with this picture?

That same year, we followed up on a guy who'd been at the draft party, J. J. Stokes. We had the guy who was the tenth pick in the draft in Jamir Miller and we had Sean LaChapelle, the all-time leading receiver for UCLA. Sean and I got to be friends off the field and he came over to my parents' house, later even giving me a dog, named Touchdown. Ironically, I didn't give him money but he gave me a dog. I thought I'd sign him after his junior year but UCLA coach Rick Neuheisal convinced him to go back as senior. For the next year, to keep other agents away from him, I moved him into my house. I'd made a deal on a distressed property in Woodland Hills, twenty minutes from UCLA, that I co-owned with Glen Walker, sports broadcaster on *Prime Ticket*, hosting the Pac 10 show. Glen lived in the master bedroom and I took the other two bedrooms, one for me and one for Sean. I even got Sean to give out my phone number for his. I'd listen to the messages agents would leave in pursuit of Sean, including Leigh Steinberg, (who claimed he never recruited players, that they just came to him). My answering machine would've proven otherwise. Sean, Glen, and I were roommates during Sean's senior year.

Doc and His Jew-Boy

Doc and I were breaking a lot of agent-player stereotypes. Other black agents were amazed that he or we had signed UCLA's white golden boy, Sean LaChapelle. He said maybe those black agents needed a "Jew-boy of their own" like me. And at the same time, I was running around with black athletes, partying, hanging out, and signing them. One night, I went to an L.A. club with a bunch of players, and the rap group Public Enemy was playing to a packed "all-black-except-one-Jew-boy" house. One of the lead singers, Flava Flav, came out with a replica of Big Ben around his neck, and with the other lead, Chuck D, started singing their hit antiestablishment anthem, "Fight the Power," from the Spike Lee movie *Do the Right Thing*: "We got to fight the powers that be / Lemme hear you say / Fight the power . . ." They were marching like soldiers in formation across the stage, in military uniforms and army boots, and I was thinking, I sure hope they don't see this one pasty white face as "the power" they need to fight.

Later, when I started dating the woman who would become my wife, I asked her to go with me to a players' picnic in a park in Pasadena. She thought a picnic would be a nice, wholesome way to spend an afternoon. When we got there, again, we were the only white people. And she was fine until someone started shooting a gun off for fun. When star wide receiver Keyshawn Johnson heard the shots, he planted a stiff arm in my chest like a Heisman pose and started the stampede to the parking lot. This was not from the world my girlfriend/future wife was used to. Nor from mine. But what was becoming my world was being as comfortable hanging with a white player like Sean LaChapelle as I was hanging with black players like Keyshawn or J. J. Stokes.

When Stokes broke Sean's all-time UCLA receiving record, he was a natural for us to sign. We were starting to gain enough credibility that giving him money wasn't the key. In fact, he made it clear he didn't want or need money. We were trying to get him to come out as a junior and we said, if you stay another year, how will you be financially and he said he'd be fine, he was only considering coming out early so he could play pro ball sooner.

One player just led to another, from Sean to J. J. to defensive backs Carl Greenwood and Othello Henderson, to offensive guard Matt Soenksen, to tailback Chris Alexander, defensive tackle Bruce Walker, and offensive tackle Vaughn Parker. First of the month, like a deliveryman, we paid whoever was on our payroll. We paid Ryan Fein, the UCLA quarterback. He transferred to Idaho and so did our payments. Bruce Walker was arrested for firing a gun in L.A., and later pleaded nolo contendere to disturbing the peace. Guess who was his bail-maker. Me. Guess who got Jonathan Ogden, star UCLA left tackle, tickets to a Janet Jackson concert. Me. He didn't take our money but he took the tickets. I'll never forget his high-pitched shrieking, "Jan-et! Jan-et!," like a teenage girl . . . a six-foot nine-inch, 345-pound teenage girl.

Trusting a College Coach: Big Mistake

In the midst of pursuing J. J. we got a call from Frank Stephens from the UCLA athletic department arranging a meeting with Terry Donahue, the Bruins head coach. I was kind of nervous but also was excited that Terry Donahue knew who I was. Frank was a guy Doc knew pretty well, and I suspected he might have a connection to Marvin Demoff, one of the marquee agents of the time (a guy whose path we would cross many times). Coach Donahue said, "Josh, you're the biggest threat to the well-being of my football program in all my years of coaching here." He said it had hurt the program when Jamir Miller had come out as an underclassman and it would hurt if J. J. came out. I wasn't sure how to feel about this. He was calling me out, as if I were in the principal's office, but he was also acknowledging that I'd become a factor to be reckoned with. He said to me, very man-to-man, that he'd appreciate the courtesy of me backing off, not putting any more ideas in J. J.'s head about coming out in his junior year. So we backed off and J. J. stayed with the program. I thought we were doing the right thing for a coach who was trying to do the right thing. I never made that mistake again.

Doc and I had done right by UCLA players, getting them drafted high and signing them to good deals. And we'd done right by Coach Donahue, not meddling with his star receiver's senior season. But despite our cooperation, the coach did nothing to reciprocate. Under Donahue, J. J. never talked to us again, and he later signed with another agent. Looking back, I guess I could chalk the whole incident up to a bad break or chance. Maybe Donahue played no part in J. J.'s decision, was never asked and never offered an opinion. Or maybe J. J., who'd been open to talking to us, woke up one day and decided not to. I *might* say it was just chance if it weren't for the Othello Henderson story, which had happened two years earlier but which I didn't learn about until much later. Henderson, a safety, had agreed to work with us and announced he was going to come out as an underclassman. (We had signed him early with a postdated contract, effective as soon as he was draft-eligible. It wasn't by the book, but by the time Donahue got involved we were officially Othello's agents.) After Othello declared himself for the draft, Terry Donahue called him into his office and introduced him to Marvin Demoff, essentially putting his stamp of approval on Demoff as an agent. We were recognized as Othello's agents of record but his coach was now presenting his own guy— very inappropriate, to say the least.

Why would a coach influence who his players sign with

after they've given up college eligibility? Sometimes it's because coaches have their favored agents. Sometimes the agent is the coach's agent. Sometimes the agent is a friend. Sometimes the agent is powerful. And sometimes, I can only assume, there might even be money or favors exchanged. Am I saying Donahue got something out of the deal? No, I have no way of knowing that. I'm just saying everybody is a commodity; everything and everyone has a price, whether it's dollars and cents or something less tangible.

After I did my *Sports Illustrated* agent exposé in 2010, Othello told his hometown newspaper the way things were back then.

(excerpts from online article)

ON THE TAKE: FORMER ELLISON STAR ADMITS HE TOOK MONEY FROM SPORTS AGENTS

Posted On: Monday, Oct. 18, 2010, 10:43 P.M.
By Alex Byington, *Killeen Daily Herald*

After last week's *Sports Illustrated* cover story named him as one of 30 student-athletes who allegedly took money from former professional sports agent Josh Luchs, Henderson said he hopes current high school and college players can learn from his mistakes.

"I wasn't breaking the law, I was breaking NCAA rules that nobody agrees with," Henderson said. "But in rebuttal to that, I was doing the wrong thing, because I knew I was doing wrong."

While still in college at UCLA, the former Ellison football and track standout said he jeopardized his amateur status with the NCAA by accepting thousands of dollars and other benefits—not just from Luchs, but from multiple agents.

"Once you put your hand in the candy jar, and you realize that candy is rotten, you can't pull it out when you're in college, because you're risking your college eligibility," Henderson said.

"If you always feel like you can win, then sometimes that's a negative," Henderson said. "It starts to feel like you're invincible. (Everyone is) pretty much telling you, everything you do is good, and anything you touch is gold."

Over a six-to-eight-month period between the end of his sophomore year and the end of his junior season (May through December 1992), Henderson estimated he took monthly payments of a "few hundred dollars just to get by" from more than one agent.

"I don't remember who introduced me to (Luchs), but within the first conversation, it was, 'If you need money, I got you [taken care of],'" Henderson said.

"I wasn't in a situation where I could call my mom and be like, 'Hey mom, I need like $500,'" Henderson said. "... It's not like I was born with a silver spoon in my mouth, and I could call and ask for 5, 6, $700."

For most student-athletes, tuition payments and on-campus housing represent the bulk of their athletic scholarships. However, the NCAA doesn't allow student-athletes to seek employment during the school year, a fact that Henderson said played into his decision to take money.

"At 17, 18 years old, you've got a one-track mind, and if I got bills to pay, if I need money in my pocket, I'm looking to get that money," Henderson said. "I don't break any laws to get it, but I'm going to find out an avenue to do it."

"Agents have been giving kids money for decades," Luchs wrote in the article. "It was more open in the 1960s, '70s, and '80s, before states passed sports-agent laws making it illegal. Now, agents still do it, but they are more secretive and use middlemen."

Henderson agreed with Luchs on the prevalence, both back in the early 1990s when he was in school, and now, stating he believes that up to 90 percent of college athletes are getting money under the table.

"When you compare your stories in the league (NFL), it was like everybody else was doing the same thing," he said.

We had investments in players, paying them, bailing them out, picking up tabs, whatever it took, flaunting NCAA regulations. But Doc rationalized, "We ain't members of the NCAA. These aren't our rules." And since we were hardly alone in what we were doing, we'd go to almost any lengths to keep our prospects away from the competition.

After LaChapelle, I had other players living with me in my townhouse. It was a good way to bond with them and our best way to shield them from other agents. We'd been paying Carl Greenwood for a while so I had him in the upstairs

bedroom of my townhouse, and at the same time I had Darick Holmes from Portland State with his baby and his baby's
momma living downstairs. (Darick named all of his babies after himself, à la George Foreman.) It was just easier this way;
despite the NFLPA rules against soliciting players from other
agents, the competition was always lurking. High-profile
agent Drew Rosenhaus has been accused of stealing players
from other agents for years but nothing has ever been proven.
He claims the players come to him because their agents have
done a lousy job (though his own book is titled *A Shark Never
Sleeps*). Either all those other agents are miraculously innocent or the rule is hard to enforce. In any case, we had an investment to protect.

We concentrated on UCLA but we also tracked down players with any ties to the L.A. area. We'd landed Chris Mims, a
local kid who was a defensive end at Tennessee, and paid him
$500 or so per month, plus we paid a high school coach who
helped us get to him, all worth it since Mims was taken by the
Chargers in the first round. We paid Greg Thomas out of Colorado and Delon Washington from USC and they signed with
us. We also paid Joel Steed at Colorado and Travis Claridge at
USC but they didn't sign with us. The cost of doing business.

Around this same time, there was Rob Waldrop, a nose
tackle for Arizona in what was called the "Desert Swarm Defense." We paid him, too, even though he later denied it. But
recruiting him and getting to the point of paying him was
one of the more "colorful" adventures of my young agent life.
Rob was short and squat, not an ideal example of what the
league wanted; but he still won an Outland Trophy (awarded
to the best interior lineman in the NCAA) in 1993. In his ju-

nior year, I went to meet with him, waiting outside the athletic facility, waiting to stumble on him like I'd gotten good at doing, talking my way into his apartment. That's where I saw two things that were indelible: his enormous white ass and the apartment's black wall. When I got there, he'd just gotten out of the shower and was talking to me while lying on his stomach, naked, with his incredibly huge, incredibly white ass sticking up in the air like a planet, while we were carrying on what was supposed to be a conversation about how I could help with his future. And then I heard BOOM! BOOM! BOOM! from the living room. His roommates were driving golf balls into the wall they'd painted black, leaving little white holes all over the wall. They asked me if I wanted to take a couple swings but I declined. The wall looked like black Swiss cheese. They were not getting their damage deposit back. The next thing I knew, they asked me to go with them in one guy's pickup truck to what amounted to a sex shop, where they planned to watch naked dancers and jerk off. Again, I declined to participate. I would do *almost* anything to recruit Rob Waldrop, Outland Trophy winner.

Eventually I convinced him to come see us in L.A. and, took him to Raiders camp to show him the guys I knew, and by then, we were paying him. On the way to training camp in Oxnard, I got pulled over for speeding and I was totally paranoid. I thought somehow the cops were going to write up the ticket and it would go into some kind of giant database that went straight to the NFLPA and they'd know an agent had a college player in his car, they'd know everything. It was total paranoia, irrational but terrifying, because I knew what I was doing was wrong and I'd be found out. In the end, Waldrop didn't sign with us. He said he didn't "feel comfortable" enough. He was comfortable enough to talk to me with his white orb of an ass in the air, drive golf balls through a wall, and take me to a jerk-off club. But that line, or some variation of it, was what all the players used. "I'm not comfortable." "I need to go a different direction." "I have to do what's best for me and my family." Stock lines out of a bad script. Still, when he turned pro, he paid us back the money we had loaned him.

In fact, almost all of the players we later lost to other agents ended up paying us back, either with bonus money from the team that signed them or with money from their new agents. There was a notable exception.

Then the Rules Changed

In 1999, the NFLPA said if a player took money from an agent while in college but that payment was revealed during or after college, the player did not have to repay the money. It was an odd rule to make, considering the NFLPA didn't allow players to take money; but it goes to show just how obvious it was that everyone was getting paid. From that point forward, agents lost their threat of suing for the money. Once a player finished his final college season, he was off the hook. It was like amnesty for the players. We had loaned money to R. Jay Soward, wide receiver from USC, who started his college career with a four-touchdown game against UCLA but had a rocky path after that, literally almost getting killed by the USC Trojan mascot horse while gesturing to the crowd at halftime, falling into a daily marijuana habit, and selling the weed for more extra cash. R. Jay's father knew the rules, so when it came time to enter the NFL draft, his father told us he was not only going with another agent, but he wasn't paying us any of the fifteen grand we had advanced R. Jay. By then, Doc was going downhill physically and we just let it go. Despite his troubles on and off the field, R. Jay was drafted in the first round by the Jacksonville Jaguars. But along the way, he had apparently taken money from other guys too—agents or agents' runners—who didn't swallow losses as easily as we did. He told me he'd once been threatened in the Jaguars' parking lot by a scary guy with a scary weapon, sent by a very prominent agent with a simple message: "Pay the money now or I'll blow your fucking face off." Rule change or not, they got their money.

All in all, it was pretty rare that a player would just flat-out turn money down, but it happened. It happened with J. J. Stokes and Keyshawn Johnson, USC wide receiver and number-one overall draft pick. It happened big-time with Dana Stubblefield, Kansas defensive tackle and first-round pick. I put $10,000 cash money on the table in front of him and he shook his head, no thanks. (What he said to other agents' money, I don't know.) And it happened with Michigan State star wide receiver Derrick Mason, who we'd connected with after representing his former teammate, quarterback Tony Banks. We bought Mason a plane ticket to come see us between his junior and senior seasons. When I went to meet his plane, he was a no-show. Derrick had never boarded; I wasn't able to get hold of him again, and we were out the price of a ticket. But for every Dana, J. J., or Derrick who said no to us, there were ten who'd take it and connect us with ten more.

So, my time with Doc was like going to grad school day and night, my in-the-field, on-the-road education. Doc was a big man, not only in size but in impact and stature. And he was quirky. He had very bad knees and would carry a huge massager with him because if he didn't rub his knees for a half hour every day, he couldn't move. And he rubbed some heinous white ointment on his bald head every morning. I don't know what it was supposed to do—grow his hair back, maybe—but it smelled awful, like funky ass. And he had this thing with hotel maids. He had his own definition of "room service." He thought maids were there to service him. He'd be sitting in his underwear on the edge of the bed—all six-seven, four hundred pounds of him—when the housekeeper came in, and he'd strike up a conversation. "Hi Baby. You married? Does your man treat you right? You get good lovin'?" Then he'd motion for me to leave the room. I think he slept with a maid in every hotel on every campus we visited. He was married, technically, but not living with his wife, and living with another woman he called his wife. His relationships with women were "fluid."

One time, at the Senior Bowl in Mobile, while Doc was enjoying "room service," I was in the hotel lobby on the house phone trying to call a player when another agent, Terry Bolar, came up and punched me right in the face. Bolar was a big black man, a former linebacker with the Oilers, who had worked with Doc as an agent and had been repped by him as a player. No warning, nothing, just pow! He smacked me in the face. He said, "Stay the fuck away from my players." Several thoughts careened through my rattling brain: 1) This guy may kick the shit out of me in a lobby full of players, which won't make me look too good; 2) This is Alabama and even if it's the early 1990s, it's not a great place to be black; 3) It's not a great place to be a Jew, either, so I'd better be careful; and 4)

I should just walk, or stagger, away. When I got up to our room, Doc was finished with his business and noticed my fat lip, and I told him what had happened. Doc went down, found Terry, and took a walk with him. I don't know what Doc said, but Terry came up and apologized, and then for the rest of the week he bought me breakfast and lunch, drove me to the practice field, whatever I needed.

On the plane ride home, I asked Doc what he had said to Terry. "I told him, nobody fucks with my Jew-boy. He's my Jew-boy." And he added, "And I told him your father is a doctor for the Mafia and he already made some phone calls and I didn't know if I could help him." I laughed my ass off. It was funny. But more than that, it showed Doc's loyalty. He had my back and I could trust him completely. So could his players. We worked on a handshake for ten years. And I was paid every penny I was owed. Even much later, after we went our separate ways in business, if there was a payment from a player we'd signed together, I always got my share.

Say what you want about Doc's practices with the NCAA rules—he always looked out for me, and unlike a lot of other football people, he never tried to screw me.

CHAPTER 5

Sudden Death

Doc and I were together through so much, even the illnesses and deaths of both of my parents. My mother had been sick on and off for ten years after a kidney transplant and rejection, and ultimately an infection that attached itself to her heart. Finally, she was in intensive care for four months and Doc and his mother, who was a preacher, would pray for my mom every morning. She died on the operating table and even then, I kept thinking she'd be okay because somehow she'd always been okay. Not this time. Then my father got sick, and Doc was there for me again. My father's death was almost too much, coming so close to my mother's. He died within days of my first Mother's Day without her. Unlike her death, his came fast. After years of practicing medicine, my father, the lifelong scholar, decided to go back to school at night to earn a law degree, to supplement his understanding of medical-legal issues and fight the HMOs. But soon after, he was diagnosed with an inoperable, malignant brain tumor.

It was an awful, crazy, emotional, horrible time. I'd be on three days, staying at his house, then my sister would be on for three, each of us taking him for chemo and radiation, and me trying to juggle these players who needed constant coddling.

There were two incidents I'll never forget. One day I was driving to pick my father up to take him to UCLA for treatment, in my Range Rover, stuck in traffic, and I acted in a way I never had in my life and never have since. A guy in a Mercedes kept edging up as the lanes merged, almost sideswiping my door, coming to a stop within inches of my car. I yelled out, "Hey, back off," and his college-age kid next to him rolled down the window and said, " Fuck your mother." Not the right member of my family to pick on, especially when I was on my way to be with my dying father. This put me over the edge. I lost it. I put my car in park, jumped on the guy's hood, pounded on the windshield, and threatened to beat the shit out of his kid, who had jumped in the back seat out of my reach, while the father yelled at him never to say anything like that. I took a breath, somehow cooled down, and got back in my car thinking, *Josh, what's wrong with you? You're out of control. Now you're screwed. Somebody's going to see that and report you.* I was doing my best to keep it together for my dad and I guess the pressure was just too much.

The other incident I remember was taking my father to make rounds at the hospital, at his sickest but still determined to see his patients, then to his office, then for his own treatments. I happened to have picked up $7,500 in cash, in a gym bag, from a player who paid us back money he owed and it was in the trunk of my father's Lexus, which I was driving

him around in. We turned down a street and there was a police barricade where they were doing random searches. They
asked me for my driver's license and it was expired. I told
them I was taking my father for chemo treatments; I had just
buried my mother in October, right after my birthday in September when I should've gotten my license renewed; and
I promised to go right to the DMV afterward, but the cop
wasn't buying it. He made me get out of the car, and he called
a tow truck to take our car away, at which point my sick father practically threw himself on the hood of his car, yelling
at the cops that he needed it to get to the cancer center. He
said they'd have to shoot him to take our car since he was a
dead man anyway (maybe jumping on car hoods is genetic). I
calmed my father down, sitting on the curb as they towed the
car, and we waited for the nurse from his office to come and
take him to UCLA for his treatment.

I went to the DMV and got a new license; my dad called
his friend at the police department to get our car released
from impound, and we got it back . . . minus a gym bag full of
$7,500 in cash. Worse yet, it wasn't my money. It was money I
owed Doc. As usual, Doc understood. And it all seemed minor compared to what my father was going through. Despite
the most aggressive treatments, with trips back and forth to
Duke Medical Center where pioneer work was being done,
he died within weeks of attending a special graduation arranged by the law school because they knew he wasn't likely
to be alive for the regular ceremony. My father had signed a
DNR—Do Not Resuscitate—order and after what had happened with my mother, we didn't try to fight it. His valiant
fight for life and for his degree were written up in several
newspapers. And Doc was with me through it all.

(Jewish) Boy Meets (Jewish) Girl

I was an orphan at age twenty-seven, too old to need a legal guardian but too much of a kid to deal with life on my own. Then came Jennifer. But neither of my parents lived to meet her. It pained me to think my mother would never know the woman who would become my wife and moral compass. Jennifer is the person my mother would have created for me if she could have—smart, grounded, beautiful—and the first Jewish girl I'd ever dated. I met her at a birthday party for a mutual friend. I was with someone else and the scene played out like a corny movie: she walked in and it was as if a spotlight hit her. The music played, and I was done, finished, off the market. Up to that time, when it came to girls, I'd been focused on such admirable goals as sleeping with a member of every pro team's cheering squad and I was well on my way. Like the Rams cheerleader who came by my parents' house one Father's Day and I wouldn't let her change out of her uniform—short skirt and fishnet stockings—because I wanted to show her off. Plus the Hooters girls. And the actresses and models and various hook-ups. Ah yes, in search of deep and meaningful one-night stands.

Jennifer was different, and I was different with her; she was my true partner. I met her family and passed the entrance exam . . . barely. I moved out of my bachelor townhouse/motel, where girlfriends and jock groupies had checked in and out (Adam Baratta, a pretty-boy actor, was one of the great wingmen and sources of beautiful girls in history, and he'd been living in my basement). Football players stopped by like it was an ATM for their monthly "allowances." Now the players stopped by my wife's place for their money, including the aptly named Phalen Pounds, the four-hundred-pound lineman from USC who made the floor shake. By this time, Doc's health was failing. The big intimidating force I had known was literally shrinking and faltering. Still, he stood by my side throughout the wedding, a long, traditional ceremony. From then on, Jennifer began to help me shape a new direction. Life was finally changing. I knew one day it would mean leaving Doc, but not yet.

Wanted: Quarterbacks

I was working with Doc, recruiting, handling a lot of defensive players, and we realized we had to broaden our representation. Kids or their parents would ask us what other running backs or quarterbacks we represented, as if there was something different about making a deal for them. Top agents, then as now, are associated with quarterbacks. At one time or another, Steinberg, Demoff, and Condon represented Steve Bartkowski, Mark Brunell, Steve Young, Troy Aikman, Warren Moon, John Elway, Dan Marino, Ben Roethlisberger, Peyton Manning, and Chad Pennington.

We needed a quarterback. Several years earlier, Doc had signed star USC linebacker Chip Banks, who went on to play for the Browns. Chip's nephew was Tony Banks, a kid from San Diego and the Michigan State quarterback. Doc set me up to meet Tony in East Lansing. I did my usual drill, working his need for extra cash into the conversation, letting him get interested, and eventually paying him. He was in his last year at MSU and was invited to the collegiate All-Star games. The most prestigious of these is the Senior Bowl, which is coached by NFL staff and attended by many NFL scouts and personnel people. If we wanted Tony, a talented QB, to crack the first round, the Senior Bowl was key.

Tony was involved with a girl in northern California at that time and she wanted him to play in the East-West Shrine Game, not far from her. We just wanted him in the Senior Bowl, fresh and healthy. Against our advice, he wanted to play in the Shrine Game first; we said okay, but get on a plane right after and get to Mobile in time for practice for the Senior Bowl too. But after the Shrine Game ended, we couldn't find him. He was out with his girlfriend, hanging with her family and friends. He was one of the only guys in the country picked to play quarterback at the Senior Bowl and he was a no-show. Steve Hale, who ran the Senior Bowl, was livid. So was I. I was so furious that Doc had to calm me down and remind me the most important thing was keeping the client— we would just have to deal with it. Tony had played well in the East-West game, which helped his cause, but he still fell short of the first round. He was picked in the second by the Rams, the first quarterback of the 1996 draft, but had probably cost himself a million dollars. That's an expensive weekend.

But we did everything we could for Tony, even giving up our marketing commission to put him into something called the Quarterback Club, a marketing organization that arranged group licensing deals for star quarterbacks like John Elway, Dan Marino, and—we hoped—Tony Banks. Still, he told Doc maybe he needed more of a "quarterback agent," someone who could get the big deal done. I kept saying, what else could somebody do for him? Doc knew the answer. If we didn't want to lose him, we needed to find that known "quarterback agent" before he did. Doc had a connection to Marvin Demoff, who represented Marino, Elway, and other superstars and had an office in west L.A. Our plan was to deliver Tony Banks to him and share the commission. Getting 33 percent of something was better than 100 percent of nothing. We made a handshake deal, like mine with Doc; no written contract. And of course, it wasn't long before Doc and I were out of the deal, handshake or not, and Tony Banks was exclusively a Demoff client.

The postscript on Tony was a classic case of what-if. A few years later, Tony was released by the Rams, Trent Green was made the starter, and an unknown Arena Football League player named Kurt Warner was brought in as his backup. When Green tore his ACL (anterior cruciate ligament), Warner stepped in and had one of the great breakout seasons in football history. He took the team to the Super Bowl and retired ten years later as a football legend. What if that had been Tony Banks? And what if I'd been his agent?

Ryan Leaf: Coulda, Woulda, Shoulda

Where Tony was a what-if, Ryan Leaf was an almost. That word says a lot about him—almost a client, almost a great player, but not quite. He was the Washington State University quarterback, a Heisman Trophy finalist, and one of the two highest-rated players in his draft year. The other one was Peyton Manning. One became a superstar; the other became a punch-line for jokes. What went wrong? It's a sad, complicated story but one incident puts it in perspective.

I'd paid my dues, literally, to get inside the program at

Washington State. We were picking up the tab on Torey Hunter, Singor Mobley, John Rushing, all defensive backs, and Leon Bender, a defensive lineman. Word was, if you need extra money, call Josh Luchs. Ryan got the word. I had my first meeting with him at a hotel near the campus, just after his sophomore season, just before his career was going to take off. Right away, he let me know he'd run up a big credit card bill, around $5,000. One thing I knew by then: Don't pay it all off. That would bring our nonrelationship to a fast halt: he'd have what he needed, and he'd have no more use for me. I asked him how much he'd need month to month to "make life a little easier." About $500, he said. I considered that a bargain for a guy with Ryan's star-potential; he was in the running to be the next number-one overall draft pick. We stepped into my office, the bathroom of the hotel, and he signed a rep agreement, undated, and a loan agreement. Then I started getting monthly money orders to him, usually around $500. And we established what I thought was a good relationship, him at age twenty, me at twenty-six, a cross between friend, big brother, advisor, and an ATM. He and other players would come to my place in L.A., raid the beer, soda, and steaks in my fridge, play my video games, and party with great-looking L.A. girls. It was heady stuff for Ryan, a boy from Great Falls, Montana, population 50,000, give or take.

Sometime before what would turn out to be Ryan's last college season, 1997, he and I were sitting in a Jacuzzi, smoking cigars, contemplating the good life that was sure to un-fold for him. He told me a story about having just been to the *Playboy* All-American photo shoot. Leaf and Manning, along with a slew of other top-rated football players, were waited on hand and foot, fed a banquet, and generally treated like royalty. And then there was the after-partying—unofficial, unsanctioned, and unpublicized. But Ryan told me that Peyton Manning hadn't partied. He had dinner, socialized a bit, and then said he wanted to "get some shut-eye." Ryan couldn't believe this country bumpkin could go to bed when the parties were just getting started. I remember thinking, this Manning sounds like a pretty solid guy, surprisingly mature and grounded for a guy who is being worshipped everywhere he goes. And I remember thinking, too bad Ryan didn't seem to have that discipline. But . . . he was going to sign with us, and he had a world of talent, so he was my guy. I just hoped the Playboy event wasn't a glimpse of the future, of the difference in two promising players. When the time came, Ryan would step up.

As good as our relationship was, it was always like dating a diva. One wrong move and you could be frozen out. Case in point: a week-long binge in Las Vegas with Ryan when I didn't pick up the tab for the two backup QBs he'd brought along, Steve Birnbaum and Dave Muir. I didn't mind spending money on this kind of thing, but these guys weren't potential clients, just Ryan's sycophants. I made a lot of risky loans, but if I hadn't limited myself to possible stars, I would've been broke in a week flat. But Ryan didn't like it. Despite the girls, the drinks, the meals, and the bad behavior I enabled, nothing I did was enough. I could tell on the ride back that I had offended the diva and jeopardized our future together. Plus, around the same time, we began to hear rumors that Ryan's coach was pushing him to sign with Leigh Steinberg.

The only guy in the business whose client list could hold a

candle to Steinberg's was Marvin Demoff. And this was during the time we were corepresenting Tony Banks with Marvin, but before he cut us out; so Doc suggested we bring Demoff in on Ryan Leaf as well. Again, it wasn't what we wanted, but a piece of something was better than all of nothing.

I was supposed to fly out to Montana with Demoff to meet Ryan's father and get his final blessing on the deal. I'd been selling Marvin hard to Ryan and his family. This was a very stressful time for me, given that I was still dealing with my father's death while spending every spare minute with Ryan. But, at the end, he had even gone with me one day and told my dying father he could be at peace knowing, "Josh doesn't need to recruit any other players. He's got me." Ryan seemed to be on board with Demoff. Then, at the last minute, Marvin bailed out on the trip. Why? He thought he had a good shot at landing Peyton Manning and didn't want to risk that by meeting with Ryan Leaf. So, suddenly, we were screwed. Doc decided to go with me but he was really out of place in redneck, outdoorsy, woodsy, very white Montana. We were done. I kept paying Ryan, even meeting up with him before the Rose Bowl. I went into the bathroom, checked to see the stalls were empty, and gave him his $500 for the month, but he could barely look at me.

Ryan Leaf ended up signing with Leigh Steinberg. Peyton Manning signed with Tom Condon of IMG. If it sounds like agents have no loyalty, no scruples, no rules, and just chase the hottest skirt in the room, you've got it.

Ryan announced he was coming out after his junior year, after his school's first Conference championship and Rose Bowl appearance in sixty-seven years. I saw him on television, having been picked number two, right behind Manning, by the Chargers. I'd like to say that I knew way back then, in the Jacuzzi, that this guy was going to be a bust in the NFL, but I didn't. I thought he was in the mold of hard-partying quarterbacks like Joe Namath or Kenny Stabler, superstars who had a good time. Sure, I had a little nagging feeling about him, but mostly I just wished he'd signed with us.

One thing I will say about Ryan: he paid us back most of the money we gave him, roughly $10,000. We had represented Chris Mims with the Chargers and a couple of others on the roster so I asked Chris to tell Ryan I was coming to collect the money he owed us. He came out and saw me and I told him we had some unfinished business. He gave me a kind of embarrassed look and we walked to his car and he handed me a stack of money. But it was short. Maybe he thought I wouldn't count it. So we drove to a gas station with an ATM and he gave me some more, not quite all, but . . . *almost*.

He lasted less than four years in the NFL and never did hold down a starting job. As of this writing, Peyton Manning is in his fourteenth season, well on his way to the Hall of Fame. So what happened to Ryan Leaf? Was it a poor work ethic? Immaturity? A shoulder injury? Or all of those factors? And why? No one really cares, sadly—not the NCAA, not the NFL, not the NFLPA—because he failed, and in American sports nobody wants to be associated with that. He remains, to this day, probably the biggest draft bust of all time.

I learned a lot that year. I'd grown up, literally, having lost my parents. I'd had some rude awakenings, from Ryan Leaf's false promise to my dying father that I was his agent . . . to watching him on TV next to Leigh Steinberg announcing he was entering the draft . . . to Damien Covington, a Buffalo Bills linebacker who we paid when he was broke during the off-season, asking me for still more money, for a nicer apartment, *while* I was caring for my failing father. And let us not forget offensive lineman Travis Claridge, whose fiancée, Tiffany, coldheartedly bragged of shopping the USC roster for a player likely to make it in the pros (which he did); and when we advised him to have a prenuptial agreement, she convinced him not to sign with us. This was the life I'd chosen. Heady and exciting—sometimes. Self-absorbed and infantile—often. Soul-eating—daily. There wasn't one aha moment. There were a thousand of them. Something had to change. When I married Jennifer, I knew it was the beginning of that change. Together, we set a new course. The business I'd known was evolving fast, becoming more sophisticated, more polished, with higher stakes, and on a whole new level of competition. It was time to stop working out of the trunk of Doc's car, hustling for every chance I had. It was time to clean up my life. And time to have the toughest conversation of my life.

CHAPTER 6

Post-Doc: Doing Things Less Wrong

My wife was running a movie theater for her family and I used to stop by and show the kids who worked there how to "up-sell" on the concessions. "Would you like a large drink for twenty cents more with that jumbo popcorn?" "Have you tried our nachos? It's a pretty long movie." It was as far from the sports world as I could get so that's where I asked Doc to meet me to discuss our future. But it wasn't really a discussion, it was a decision, the most difficult one I'd ever made. He showed up with a young girl he was seeing, so we asked her to wait in the theater and went off to talk. I told him I had something difficult to say and I think he knew what was coming. I said I'd loved working with him but I had to take my life in a different direction. (I guess I sounded a little like the players and their clichés telling us why they'd decided to go with another agent.) I was married, about to raise a family. I had to make this change. I told him I loved him. He nodded and said he understood. And we both cried.

I had been talking to Gary Wichard, by then one of the bigger agents in the business, to see if he had a place for me in his company. I'd met him at the Senior Bowl, which was like the annual convention for agents—you could meet anyone, do business in hotel lobbies, discuss trade secrets, spin stories, and maybe make your next career move. Gary was in the lounge of the hotel, sitting at the table next to me, talking to the mother of Darren Howard, a defensive end out of Kansas State who was going to be in the 2000 draft. I had already been thinking about which agents it made sense to hook up with. I wanted someone who would value my ability to recruit on the West Coast and Gary was at the top of my list. Even though his office was in Pacific Palisades, ten minutes from UCLA, he had few to no West Coast clients. His players were from places like Syracuse, Oklahoma, all over the place really—except in his own backyard. I'd studied Gary and I knew I could fill a void in his business. In fact, I collected marketing material from other agents, stuff other players would throw away, all part of my obsessive research—names, addresses, client lists, anything I might need someday.

I leaned over to Darren's mother, right in front of Gary, and told her how fortunate she was to be working with such a great agent—Gary Wichard. I regurgitated his own marketing pitch from his printed promos, complimenting him more effusively than he could himself—an A.P. All-American quarterback out of C.W. Post College, who was drafted by the Colts; Seahawks linebacker Brian Bosworth, Cardinals receiver Rob Moore, Pro Bowl tight end Keith Jackson; his role in pioneering free agency—all parts of Gary's spiel. I wasn't trying to sell Gary to Mrs. Howard; I was selling Josh Luchs to Gary. Then I got up and said good-bye. I didn't say a word to him the rest of the week of the Senior Bowl.

But when I got back to Los Angeles, I called and asked if we could talk about a big move I might make. I sat in Gary's office overlooking the ocean, with his framed articles, pictures with players, and awards everywhere, all very impressive. And he knocked Doc as we talked, saying Doc was a dinosaur, an old-time hustler at best, ill-equipped to land big-name players in the modern game. I explained to him I'd been selling Doc more than myself because I was a kid in my twenties and the best way to build myself was to build on someone else. He acknowledged I had been able to get some good players. "You've been hitting singles with a twig for a bat," he told me. "If you were selling me, you'd have a real piece of lumber. Let's see what you could do then." He was cautious, saying I'd have to meet John Blake, the guy he referred to as his "partner," which eventually turned out to be a subject of controversy. Much later Blake would become defensive line coach at the University of North Carolina. And then, later still, he resigned from that job after—guess what—being accused of funneling clients to Gary Wichard (his former partner?) in exchange for money. None of this had happened at the time, though. I was just making a career move, and meeting a future colleague.

I spent the afternoon with Blake and it was great. He had a Super Bowl ring for coaching the defensive line for the 1993 Cowboys; he was the former head coach at Oklahoma; and he was an incredibly persuasive communicator. I could sell this guy. What a mentor he'd be for players, working on technique, going over game films, grading their skills, telling them how the pros were going to size them up. Instead of having to give a kid money, I could give him something better: John Blake. He could be worth a fortune to a kid's career. And we hit it off right away. Gary dragged his feet but finally agreed to take me on to start recruiting. He made it clear from the start that he didn't recruit the traditional way, cold-calling, going to games, hanging out in tunnels. He had relationships with coaches, assistants, and trainers who were influential with players and created a pipeline for him. And he had been a Heisman Trophy candidate (even if he only got one vote) and had the ballot hanging on his wall. He made it clear he wouldn't be associated with giving money to players. He referred to other agents as "scumbags" and "slapdicks" and said he'd never do the things they did to get a client. (Of course, his "pipelines" from coaches and agents were every bit as improper as paying college kids, but he didn't see it that way, at least until he was investigated for it.) He was closing 40 to 50 percent of the players he talked to, way above the 10 percent I was used to. Gary said I had talent and ability but needed to be "completely reprogrammed" to do things his way, which was fine with me.

I didn't get an office. Gary had a guy, Mike Sasson, trying to build a baseball business, and Jeff Friedman, a PR and marketing guy, plus John Blake, and they each had offices and paychecks. Not me. I made my calls from the conference room, a step up from the trunk of Doc's car, and I didn't get a salary or benefits. I got 25 percent of anybody we signed who was in the Pacific and Mountain time zones, except for Utah, where Gary had some history and a contact in the football program. If I got somebody from farther east, it was on a player-by-player basis and had to be approved by Gary ahead of time. I was going from 50 percent of the commissions down to 25, but I also knew that Doc's style of doing business was on its way out so my cut could soon be 50 percent of very little. Marvin Demoff had taken Tony Banks, and he would've taken Ryan Leaf if he'd had the chance. Leigh Steinberg was the king of quarterbacks, IMG was the sports rep powerhouse, and Octagon had reinvented sports marketing. The era of Doc Daniels types was coming to an end.

And Doc himself was coming to the end. He got very sick in the next year, developing an infection in his leg, and kept traveling anyway. Between trips he'd go to the hospital for treatment and I visited him pretty regularly. He kept deteriorating and was ultimately put into the ICU. The day I was to go to my first Senior Bowl with Gary, I got a call from Doc's first wife, Patricia, who I barely knew, to tell me Doc had died. I was supposed to leave for Mobile, Alabama, for what amounts to the second most important event of the football year, just behind the draft. That year we had Willie Howard from Stanford and Adam Archuleta from Arizona State, plus Todd Heap, who wasn't playing because he was still a junior. But there was Doc's funeral. I thought about what he'd have told me to do . . . and I got on the plane to Mobile for the game. He'd have told me to take care of myself and take care of my players.

As soon as I got back from the Senior Bowl, I went to the cemetery and had my own private memorial for Doc. I put flowers at his gravesite and reflected on our time together, as unlikely a pair as there had ever been. I'd never had a friend like him and may never again. I thanked him for his love and guidance. And I said good-bye to him.

Doc took care of me right up to his last days. Even beyond. A couple days after he died, I got an envelope with a check for $16,000, my share of the commission for Carlos Jenkins, who'd been a veteran free agent we signed with the Rams. I'd never met Jenkins but we'd signed him when I was Doc's fifty-fifty partner, so I got the payment even after Doc was gone. And, in all my time with Doc, we never had a written contract between us, just a handshake. You could say he taught me how to do things wrong, like paying players, or you could say he taught me how to do things right, like being fair. Nobody else I worked with treated me like Doc did. I learned that the hard way.

Pro Tect Management:
Gary Wichard's Way of Doing Business

At this point, I was working with Gary at his company, Pro Tect Management. No more greasing palms to buy players' loyalty. I was learning to do business the way I imagined big-time NFL agents did it, more respectably, maybe not exactly right, but at least less wrong . . . if there is such a thing. Right away, I coupled Gary's reputation and approach with my local skills to get us meetings with Pac 10 players, West Coast players, any kid who called California home. They were all untapped by Gary, and they were all gravy. I'd get a player on the phone and say, "Gary Wichard wants to say hello" and put them together on the speakerphone and it was working. My job was bird dog. His was pitchman and closer. I set them up; he went for the kill.

One of my first meetings for Gary was with Freddie

Mitchell, a wide receiver from UCLA who was a first-round draft pick by the Eagles. I got him on the phone and he sounded very bright, sharp, charismatic. I went to his neighborhood to pick him up. That's a violation—giving a kid transportation to meet with an agent before his eligibility—one of those things that's wrong but not *so* wrong. I had no idea what he looked like and when I got to the right place, I saw this kid on the street who looked scrawny and disheveled, almost like a homeless person. *That can't be Freddie,* I thought, but it was. I drove him to our office and we went into our routine. It was a beautiful performance.

First thing, Gary came in, introduced himself, and made some small talk, and in a couple of minutes the phone rang. Gary hit the speaker button, said hello, and there's Mel "the Viper" Kiper, the ESPN football analyst who can single-handedly put a guy on the NFL radar, just by repeating his name on the air. Gary said something like, "Hey Vipe, I'm sitting here with the best wide receiver in college football." And Kiper said, "You must be with Freddie Mitchell." That got Freddie's attention. Wow, he must've been thinking, Mel Kiper thinks I'm the best. And he's tight with these agents. Of course, it was all set up in advance. Gary would call Mel and ask him to call in at a certain time. Then he'd tell his assistant, Beth, to put Mel's call through to the conference room. Mel would talk to the player—Freddie in this case—about the season he'd had, the upcoming All-Star games, inside-football talk. He'd never say, "Hey, you ought to sign with these guys"; that would have been blatantly inappropriate. It was just an endorsement by association. *I know about you. And I know Gary. Good luck.* In fact, Gary would tell the players that he represented Mel. In what way, I'm not sure; as far as I knew, he didn't do Mel's contracts. But just saying it carried a lot of weight.

Then Gary would follow up with another call—Steve Hale, Executive Director of the Senior Bowl. Gary would say, "Steve told me he saw your last game and he wants to talk to you." And then, if the timing was right, and the player was about to be invited to the Senior Bowl, Steve would tell him, "You're going to be getting your formal invitation as soon as you get back to school." It was like a great sneak preview. Hale never said a player should sign with us. We would let them connect the dots on their own. *These guys know Mel Kiper; they know Steve Hale; they'll take care of me.*

Did Mel personally talk to other players or other agents? I don't know. In 2010, Kiper went on a variety of sports radio stations across the country, responding to allegations that he was being used by Gary Wichard. As quoted from a station in Kansas City, he said, ". . . Well, I guess I'm being used by a lot of agents. I guess in life you're used by a lot of different people without your knowledge. If that's the case so be it. I'm also not 'using' them, but I'm using them as a vehicle to get to a player and ask questions and get to know that player . . . I'm not going to cut off that avenue to get to know a kid because somebody says I'm being used." That sure doesn't sound like a denial to me.

Kiper, who is well known for his ability to rank players according to talent level, also defended his position on ESPN's *Mike and Mike Show*, saying Wichard's players were frequently drafted higher or lower than where he'd ranked them. "So, in terms of my relationship with Gary, it has allowed me to make some of the best calls, good and bad, that I've ever made in this business." Kiper has said he would advise players as to where they stood in the draft, what all-star games to attend, if they should work out at the combines—all of which is a lot like what an agent does. Still, he insists his access didn't influence his ratings and he didn't knowingly use his influence for agents. Maybe. But his ratings and analysis are broadcast nationally, over and over, and like anything that gets a lot of air time, it can eventually sink in, especially if it comes from an "expert." Fans hear it, agents hear it, and most importantly, NFL team decision-makers hear it. Let's say, they hear him repeatedly say a given player is being neglected, has great talent, and should be ranked higher. Instead of that player sneaking under the radar and getting "stolen" by a smart team, as a result of the Kiper drumbeat, maybe he gets bumped up just a little in the rankings. Let's say Mel's influence only helps move the kid up one notch. How much difference can it make? Well, if that notch is from the first pick of the second round up to the last pick of the first round, a lot. In the 2010 draft, the first pick of the second round signed for an overall average income of $1,027,500 per year versus the last pick of the first round who got $1,617,000 per year. That's a difference of almost $600,000 a year over five years, for about $3,000,000. Sprinkle that throughout the draft and Mel Kiper can be a powerful "influence" to contend with.

As for Steve Hale, sometimes we'd have players tell us they'd already heard from him, by way of another agent, that they'd been selected for the Senior Bowl. Then I'd play it down. "That agent didn't help you get invited. You earned it.

The agent just told you what you were going to find out anyway. In fact, your school's athletic department should have told you already." This last bit is true; athletic departments hold back the information because they say it distracts players from concentrating on the season. Which of course shows the players that their school is protecting the self-interest of the school and the team, not the interests of the individual kid hoping for a pro career, who could benefit from knowing where he's been invited to play. Agents like me use it as a wedge to create doubt about who's really looking out for them—evidently not their coach or college—and to demonstrate why they can trust us more. If we're the first to get the invitation info to the player, we tell him we saved the day because if the bowl doesn't know he's accepted, they may give his spot to another player. And these are the games NFL decision-makers rely on, so we've shown we're there for the player's future.

Game Plans: We're Holding Your Future in Our Hands

Whatever happened, my job was to spin it our way. That applied when we were meeting with a player who'd been pitched by other agents and in prepping what Gary called our "Game Plans." They were bound books, custom-assembled for each prospective player, laying out our plan for his future, complete with stats on him, on other players, on pro teams, and where we would almost promise he'd come out in the draft. Gary had been putting them together for years.

The books were very impressive, but telling the truth was

less important than selling the prospect. If the player ratings didn't serve our situation, we "adjusted" them. He taught me how and then I surpassed my teacher. I'd graduated from First National Bank of Player Loans to Truth Embellisher. I stretched and massaged data with the creativity of an artist. Sexy embellishment is more persuasive than dull facts. Everyone wants to believe things are better than they are. Promise a college player success in the NFL draft and you have a shot at becoming his agent. Back it up with what looks like data and case studies and you have an even better shot. Before me, Gary did it with scissors and tape. I introduced him to the magic of the computer: Internet search, copy-cut-paste, data seamlessly lifted from here, dropped over there, altered, enhanced, embellished with digital perfection.

Before we ever met with any player, I'd talk to him on the phone and send out a Pro Tect brochure and cover letter from Gary and me. The brochure was very slick, very expensive, splashed with color shots of our clients—Brian "Boz" Bosworth, Seahawk and movie star; Jason Taylor, Dolphin Pro Bowl defensive end; Keith Brooking, Cowboy Pro Bowl linebacker; Mark Gastineau, Jets Pro Bowl pass-rusher; Rob Moore, Jets wide receiver; Darren Howard, Saints and Eagles defensive end; Keith Jackson, Pro Bowl tight end; Kevin Dyson, wide receiver drafted ahead of Randy Moss; Keith Bulluck, Titans Pro Bowl linebacker; Jim Druckenmiller, 49ers first-round quarterback—plus company bios and history. I'd go back through old cover letters and make changes suited to impress the players. If it was for a safety, I'd reference defensive backs. If it was a linebacker, I'd note that we represented Bulluck or Bosworth or Ken Norton Jr. Gary was compulsive about the language in the letters, changing "a" to "the" and back again. He was a control freak, but it had been working for him.

I got us an audience with Adam Archuleta, the safety from Arizona State. I tracked down a phone number, talked to his stepfather a couple of times, and, most importantly, persuaded his mother, Vange, that it was a good idea for us to meet. Then I got Adam on the phone and put Gary on and we arranged to go to Arizona. On the same day, we'd set up meetings with Nijrell Eason, a cornerback, and Todd Heap, who was a great tight end. Todd was a junior, which these days—post–Junior Rule—would make it an NFLPA violation for us to talk to him. (The Junior Rule now stipulates agents cannot contact players until they have completed three years of college eligibility and have declared their intention to turn pro.) But in 2000, when the meeting happened, it was still legit. I had called Todd and told him we (really Gary, before I worked for him) had represented Stephen Alexander, a tight end from Oklahoma, who'd been a second-round draft pick and was having a good year with the Redskins, as well as Keith Jackson, one of the best tight ends in NFL history. Representing such talented players, at Todd's own position, really got his attention.

We had three meetings scheduled back-to-back, at the Tempe Mission Palms Hotel. Gary thought three was too many so he called Kiper on the speakerphone and said, "Mel, I have three guys—Heap, Eason, and Archuleta—and I only have time for two. Who should I skip?" Mel said, "Don't meet with Archuleta." Gary hung up the phone and told me to cancel the meeting with Adam, but I was adamant about it. We butted heads, but I kept at him until finally I got him to do it. In the end, Adam was drafted the highest of the three. I'd like to say I knew it then but I just thought he was good. And Adam ended up being very close with Gary over time.

We met with all three guys, an exhausting day in a suite, each meeting two or two and a half hours. We'd have a tray of cookies and sodas—also technically illegal—but what two-hundred-plus-pound football player could talk for two hours without something to eat or drink? And all three showed up, Todd Heap, Adam with his stepfather, and Nijrell Eason, a great turnout. Sometimes you'd schedule a meeting and just get a no-show—no reason, no call, just a player who was suddenly impossible to track down. We had a video player to run films or training tapes and we had our Game Plans.

I'd seen agents go through their pitch with players, talking about who they represented and what kinds of contracts they'd signed. But the Game Plans elevated the process to a whole other level. They made it formal, official. *Here is a bound book devoted to you. Here's your Game Plan. We focus on your position, what we can do to raise your draft stock to the maximum, how we've done it and will do it for you. Here are the stats to back up what we say.* It wasn't our word, it was written in a book . . . even though we had written the book. It was genius.

I remember the first time I saw Gary change the information to make a book look better. He took an article with a sentence he didn't like and he put white-out tape over it, cutting and pasting, and then photocopied it again. He'd hold up the final result and say, "Magically, no longer there." This was before I introduced him to the real magic of a digital OCR program—to convert a scanned image into a document you could edit. Gary wasn't good with computers, but I was good enough.

That year, of the three back-to-back meetings, we landed two—Heap and Archuleta, but not Eason. Both went high in the draft, both signed big contracts. Not bad.

The next year, capitalizing on those successes, I connected with Terrell Suggs, the defensive end/pass rusher from Arizona State, a prized prospect. His case is a real demo on how we used the Game Plans. We'd meet in a hotel room with the player's family (in Suggs's case, it was a hotel a few blocks from his school), and we would carefully walk them through the reasons they should go with us, step-by-step. At the end, Gary would hold up two Game Plan books, one in each hand. Book one was filled with data assembled by us on a former draftee who had signed with us and had a great career; and book two was filled with one who had signed elsewhere and failed. One success, one loser—which did you want to be?

For the Suggs meeting, our success story was Adam Archuleta, who, like Suggs, had played at Arizona State. Our Game Plan showed he'd been ranked to go in the fifth round by BLESTO, the NFL's first scouting organization, which was named the Lions, Eagles, Steelers Talent Organization for the teams that set it up in 1963 and was later modified to include Bears. The National Report, another prominent ranking service, projected him to go in the seventh round. But, according to our Game Plan books, Adam Archuleta made the smart move: he worked with us, worked with a strength coach and with our position coaches and nutritionist. He watched films and did drills with an NFL position coach, and he ended up being picked in the first round, by the St.

Louis Rams, who just happened to employ the very same position coach he'd worked with to prepare for the Senior Bowl and the NFL Scouting Combine. Adam signed a contract with guaranteed upfront money totaling $4.2 million.

The second book's "loser" was Nijrell Eason, the defensive back and teammate of Archuleta we'd met with but hadn't landed, who our plan said had been graded a second-round pick on the National Report. But he walked away from us and fell out of the draft entirely, and was then picked up by the Cleveland Browns with a contract that guaranteed him only $5,000 as an undrafted free agent.

After presenting the two plans, Gary asked Suggs and his family, "Next year, which hand do you want us to be holding your Game Plan in—the Adam Archuleta hand or the Nijrell Eason hand?" Suggs signed with us. Terrell Suggs went in the first round of the 2003 draft to the Baltimore Ravens and signed a contract with upfront guarantee of $7.3 million. Suggs is now a four-time Pro-Bowler on a very competitive team. Happy ending.

Just one thing: The facts weren't facts. They were stretched, altered, or just plain changed if necessary. Archuleta was *always* ranked to go high in the draft. Our services may have bumped him up a round . . . or his performance may have improved between spring, when the prospect rankings were released, and the actual draft almost a year later. Nijrell Eason had rated high in the spring and had fallen off in fall during the season. By the time the season ended, he was no longer an elite prospect. And when the winter report, released sixteen weeks before the draft, came out, he was graded seventh round or "undrafted." It had nothing to do with not working

with us. In fact, he didn't even turn us down, we'd lost interest in representing him and walked away. And Suggs? We
were talking to him when he was a junior, still unranked
but already highly touted by experts. By the time he declared himself eligible for the draft, the reports had him in
the top five to ten in the first round . . . but we didn't make it
happen.

The next day or next week, if we had a meeting with a
second-round ranked defensive back, we'd highlight and adjust based on the player, the school, and the agents we were
competing with, complete with stats and scouting reports
adjusted just for him. If we had a cornerback, I created numbers that would sell him. We made sure we didn't make claims
that were outrageous, such as raising someone from the seventh round to the first. We stuck to credible embellishment
and made sure we never fabricated a number that could
easily be checked—actual draft outcome, professional stats,
or anything too visible. Those numbers were often common
knowledge or could be found. But smaller stuff, like predraft
rankings or scouting reports, that stuff you could invent, and
we did so often.

Did other agents do it? Yes, absolutely. *I have the presentation material that three of the most successful agents used to recruit the top seven picks in the 2005 and 2006 drafts. I have audio
recordings of two of them in their pitches citing client contract
details of 40 percent incentive bonuses for making the playoffs,
$1.5 million for being named All-Pro, and deferred comp pack-
ages of $3 million tied to playtime performance bonuses. I have
proof of inflated and/or false statements of guaranteed money in
contracts they negotiated for players.*

Okay, actually—I don't have any evidence of what others did. But note how the supposed figures and facts I rattled off above—three agents, top seven picks, draft years, percentages, incentive bonuses, deferred comp—made my story seem credible. That's how our Game Plans worked. As for actual BLESTO and National Reports, we weren't supposed to have them but we did. How did we get them? Well, I can put two and two together. The fax number from where the reports were sent was the Redskins front office and Gary had at least one close friend (GM Vinnie Cerrato) in Redskins management. I still have our Game Plans with real names, real and altered grades, real contract numbers. They worked.

And Gary was a maestro. I had been in meetings with Doc Daniels and with Marvin Demoff. I'd seen them in action with dozens of prospects. I'd taken Flozell "the Hotel" Adams (also known as "Roach Motel" and "False Start" Flozell for his dirty play), the massive offensive tackle from Michigan State, on a trip to see the Super Bowl. We thought, with Demoff and his partner, former Raider Sean Jones, we had a shot at him. Demoff represented Jonathon Ogden, maybe the best tackle in the game. Marvin was big-time. I'd been with Mike Trope, as smart a guy as there ever was at handling players and deals. Gary was better than all of them at a pitch. He performed at the meetings as if he were conducting an orchestra.

And then, once we signed a prospect, Gary was a master at identifying a hole in a player's game and setting out to plug it—on-the-field issues like times in the forty-yard dash or off the field behavior issues. Once agents took action to address a problem, we could get scouts to check it off their list. We would take what the players offered to work with, build on it, enhance it, and and try to minimize or eliminate the negatives. Sometimes a player didn't give us enough to work with and we couldn't raise his stock much. We signed Joe Tafoya, defensive end out of the University of Arizona, and he just wasn't generating much buzz and there wasn't anything we could do. After the Senior Bowl, Joe fired us. In the 2001 draft, he was picked up in the seventh round, which was about right. It was the same story in 2003 for Cal pass-rusher, Tully Banta-Cain, also taken in the seventh round by the Patriots. After the draft, he fired us. Sometimes no magic would change the outcomes.

Joe Tafoya thought we were giving our attention to Adam Archuleta and Willie Howard, which was true. Gary was cultivating interest in Adam through his relationships with Mel Kiper and other sports writers at *ESPN the Magazine,* and *USA Today*. He even hyped his media contacts in the Game Plan. He'd say, "See this writer, good friend of mine. Notice almost every year, he does a feature on one of my players." Gary helped the writer get access to the player and the story helped the player. The scouts were traveling around the country, staying in one hotel after another, and what was on the floor outside every hotel door, on every airplane? A copy of *USA Today* with a story on our player.

And Gary could spot the stories. Like when Adam Archuleta was making a position change. He was an undersized linebacker in college, the Pac 10 defensive player of the year, in fact. But he was switching to safety. And we knew he had better speed than he was getting credit for. In the BLESTO report, they had him estimated at 4.7 in the forty. But if, at the

Combine or a private workout, he ran a 4.4 or even 4.3, the
next thing you knew, people were saying, "Maybe we under-
estimated this guy. He's fast." Now the question was, could
he make it as a safety? Did he have the athleticism, the hips?
So Gary leveraged his relationship with Ron Meeks, at the
time the secondary coach for the Rams. Before the Senior
Bowl, Meeks flew into L.A. and did ten days of defensive
back drills with Adam. Meeks taught him techniques like
backpedaling, flicking his hips, and changing direction, so
when Adam was on the field during Senior Bowl week, he
showed off moves and techniques that the scouts were looking for, moves they hadn't seen on college films.

These private workouts with NFL coaches are strictly
prohibited by NFL rules. Gary had lots of NFL assistant
coaches do it, at least one of whom has gone on to become a
head coach. Coaches are not supposed to even see a player
until the Senior Bowl, let alone be training him. So, besides
training Archuleta, we were building more buzz around his
unorthodox workouts with trainer-guru Jay Schroeder (later
we had Jay and Archuleta make the video *Freak of Training*).
The result of all this? Adam Archuleta was drafted twentieth
overall in the first round, higher than anyone believed he'd
have gone otherwise.

Willie Howard, the defensive end from Stanford, was another case where there was simply no rabbit to pull out of the
hat. I was tight with Willie and with his mom, Deby. Willie
was originally projected to be a first-round pick but he had
a history of knee injuries. Medical red flags are tough to beat.
Even with a clean bill of health, some players just get labeled
as "injury-prone." Willie fell to the second round, number

fifty-seven overall, was picked by the Vikings, played two years, and then suffered a career-ending knee injury.

Then there was Todd Heap. By the time we were leaving for the Senior Bowl, we didn't have him signed. It was a competition between us and another agent. Gary flew to Arizona on the way to the game to meet with Todd and his parents, while John Blake and I went straight to Mobile, Alabama, for the Senior Bowl. Gary closed the deal. We now had the number-one-rated tight end in the draft. He hadn't played in any all-star games because he was a junior so Gary brought in Richard Mann, tight-end coach for the Chiefs. "This is the coach who works with Tony Gonzalez, the Pro Bowl tight end with Kansas City," Gary said. "And now he's going to spend a week or two with you." By working with these coaches, we were giving players training in what the actual drills would be at the Combine. The NFL Combine is a skills competition, where players are tested for strength and speed and a variety of football techniques, agility drills, passing, and so forth. These days it's televised but back then it was very secretive; the official results just leaked out, little by little. Everybody knew about the forty-yard dash, vertical jump, broad jump, and long and short shuttles; they could prepare for those. But we were selling access to training on the position drills, the specifics of exactly what coaches would be looking for at a given position, so Todd wouldn't be surprised or unprepared. He would have a competitive advantage . . . thanks to Gary and me. Todd was projected to be the top tight-end pick and in the end, he was. Number thirty-one in the first round. We didn't add value; we maintained it.

Two years later it was Terrell Suggs's draft—the happy

ending from the Game Plan example. But what happened before the happy ending? Suggs, a linebacker at Arizona State, was another underclassman, so he wasn't going to be in any all-star games. Gary had done his magic with a *USA Today* story and Mel Kiper was saying Suggs could go as high as number three in the first round. But then two things happened. One, Suggs didn't run a great forty. When you run slower than expected, you can shoot firecrackers out of your ass and you're still going to fall in the draft. And two, there was what we came to call the basketball incident. He was in a pickup game and somebody started a fight with his cousin; they went out to a parking lot, somebody hit somebody with a crowbar, and not too long later, a letter arrived from an attorney asking for money to settle damages or they'd file an assault charge—fancy language for extortion—all conveniently before the draft.

Suggs said he had been defending himself and wasn't afraid of the incident going public. We didn't feel the same way—even if he was innocent, it could still have affected his draft status—but the story came out anyway, and Gary handled it very well with the NFL, and Terrell was acquitted. The slow forty time, coupled with the "off-field issues," caused Suggs to drop to number ten in the first round. We did what we could for every player, sometimes moving them up, sometimes maintaining their position, sometimes trying to make problems go away.

Despite Suggs's problems, he was a top pick, and though Gary had represented many great players, this was the first time he was invited to the draft in New York. And, I figured, it would be my first time too. I'd made the first contact with Suggs, through another Arizona State player; I had cultivated the relationship, attended almost every day of his training, and kept in touch with Suggs as his lawyer talked him through the basketball incident. But Gary wouldn't let me go. He said I needed to stay back and take care of Kevin Curtis from Utah State and "man the ship." It wasn't as if we had a complex business. It was Gary, me, Blake, and a couple of others. No ship—barely a rowboat, really. I was disappointed, and angry. It was an early sign of how he'd treat me, keeping me from getting too close to players or from getting too important. I was selling him, but he wasn't grooming me.

Mixed Signals

From day one, I was getting both pats on the back and slaps in the face. After our first season, Gary called up my wife to tell her what an incredible recruiter I was. In the office, I'd overhear conversations through the walls, like Gary telling a young guy who was starting the baseball division of the agency, "Look what Josh came in and delivered. If you deliver like he did, we can talk about paying you more . . ." But I got my first real wake-up call around the time my wife was pregnant, when I found out my name wasn't going to be on the rep agreements. With Doc, we always put both of our names on them, so I assumed it would be the same with Gary and Pro Tect. I had prepared a rep agreement for Willie Howard, the first player we'd gotten together. Gary signed; I thought I was about to sign; and he said, "No, you don't sign those. This is my company. My name is on the door." I remember thinking, *So this is how it's going to be?* We'd had a really good haul this first year—Adam Archuleta, Todd Heap, Willie Howard,

Joe Tafoya. We'd scored at Arizona, Arizona State, Stanford, the West Coast, the Pac 10—all the places I'd promised to help him with. But he wanted me to be invisible. I had a child on the way, and I'd developed strong relationships with players, especially Willie Howard, but I'd only worked there a year, so I was in no position to walk. When I brought up my concern about not signing agreements, he'd say, "It's not about ego. Take care of your family. What do you care if your name isn't on the contracts as long as the check clears?" I didn't like it, but I had diapers to buy.

Around this time, the NFLPA passed a new regulation that stipulated if you went more than three years without representing an active player, you couldn't remain a registered agent. If Gary kept my name off all the contracts, I would soon lose my registration, and then I would find myself essentially a "runner," a dirty word in the agent game. (More about this later.) So, in order to keep my certification alive, Gary let me negotiate and sign the contract for Keenan Howry, a wide receiver out of Oregon. He was a seventh-round pick in the 2003 draft, so it was a bone Gary thought he could throw my way with no skin off his hide. Gary would even say that dealing with a player drafted in such a late round was bad for his image, because it made him look small-time. Howry would later become a very important player in our business relationship, but that's another story that can wait for now.

Besides the issue of my name on contracts, there was something else that haunted me: a comment from fellow agent Kenny Zuckerman, who had worked for Gary in the same role I had. I bumped into him at my first Senior Bowl with Gary and Kenny said, "Watch your ass. Gary's got his people in New

York—the Rothmans. Don't trust him or them. It's only a matter of time before he fucks you." I didn't yet know much about
the Rothmans—Gary's favorite financial advisors—but when
I looked down our roster, I saw that Kenny had been active in
the recruitment of a lot of players but hadn't been their agent—
maybe because he hadn't been allowed to sign the contracts. I
shrugged it off because I knew Gary despised Kenny after litigation and a settlement when Kenny left Pro Tect. I chalked it
up to bad blood on both sides . . . but I didn't forget it.

And something else happened, something that shook the
sports agent business and Gary in particular. David Dunn, a
partner of Leigh Steinberg and Jeff Moorad in one of the largest sports agencies in the country, left the firm. The company
had recently been sold for more than $70 million to Cana-
dian conglomerate Assante Inc., but when Dunn left, he took
with him somewhere between forty and fifty clients, including some of the highest profiles in sports. Steinberg coun-
tered with an enormous, very public, very ugly lawsuit. A
Business Week article written after the suit recounted some of
the accusations and testimony that had come out, including
Steinberg's drunken and erratic behavior in public. There was
one incident, at a social event, where he was said to have licked
women's faces; and he was once quoted as saying to a woman,
"I want to eat your leg." The case was eventually decided in
Steinberg's favor, with a $40 million–plus judgement, but his
personal reputation was damaged, perhaps beyond repair.

(That story hadn't happened yet when *Jerry Maguire* was
made. If it had, and had been included, the movie might not
have been so popular.)

When the story came out, Gary vowed that a defection

like that would never happen to him. He had total disdain for Dunn, believing that regardless of Steinberg's questionable social behavior, Dunn was greedy and would have been nothing without Steinberg. And Gary was either cautious or paranoid, depending on your point of view, to prevent an insurrection like that. The only way to assure it couldn't happen was to keep his employees out of the spotlight and prevent them from having any real influence with clients. In this case, "them" meant me.

Over time, the better we did, the more tension there was. We had a strong 2002, thanks in part to John Blake's magic. The Super Bowl Cowboys' defensive line coach went with us to Fresno State to meet and sign defensive lineman Alan Harper. On the ride home from Fresno, we had a particularly unpleasant conversation. In front of Blake, Gary felt the need to explain the key to my success. "Josh, you're smart enough to realize your limitations," he said. "Without earning your college degree, you have to make sure you keep yourself surrounded by people more capable than you, with better credentials. If you continue selling accomplished people like me, maybe someday you can hope to achieve a small portion of the success that I have." Instinctively, I responded, "Why would I ever choose to limit myself to your accomplishments?" Gary nearly drove off the road, screaming that he had represented all these great players, and produced movies, and I could never be as successful as he'd been. Between the car swerving and Gary screaming, I could hear Blake laughing in the back seat. I never understood Gary's thinking. Why put me down? The better I did in the business, the more he'd benefit.

In 2002 we had Blake work out defensive end Kenyon Coleman and defensive tackles Rodney Leisle and Kenny Kocher of UCLA prior to their senior year. I would pick the guys up from Kenyon's apartment or meet them at the bottom of a service road right near the UCLA locker room and practice field. This was clearly a violation of NCAA rules but I could rationalize it: no money changed hands and the kids were improving their conditioning. Gary also took credit for getting Kenyon on the back cover of Kiper's preseason draft preview. We were helping the players. Wasn't that what we were there for? That same year, Gary signed Dwight Freeney out of Syracuse, and some Oklahoma players, who were also in Gary's territory, but with a big assist from Blake.

Then I got us in contact with Larry Tripplett, a defensive tackle from the University of Washington who was touted as a top pick. We'd had Willie Howard, one of the premier defensive tackles out of the Pac 10 the year before, and now I had a formal meeting set up with Tripplett and his family, right after a bowl game in San Diego. Bowl games are major events, with lots of demands on players' time, so if a prospect wants a meeting, it usually means he's ready to sign, or at least that we're one of his final two or three. I had a great rapport with Larry; he was really smart, personable; he was one of my big fish for the year. It happened to be the same year elite safety Roy Williams was coming out of Oklahoma. If we signed Tripplett, I would get my 25 percent. If we signed Williams, Gary would get 100 percent. But I didn't think it was either-or. Why not sign both of them? I made an appointment for Blake, Gary, and me to see Tripplett. Gary canceled at the last minute, saying he was going to see Roy Williams and I could forget about representing Larry Tripplett. He did essentially the same thing the next year in passing up a meeting with Nnamdi Asomugha, a Cal cornerback. These were big-time prospects, guys who were ultimately drafted high and well compensated in their pro careers. Why miss a chance at possible first-round picks? I began to realize Gary was competing with me, making sure I didn't get too much.

The same was true when I orchestrated the meetings with running back Justin Fargas, who was transferring from Michigan to USC, and his father, Antonio, who had played Huggy Bear in the *Starsky and Hutch* television series and who eventually represented his son in the 2003 draft. But I got no accolades from Gary. Despite all of our successes, he was determined to keep me on a short leash. But he still wanted those big West Coast players I was getting him. So, eventually, he was going to find an avenue into my geography, to get the players I was bringing in. He got it when his former client Ken Norton Jr. won the linebacker coach's job at USC. Between that and the doors I'd already opened for the agency at Arizona State, Stanford, and UCLA, he now had his own entrée into my territory.

To add to his West Coast presence, with less reliance on me, Gary decided to use an outside "street runner." This meant a person who was not certified as an agent, was not a financial advisor or marketing expert, just somebody who was paid to connect the actual agent with a player. It could be a former teammate, a guy from the old neighborhood, a cousin, a girlfriend, even a player's mom. An agent like Gary didn't want to know how the runner got a player's attention. Maybe he invited the player to a party, or hooked him up with a girl, or got him the use of a car, whatever—it's better not to know.

And he was only paid, on or off the books, when and if the player signed with the agency. One thing Gary and every other agent did know was that if any of this took place while the players were still considered student athletes, it was strictly forbidden by NFLPA and NCAA rules, and by forty-two individual state laws.

For recruitment at USC, Gary brought on Wade, a young guy who he said had the right "paint job," meaning he was black. Wade was a former Fresno State player, so Gary tried to convince me he'd add value to our West Coast recruiting and I should reduce my piece of the commissions to offset Wade's fee. No way was I buying that. Wade recognized me from my days with Doc; we'd represented, and funded, his teammate Tony Brown, a defensive back who was picked by the Houston Oilers in the fifth round in 1992. Wade knew me and my street reputation with Doc and I knew a lot of Wades—street runners.

Gary was out of his element. I had a pretty good handle on how this new venture was going to work out—not well—but I figured Gary wouldn't want to hear my take anyway, and I decided to just let it play out. After all, he was using this guy to try to replace me, so why should I help him? Wade promised to deliver a player, his "cousin," Kassim Osgood, a San Diego State receiver. Wade convinced Gary to front him some cash, pay his cell phone bill, and rent him a car so he could drive down to see his "cousin." Kassim, of course, was no more Wade's cousin than he was mine. I'd seen this movie before and I knew how it ended. A week later, Gary couldn't reach Wade, even on the cell phone he was paying for, and now he thought Wade had stolen the rented car. That was the end of Gary's "street runner," but it sent a clear signal to me. He had always bragged he wouldn't bring a certain type of recruiter into his company, but now he'd gone down the low road to try to assure he never needed me the way Steinberg had needed Dunn.

I talked to my wife, Jennifer, about the episode but we agreed I should swallow it for the time being. We'd planned our life around family and my career. It wasn't a good time to rock the boat. We even went so far as to plan her pregnancy so she'd deliver after the draft, and before the start of the season, so I'd never risk missing a birthday party. The draft was in April and her C-section date was May 15.

The Wonderlic Test: The Test Nobody Should Fail

So, I just put my head down and did my work. Sometimes it was more like homework, like when we prepped players for the Wonderlic test. In addition to all the strength and speed tests at the Combine, the Wonderlic is given to every player in each year's draft, supposedly to provide an objective evaluation of their intelligence as another of the tools they will need to excel in the pros. In a word: bullshit. What it really provides is an evaluation of agents' ability to get their hands on the test in advance and teach players how to answer the questions. It's all about cheating—agents cheating to help players pass a test. (Not that the players should need our help, of course, because they were getting a college education while they played football, right?)

We had copies of the Wonderlic, every year. So did a lot of other agents. In fact, I'd say, if your agent couldn't get you a Wonderlic test, you needed a new agent. We got them from people who got them from people . . . I don't know where it started. There were five or six versions of the test, same concepts, same format, fifty questions of increasing difficulty, taken over twelve minutes. We drilled the players to memorize the questions and answers, if not verbatim then at least the concepts, which were the same from year to year. Sometimes the order of questions would change, and number six became number twenty-two, or sometimes in a math problem the apples one year were lemons the next, or sometimes Betty became Nancy, Nebraska became Texas, or June became September. But overall, not much changed. Even if you didn't understand the questions, you could still memorize the answers. But plenty of players, even after we'd been spoon-feeding them the answers, quizzing, and repeating, still couldn't get them right. Some refused to learn. Some had almost no experience of actually learning other than Xs and Os on a chalkboard. Some never had to go to class or had tutors who did all their work for them. A score of twenty is acceptable. Still, plenty—too many—can't score a twenty or even close.

I watched Mike Sasson, a guy who worked for Gary building a baseball practice, who'd also been coaching players on the Wonderlic for years, learning his techniques and adding some of my own. It was as important how many questions were answered as how many you got right. The teams wanted to make sure the player could make his way through the test. Our goal was that the player would get a decent, respectable score . . . but not get them all right and raise suspicion.

Plenty of scouts, general managers, and coaches know the players are getting tutored—that is, memorizing questions and answers they've been fed—and some are okay with that. There even are some people in the NFL who say they don't want players who are *too* smart, just enough to do what they're told, run a pass pattern, or cover an opposing player. On the Internet site ProFootballTalk.com on February 13, 2004, in his "Daily Rumor Mill," Mike Florio wrote, "With as many as six versions of the [Wonderlic] test floating around, there are some league insiders who think that if the players are smart enough to memorize the answers, they're smart enough to memorize their plays."

According to Charlie Wonderlic Jr., president of Wonderlic Inc. and grandson of the founder-inventor of the test, "The closer you are to the ball, the higher your score." That axiom is commonly accepted knowledge in the game—though never logically explained—but it was corroborated by a chart published after the 2004 Combine:

WONDERLIC SCORES BY POSITION, 2004

Offensive tackles 26	Defensive line 17
Centers 25	Linebackers 19
Quarterbacks 24	Cornerbacks 18
Guards 23	Wide receivers 17
Tight ends 22	Fullbacks 17
Safeties 19	Halfbacks 16

For comparison, here are scores for some other vocations: chemists—31, programmer—29, newswriter—26, sales—24, bank teller—22, clerical worker—21, security guard—17, warehouse—15.

Our job was to get our players up to the acceptable level, high but not too high. Ironically, I wasn't a great student and here I was tutoring these guys. Maybe I could relate to them. In any case, we got our players through the test with respectable scores. Kevin Curtis from Utah State got forty-eight out of fifty even though I begged him to miss more. Willie Howard was the same way. He figured he went to Stanford so he should get a high score. Adam Archuleta scored in the higher range, smart enough to learn the plays but not too smart to be coachable. Later on, we had trouble with J. P. Losman, the Tulane quarterback. The first time he took the Wonderlic, he had a ridiculously low score, but we managed to get him into the low twenties the second time. Then it was our job to explain the big difference to the scouts. We said he just hadn't taken the test seriously the first time, had got up and gone to the bathroom and not even finished the test. Not a great excuse, but good enough. He was drafted in the first round by the Bills.

In the end, the Wonderlic is another box to be checked. Time in the forty-yard dash—check. Vertical jump—check. Shuttle drills—check. Interview—check. Our players could all check the Wonderlic box. And we never had to worry about disasters like what happened to Vince Young. In 2006, the National Champion, Heisman-winning University of Texas quarterback got a score that made national headlines, but not in a good way. He scored a six out of fifty.

(Excerpt from story posted on USA Today *after Vince Young's score became public)*

WONDERING ABOUT THE WONDERLIC? TRY IT.

By Mike Chappell, the *Indianapolis Star*

INDIANAPOLIS—Wonder why there's so much fuss at the NFL Scouting Combine regarding the Wonderlic test, the one Texas QB Vince Young purportedly bombed? . . .

The Wonderlic has been part of the NFL's player evaluation process for nearly three decades. It consists of 50 questions and must be completed in 12 minutes. The average score is 21 correct answers . . .

Michael Callans, the president of Wonderlic Consulting, describes the examination as a "short-form intelligence test." Others consider it an exam to assess an individual's problem-solving skills.

The test starts off with simple questions, perhaps pertaining to the days of the month or, according to Callans, "adding 2 plus 3. As you go through the test, it gets more and more challenging, and we begin to add more content and types of questions."

The key is for an individual not to dwell too long on one question . . .

TEST YOURSELF

Here is a sampling of questions included on a Wonderlic Personnel Test:

1. Assume the first 2 statements are true. Is the final one: a) true, b) false, c) not certain?

   The boy plays baseball.

   All baseball players wear hats.

   The boy wears a hat.

2. Paper sells for 21 cents per pad. What will four pads cost?

3. How many of the five pairs of items below are exact duplicates?

   Nieman, K.M./Neiman, K.M

   Thomas, G.K/Thomas, C.K.

   Hoff, J.P./Hoff, J.P.

   Pino, L.R./Pina, L.R.

   Warner, T.S./Wanner, T.S.

4. PRESENT, RESENT—Do these words: a) have similar meanings, b) have contradictory meanings, c) mean neither the same nor opposite?

5. A train travels 20 feet in 1/5 second. At this same speed, how many feet will it travel in three seconds?

6. When rope is selling at 10 cents a foot, how many feet can you buy for 60 cents?

7. The ninth month of the year is: October, January, June, September or May?

8. Which number in the following group of numbers represents the smallest amount?

   7, .8, 31, .33, 2

9. Three individuals form a partnership and agree to divide the profits equally. X invests $9,000, Y invests $7,000, Z invests $4,000. If the profits are $4,800, how much less does X receive than if the profits were divided in proportion to the amount invested?

10. Assume the first two statements are true. Is the final one: a) true, b) false, c) not certain?

Tom greeted Beth. Beth greeted Dawn. Tom did not greet Dawn.

11. A boy is 17 years old and his sister is twice as old. When the boy is 23 years old, what will be the age of his sister?

Answers: 1. a; 2. 84 cents; 3. 1; 4. c; 5. 300 feet; 6. 6 feet; 7. September; 8. .33; 9. $560; 10. c; 11. 40 years old.

There was a brief but temporary outrage over Young's score and the education, or lack of it, that college athletes were getting. You'd think if a college quarterback can get the snap count under center, he'd be able to answer a reasonable number of questions. The colleges squirmed. The NCAA squirmed. The NFLPA was silent. The NFL wanted the story to just go away. And eventually it did. Young was the number-three pick in the draft. Would he have been number one or two with a higher score? Who knows? He got a big signing bonus and contract, the Tennessee Titans got a quarterback, the fans sang the national anthem, and the game went on.

Was It Wrong? Not If It Worked

From the time we began wooing a player to the time he signed with a team, and throughout his career as a pro athlete, we were a full-service agency, offering Game Plans, test tutoring, strength and training coaches, media management, contract negotiation, financial advisors, even insurance agents. Gary had the connections with coaches in the business. No matter the position, he could hook up a player with the expert. Gary had a media network that was unmatched—from Mel Kiper and Tom Friend of ESPN to Larry Weisman of *USA Today*. And when it came to financial advisors he had the Rothmans, Judd and his son Erik, the guys Kenny Zuckerman had warned me about.

A twenty-two-year-old kid who wakes up one day with a seven-figure signing bonus and a multiyear contract has no idea what to do with his money. Gary sent them to the Rothmans. Even if they weren't NFLPA-certified, and therefore not legal to recommend, they were Gary's pick and that was good enough for most players. (Though later on, Brian Bosworth sued Gary for sending him to someone Gary allegedly knew had been involved in fraudulent activities—Judd Rothman—and for allegedly getting a kickback from Rothman.) Gary also had his favorite insurance agent who got all the business we could send him. I had my insurance license at the time, so I'd work with the players on getting their policies, then run them through Gary's guy, who would give us half the commission in return. As an agent, Gary was not supposed to receive any referral fees without full disclosure to the players, which Gary did not provide. But since I was not the agent of record on most contracts, I could receive referral fee checks, which I then cashed and split in half with Gary. Anything was okay if he could rationalize that it was in the name of taking care of the client.

Was it wrong, what we were doing and the way we were doing it? Hyped-up Game Plans with fake data? Bootlegged Wonderlics and spoon-fed answers? Financial advisors that weren't NFLPA approved? Splitting insurance commissions without disclosure? It was all certainly against the rules, but was it wrong? I didn't think so. I didn't think too much about the right and wrong of it. I did what I always did in working for someone else: increased my value by doing things his way, learning his methods, improving on them where I could, and mostly by helping the clients. Gary knew how to create these Game Plan books and they worked. I knew how to take the books up a notch with computer skills. He was a good recruiter in the Midwest and East. I was good at recruiting in the West. Added value. And every agent out there was telling his story as persuasively as possible, bending the truth, buying dinner, wooing relatives, saying and doing whatever it took to close the deal. We were doing it with Game Plans and Wonderlics. And we weren't handing out cash to players. In my mind, I was getting clean . . . or at least cleaner. The lesser of two evils? Maybe. Where does salesmanship end and deception begin? When does embellishment cross the line into lying? It's a gray world we work in.

The Way Other Agents Were Doing Business

Manning Money: Brothers Carl and Kevin Poston, agent-partners in Professional Sports Planning Inc., made outrageous demands for their clients—mostly defensive players—that NFL insiders referred to as asking for "Peyton Manning money." Carl Poston denied using that term but he and his brother did push teams to the brink and beyond, sometimes failing to make deals at all. Carl Poston once allowed LaVar Arrington to sign a contract with the Redskins, the final version of which they had not read and did not contain the $6.5 million bonus they thought they'd secured. That negligence resulted in NFLPA fines and suspension.

Cover Your Assets: Steve Weinberg, one of the leading agents in the game since 1982, allegedly hid assets from a judgment creditor, the result of which was that players he represented were being served with writs of garnishment—to collect those assets. The judgment creditor happened to be Weinberg's business associate and co-agent, attorney Howard Silber. Silber went to the NFLPA to intercede, supposedly to protect players' interests, but ultimately to destroy Weinberg. It was a preview of the tactic that Silber would use as a lawyer representing Gary Wichard in my lawsuit years later.

Who's Wooing Who: Agent and author of *Winning with Integrity*, Leigh Steinberg, continually insisted he was above the fray, never soliciting players, always waiting for them to come to him. But Sean LaChapelle, among other players (see story in chapter 4), was said to have received repeated phone calls from Steinberg offering his services. And every year, Leigh's company threw extravagant Super Bowl and Pro Bowl parties, inviting not just their own clients but plenty of other high-profile players, the ones they wanted to represent. The rules say an agent cannot "initiate communication" with another agent's client. But they don't prevent an agent from being a good host.

The High Five: John Blake left Gary Wichard and returned to coaching, first at Mississippi State, then at
Nebraska, then at North Carolina. He had historically
used his influence to help steer players to Wichard's company, Pro Tect, and in return would get what he called
a "high five," meaning money or something of value.

I was with Gary Wichard and Pro Tect from 2000 to May
2004. In hindsight, I'd like to say I left because I was uncomfortable with the way we were doing business, but to be honest, I didn't think we weren't doing business any cleaner or
dirtier than any other agent. We just worked the way that was
most effective for us. The truth is I left because no matter how
well I did my job, Gary made it clear that I'd never be an important player in his company. The better I did my job, the
more he treated me like a threat.

When I had the chance to hook up with another big agent,
Steve Feldman, I grabbed it. I had talked to other agents, including the infamous David Dunn at his new outfit, Athletes
First, but I got wind that he was trying to steal Todd Heap
from Gary. I declined to pursue working with Dunn for two
reasons: My arrangement with Gary was that I'd be paid for
as long as Pro Tect represented a player, so I didn't want any
part of Dunn's poaching Heap; and Dunn verbally proposed
a deal to me but the papers his lawyers later sent bore no re-
semblance to the deal he'd discussed. In August 2004, I went
in to see Gary and resign. He told me two things. He said I
was "a great salesman," but I should pursue a new profession.
And he said, "You'll never sign anyone. No one without me."

He offered to hook me up with a friend of his at Mattel, the toy company. I thanked him and swallowed my real thoughts, and we parted. Not exactly like my emotional departure from Doc Daniels. Ironically, after I left the agency, and in some ways because of his actions, I eventually became just what he didn't want me to be: a threat.

CHAPTER 7

Going Hollywood

Steve Feldman was a former sports law professor at Cal State who now looked to me like a cross between Harvey Keitel's character, the Wolf, in *Pulp Fiction* and Sean Penn's Jeff Spicoli in *Fast Times at Ridgemont High*—a middle-aged guy wearing surfer's board shorts. At one time, Steve had represented a powerhouse list of young prospects, but now he focused on recruiting mostly established NFL veterans. His roster had included All-Pro defensive end Lee Roy Selmon, for whom he had negotiated a contract that made Selmon the highest paid defensive player in NFL history; Rickey Dixon of the Bengals, the highest paid defensive back; future Hall of Fame offensive lineman Jackie Slater of the Rams; Redskins Super Bowl quarterback Doug Williams; and all-world linebacker Junior Seau of the Chargers. Steve was smart, aggressive, and highly effective, with a reputation for successfully navigating controversial player negotiations, like the deals that brought Carl Pickens to the Bengals, Andre

Rison to the Colts, Corey Dillon to the Patriots, and Lawrence Phillips from the Rams to the Dolphins. What Steve
didn't do was go after rookies anymore. He had soured on
the whole sordid process, the minefield of families, friends,
hangers-on, and oversized immature egos—the stuff I was
good at.

When I met with him, I put on a mock presentation, as if I
was talking to a player and his family. I had morphed the
Game Plan from a bound book into a PowerPoint, the digital format of the moment, and renamed it "the Playbook." It
showed off the key stats, player histories, Wonderlic tests, copies
of the classified interview process, even video—clips of the
drills players would be run through, Senior Bowl clips, confidential NFL video from the Combine, and so on. I was proud
of my changes; the whole presentation could be altered with
the click of a button, plus there was no book left behind to be
fact-checked, or shared with another agent. The bottom line
was: Here's how we're going to help you, the player, do better
on these tests and impress pro teams. Here's how we're going
to handle the media to get buzz, and how it's all going to get
you drafted higher. Here's our competitive edge. Steve sat in
the darkened home office at my house and watched, totally
mesmerized. When I finished, he stood up, gave me a bear
hug, and said, "We're going to make a shitload of money." He'd
been old-school, nondigital, paper and ink, printed fliers,
concentrating on negotiating contracts, which he was very
good at. I'd taken what I'd learned with Gary to a higher level.
Together we were going to be a force to reckon with.

On day one, I reached out to some of the people I knew
could open doors for us in recruiting. My first call was to the

best recruiter I ever knew, John Blake. He was, at the time, a coach at Nebraska.

Back when I was still with Gary Wichard, John had briefly coached at Mississippi State, just long enough to help Gary sign his first Mississippi State player, Tommy Kelly, who went on to become one of the highest-paid defensive tackles in the NFL with the Raiders. Kelly had been a top-rated defensive lineman in college but due to his failing a drug test, he tumbled hard on draft day, ultimately not getting picked at all. After the draft, Gary hadn't secured a free-agent contract for Kelly and had been ready to give up and go home. I told him that if we didn't find a home for Kelly within a few hours of the draft, all the rosters would be full and he'd be lucky to get into anybody's training camp. Gary said he had dinner plans but if I wanted to, I could get on the phone and try to find a spot for Kelly. I called my old buddy George Karas and cut a deal to bring Kelly to Oakland. Gary came in the next day, made a few tweaks to the contract so he could say it was his, signed it, and Tommy Kelly had his chance to play in the NFL. Since Tommy was from outside of my territory, I wasn't entitled to payment and, as expected, Gary didn't offer.

Wherever John Blake coached, Gary signed players. In fact, it started back before Blake was officially a coach, when he was working for the Oklahoma Sooners as a graduate assistant to the coaching staff. He cultivated relationships with some of the players and then helped steer them to Gary, guys like linebacker Brian "the Boz" Bosworth and tight end Keith Jackson. Later in his coaching career (including his ill-fated stint as Oklahoma head coach, in which he was a great recruiter off the field but on the field could never measure up to

the Sooners' legendary Barry Switzer), he connected Gary
to defensive end Cedric Jones, tight end Stephen Alexander,
and cornerbacks William Bartee and Jacoby Sheppard. After
he was fired from Oklahoma, he became a full-time employee
at Pro Tect. Blake used to tell me that without his delivering
players to "G," his nickname for Gary, Wichard would never
have made it in the business. Blake is a colorful guy, full of
colorful phrases and his own country-boy humor. I'd talk to
him about how we had to recruit a certain player and he'd
make his favorite bad pun, "You got to cruit him before you
can re-cruit him." Once when he heard Gary and me tell a
joke that happened to involve cunnilingus, Blake said with
his slight lisp, "Cunnilingus? I don't know nothing about no
cunnilingus. Why you guys always got to use all them big
Jewish words around me?" Blake is a true original, charming,
disarming, and as good as they come in the game. I hoped to
follow the same path Gary had and have Blake endorse me so
that I could get a kick-start in recruiting in my first year with
Feldman.

Once I'd started working with Steve Feldman, the first
guy John connected me with was another player from back
when he was at Mississippi State, nose tackle Ronald Fields.
When Blake had moved to Nebraska, safety Josh Bullocks,
one of his players, called him for a reference on me, and Blake
said, "Yeah, Luchs is a good guy. He'll take good care of you."

In our first year together, Steve and I signed both Bullocks, who went to the Saints in the second round, and Fields,
who was picked in the fifth round by the 49ers. We also had
Claude Terrell, an offensive guard from New Mexico, picked
by the Rams in the fourth round; James Sanders, a safety

picked by the Patriots in the fourth round; Ryan Riddle, a linebacker out of Cal Berkeley, who went in the sixth round to the Raiders; and David Bergeron, a Stanford linebacker and seventh-round pick by the Eagles. (Willie Howard, by this time no longer in the NFL, was technically Gary's former client, but we had stayed close. I helped hook him up with the East-West Shrine Game as a D-line coach and he helped hook me up with David Bergeron.) All that, plus Maurice Clarett, the notorious and superathletic Ohio State running back, a story unto himself, who went—miraculously—in the third round to the Broncos. We didn't have a first-rounder but we represented players in six out of seven rounds, contrary to Gary's prediction of my future.

I got so much help from Blake that now it was my turn to get the call from him like Gary got, asking for a "high five" in return. Around Christmas, John Blake reminded me of the favors he'd done and said he needed a "high five" in the form of a $1,500 flat-screen television for his family. He called me from the electronics store and I gave them a credit card number. No problem.

I never forgot that Gary told me I'd be nothing without him, and it was sweet to prove him wrong. And it was especially sweet that I got key leads from people I'd met and worked with at Pro Tect, Gary's people, like John Blake and Willie Howard, and even Wade, the street runner.

Recruiting Big Samoans: Is That Redundant?

During the 2006 college football season, I reconnected with Gary's runner, Wade, and he offered up connection to

Tennessee Volunteers players, by way of a man called Navy, a gigantic Samoan who had connections to a couple of other gigantic Samoans, two Tennessee players. When Navy walked into our hotel room in Knoxville for our first meeting, I realized that he was a former offensive lineman Doc had represented, whom I hadn't seen in years. He explained how he was "involved with the agent selection process" (any deal would have to go through him) for star defensive tackle Jesse Mahelona and offensive tackle Albert Toeaina. Albert was a lesser-rated prospect but a superb athlete with enormous upside . . . and an enormous backside. He also had a temperament issue, having been suspended by Coach Phil Fulmer for the final game of the regular season for spitting on a cameraman on his way off the field.

After Steve and I had good initial meetings with both players, they made it clear they both wanted to work with the same agents—us—provided we got the blessings of their parents. Steve and I flew up to northern California to meet Albert's father, Pastor Alex Toeaina. After a warm Samoan greeting—"Talofa!" and a full-body hug—and the presentation of our "Albert Toeaina Playbook," Pastor Alex proclaimed he and his family had prayed on it and determined we were the agents sent from God . . . with one catch. Obviously, God would not want his son to get anything less than what other agents were offering. (I hadn't realized God even got involved in these negotiations.) Pastor Alex then showed us an e-mail from a financial advisor who worked with another agent, which promised a credit line of $250,000 for Albert if he signed with them. The pastor asked if we would match that offer. I diplomatically explained that, as good as Albert is, he wasn't rated high enough to justify that much, and more importantly, that that amount of money would put his son too deeply in the hole to start his career. But I told him we could arrange for a $25,000 credit line, more than enough for the next few months since we'd be covering his living and training expenses in Long Beach, preparing for the Senior Bowl and Combine.

They went off to consider the offer, and, after what we assumed was more praying, we ended up signing Albert. Evidently Jesus gave us the nod. Then, a few days later, I got an emotional phone call from Pastor Alex, confessing that he had altered the e-mail from the other agent, adding a zero to the $25,000 credit line offer. Steve and I had already suspected this; I'd personally heard from that same financial advisor earlier, offering to create a credit line of $25k for players we signed, provided we worked with him. No doubt this was a financial advisor of great integrity. I knew that game. And anyway, it didn't matter; we were fine with the $25,000 credit line since we weren't on the hook for it; the financial planner was. The pastor just had one more request. He said his son would work even harder to get ready for the draft if he had a custom Escalade with chrome rims and every option available including having his son's name, "Albee," embroidered on the headrests . . . and to please have it delivered during his sermon to inspire his congregation. Amazingly, the financial advisor agreed to make the arrangements, put the car in Albert's name, and had it delivered. We can only assume the congregation was uplifted. One gigantic Samoan down, one to go.

For us to meet Jesse's father, Mr. Mahelona, was a little

longer excursion, twenty-five hundred miles from L.A. to Kona on the island of Hawaii and back again in twenty-four hours. It was a trip, in every sense of the word: an expedition, a journey, and a bizarre experience. First, Mr. Mahelona said that no business would be conducted until we had dinner together, which he would arrange. He selected an Italian restaurant that we assumed was very good because it was packed. We made small talk about Hawaii, family, and football, and had what at best would be a less than mediocre meal. At the end of dinner, the waiter brought the check toward Mr. Mahelona, who executed a perfect last-second body-feint, steering the waiter and the bill to us. To eliminate any doubt about who was paying, Mr. Mahelona thanked us for taking him and his family to dinner. I looked at the check and it seemed to have one too many zeroes, like the credit line offer for Albert. When I looked a little closer, I realized that most, if not all, of the people in the restaurant were supposedly part of the extended Mahelona family, which explained why, despite the bad food, it was packed.

A thousand dollars or so later, it was finally time for business. We followed Jesse's father to his home perched at the top of a hill with breathtaking views of the Pacific Ocean. This barefoot Jabba the Hut plopped himself down in his huge chair and grunted, his signal for me to begin the pitch. I told him about our company, Steve's history and mine, and began to explain that we had a track record of managing the draft process so that our clients got drafted as high as possible. He interrupted me, screaming, "You don't get my son drafted; my son gets my son drafted." He hoisted his enormous body out of his chair and demanded we leave his house and never come back. Steve and I looked at each other with the same disbelief as when we had seen the dinner bill, only this time I didn't just swallow it. I got up in his face and yelled back, "We flew all the way here, six hours from the Mainland, to meet you, to get your blessing, to do our best to represent your son, and we are not leaving until we at least get through our presentation."

Mr. Mahelona was stunned but unrelenting. Steve, always the cooler head, pulled me outside while he calmed Mr. Mahelona, making small talk about anything but football, picking through their garage full of old surfboards, buying time, letting Mr. Mahelona cool down. He let us back in, and over the next few hours, we laid out our plan and he seemed to warm to it, and even to me. At the end, he proclaimed that we had his blessing. We took out a representation agreement for him to sign (meaningless and nonbinding without his son's signature, but getting a player to sign is almost always easier if his father has already signed). He then called Jesse in Knoxville and told him he was giving us his blessing. From a total disaster to a save—miraculous. Two for two, a Samoan Sweep.

Mr. Mahelona listened a little on the phone, and hung up. We were ready to celebrate when he explained that Jesse had decided to sign with an agent in Tennessee, Chad Speck, who said he was representing players with a philosophy of "Christian ethics," according to Mahelona. All I knew about Speck was that he represented the feared and brutal Titans defensive tackle Albert Haynsworth, who later that year would become infamous for his suspension for stomping another player's head at the end of a play. Where ethics fit into this picture was a mystery to me. The father gave us both smothering bear hugs, thanked us for making the trip, and for dinner, and said good-bye. Our miracle was short-lived. We flew all night and arrived back in California wiped out, in every sense of the word. I called Jesse's dad—why, I don't know. He said hello, and without even identifying myself, and for no particular reason, I sang, "No New Year's Day . . ." There was a long pause and then Mr. Mahelona completed the lyric in his deep, island-accented voice, ". . . to celebrate . . ." and together we went into the chorus of Stevie Wonder's "I Just Called to Say I Love You." Steve Feldman was looking at me as if I were nuts which, after no sleep, a thousand-dollar dinner for a village-sized family, being thrown out of the player's father's house, begging our way in again, bringing a deal back from the dead, and then losing it to an agent who they said claimed to have "Christian ethics" and they all bought it . . . well, maybe I was nuts at that moment. I hung up the phone and Steve and I just laughed. What else could we do? That's the business we were in.

It would just be an expensive but funny story if it weren't for the ending. Albert was signed as an undrafted free agent by the Panthers, went to the Raiders, then went to the CFL, then the UFL. Jesse was drafted in the fifth round by the Titans in 2006 but died in an alcohol-related car accident in 2009 at the age of twenty-six.

Close Encounters of the Sleazy Kind

Maybe the reason I find most agents claiming "ethics" laughable is that despite my own long and convoluted path to reform, I never ceased to be amazed at how low some guys could go. Before the start of the same season we tried to sign the Samoans, Steve Feldman and I were approached by a wanna-be agent peddling a player like a hot watch on a street corner. I got a call from a guy named Chuck Price, who'd been in-volved with a company called Air 7, an academy for quarter-backs run by a great QB coach named Steve Clarkson. Price, who wasn't yet an agent, was dangling Matt Leinart, the quarterback from USC, the 2004 Heisman Trophy winner as a junior, and the odds-on favorite to win it again. USC was the preseason number-one team in the country, and Leinart was basically the hottest guy in football at the time. Price had talked to other players including Manuel White Jr., whom we'd also talked to and White supposedly told Price I claimed to have represented Terrell Suggs, which evidently impressed Price enough to come see us. He sat in our office, going on and on about how he hated Gary Wich-ard and just wanted the best representation for Leinart. Oh, and one other thing—he also wanted over 50 percent of the commission for himself.

Later, much later, we came to find out that Price also dan-gled Leinart in front of Wichard, during which he relayed the story that I claimed to have represented Suggs, which led to Gary going ballistic, calling me up yelling and screaming that I hadn't represented anyone (and the Suggs story would reappear later in my legal battle with Gary). Price was pitting one agent against another to squeeze out the best deal he could, not for the player, but for himself. Nice business. Even-tually, after a lot of agent-shopping, Leinart ended up with Tom Condon of CAA (after hiring and firing Steinberg) . . . with Chuck Price, not surprisingly being named as co-agent.

One other thing: Not only was Price an officer of Air 7 academy, but as of 2005, so were Gary Wichard and Bob Leinart, Matt's father. That's the year *before* Matt Leinart, the country's number-one player, played his final season at USC. Are all of those intertwined relations okay? Do they constitute possible conflict? Or at least warrant close scrutiny? It's not as if the corporate papers are hard to find. They're public record and I found them in preparation for my lawsuit with Gary Wichard. I wonder why the NFLPA, the NCAA, or USC never found them. Or if they did, why they didn't raise an issue. But at that point, nothing should have surprised me. Because there's always a more sordid, more twisted, more bizarre story.

Maurice Clarett: Shooting Star

I got a call one day in the fall of 2004 from my wife's brother, who, like the rest of the family, worked in real estate. In his work he'd come across someone named Hai Waknine, an Israeli "businessman" (later referred to as a "mob figure," "mobster," or "gang member" by the L.A. *Times*, ESPN, and various online news sources). My brother-in-law said, "Have you ever heard of a guy named Maurice Clarett?" and I started laughing because nobody who does what I do within five hundred miles of a college football game *hadn't* heard of Clarett. After Ohio State won the National Championship, he attempted to declare his eligibility a year earlier than the NFL allows. His decision wasn't so much trying to set a groundbreaking legal precedent, as it was a practical one. He'd been suspended by OSU for the 2003 season for misconduct, so his choices were to sit out a whole season, then play another year as an amateur, or go pro and get paid. It wasn't a tough call.

Clarett won the first round in his legal battle for eligibility but lost round two in a higher court. Once he lost, and his attorney Alan Milstein reported to NBCsports.com that he'd hired an agent, he forfeited all his remaining college eligibility. At that point, he had no choice but to wait for the next draft, which was what he was doing. My brother-in-law said that Hai Waknine was taking care of Clarett—who was living at Waknine's house—and they were looking for help in representation. Wow! Clarett was not exactly an ethics major, but he was the kind of high-profile player that could really put us on the map. It was a chance to start recruiting big-ticket prospects again. So my brother-in-law made a call and patched me in to Hai Waknine, and other than him being a little scattered, a little ADD maybe, the opportunity seemed legitimate and I started thinking I could end up representing this kid. I told Steve and even though we'd only been together a few months, he trusted me and said he was all in.

I put together a Playbook on Clarett. Even though we were going to meet with Hai first before we could get an audience with Maurice, I took a page from Gary. I came prepared in case Hai wanted to see what we'd do, in case we did meet with Maurice, in case whatever. Gary was always prepared. He had "preparation" written at the top of every day of his pocket calendar book. He preached never, ever going anywhere unless and until you're ready for whatever eventualities may come. I made preparation my mantra like he had.

We arrived at Waknine's house, or rather compound, in Marina del Rey, right on the water. As we drove up, helicopters hovered. I just figured they were checking traffic, but later I realized they were checking Hai. We rang the bell and an enormous black guy opened the door, big enough to play defensive lineman, with a big gun in his belt bulging out of his sports jacket. He showed us to this expansive sofa facing a wall of glass overlooking the ocean. After a few minutes, Hai Waknine entered—a heavyset, dark-skinned, balding Israeli with a tic, sort of a mild case of Tourette's. He sat on the sofa flanked by gorgeous European models, crossed his legs, and revealed an ankle bracelet. The kind that notifies the Feds if you leave town. He gave us a tour, as nice as could be, and told us to try his special espresso. I don't drink coffee, but I know enough to drink it when a guy with an ankle bracelet tells me to.

He told us Maurice was working out with Charles Poliquin, who, according to *Body Builder* online magazine, was known for "producing faster athletes," having trained several Olympians, NHL players, and NFL wide receiver David Boston, of whom Maurice Clarett was enamored. On the one hand, we were salivating because Clarett had superstar potential, but on the other hand, he wasn't doing this right at all. First, living with an alleged Israeli mobster, likable or not, isn't good. Second, David Boston had tested positive for GHB (gamma-hydroxybutyrate), a banned drug associated with bodybuilding, and had been dropped by the Tampa Bay Buccaneers. Whether they were true or not, rumors of steroids swirled around Poliquin's techniques, and Boston had done nothing to distance himself from them. It seemed a distinct possibility that Maurice could run the risk of being "juiced" and maybe test that way.

I told Hai about Steve and his credentials. Hai told me he'd met Maurice through his relationship with Fizz and Boog, two rappers of the group B2K, and now had a contract giving him a big piece of Maurice in exchange for providing him trainers, lending him a new BMW, and giving him a video game console for Madden Football and a roof over his head—with a stunning ocean view. Hai had control over who would be Maurice's agent, along with everything else in Maurice's life, and set us up for a face-to-face meeting.

When we all got together, I showed Maurice our Playbook. Maurice made it clear that he wanted more than anything to play in the Senior Bowl. I'd already contacted Steve Hale, who runs it, and I knew they didn't have a place for Maurice. It just wasn't happening. Having tried to come out as a sophomore, Maurice was still technically in his junior year and the Senior Bowl had one overriding rule: like the name says, you have to be senior.

For the next meeting, I arranged for my old acquaintance Jack Hart, the director of the East-West Shrine Game, to fly out to L.A. and personally pitch Maurice on playing the Shrine. The Senior Bowl is more prestigious but playing in the Shrine would fill a hole in his story. If he could break off a run or two in practice, then pro scouts could see how good he still was, even though he hadn't played football in two years. It would answer the question, "What has Maurice Clarett been doing for two years out of football?" If he played well, we could say he'd been working out, training, practicing. We could say he was ready, and even if he'd been playing Madden for six months straight, as long as he performed well, we'd be right. Jack shared my vision of taking Maurice around to Shriners hospitals, looking for PR opportunities, and rehabbing his image as a guy who cared about kids. We'd put his face on the Shrine Game ads on buses and billboards, give him his chance to be *the* star in the game, a win-win for everyone.

I prepped Jack, the Shriner, the best I could for what he was going to see—the guard with the guns, maybe helicopters, foreign models parading around in almost nothing, the alleged Israeli mobster (I called him a "real estate investor"), an oceanfront palace. We walked in, sat down, and waited until they ushered Maurice in as if he were royalty. Jack made his earnest pitch: the history of the game, the hospitals, the good work the Shriners do for kids, their role in the community, the photo ops, how well it reflects on the players, some of the high draft choices who've played.

Maurice listened and then asked what other big-name players were committed to being in the game. The answer was, so far, none . . . there were a lot of good prospects but it was too early to send out invites. Maurice asked Jack to give him the phone numbers of the players he wanted so Maurice could call them and convince them to play. Jack couldn't do that, and said so. It would break every rule of confidentiality. He offered to show Maurice some of the names but not their personal contact information. This didn't sit well with Maurice. He'd been living with an Israeli Larry Flynt for months, absorbing the house culture, operating by the house rules. Maurice had seen that every Friday night, when the sun went down, no matter what they were doing, all work ended. Hai, his entourage, and his family lit candles and said their evening prayers. So, at that moment, when the discussion wasn't going his way, Maurice suddenly stood up and said, "This meeting is over. It's Shabbat." He walked out of the room. Jack turned to me and said, "What's he talking about?" I said, "I have no idea. Today is Wednesday." I rode with Jack to the airport, apologizing, and he was very understanding. The whole ride, I was thinking, *What can we possibly do to reshape this kid's image?*

During my time with Gary, I'd gotten to know Tom Friend, a writer with *ESPN the Magazine*. He'd done several pieces on Gary's players and I thought he would be ideal for a puff piece on Maurice. I set up a preliminary meeting for Friend, Hai, and Maurice at my house. That led to a second meeting, held at the office of David Kenner, an associate of Hai and coincidentally the attorney for the infamous gangster rap label Death Row Records, founded by Suge Knight and Dr. Dre—just to add to Maurice's wholesome entourage. My goal was to get a story written about how Maurice was preparing for the draft, his training and conditioning, as the only player ever to go through the NFL Combine twice, a pretty juicy story for Friend and *ESPN the Magazine*.

Hai and his people had a different agenda. He and Maurice thought it was a good opportunity to tell his side of the story of his troubles and suspension at Ohio State. According to the official reports at the time, Maurice had publicly criticized OSU officials for not paying for his airplane ticket home for a friend's funeral. A few months later, a teaching assistant at Ohio State told the *New York Times* that Maurice had been given favorable treatment by a professor, but upon investigation there had not been adequate evidence for academic misconduct. However, in the 2003 athletic year,

Maurice was suspended for filing a false police report, claiming that in excess of $10,000 in goods had been stolen from a car he'd borrowed, and for having misled investigators. In addition, Maurice had pleaded guilty to a lesser criminal charge.

Now refuting the official version, Maurice told Friend that when the misconduct investigation took place, he didn't tell the whole truth in the police report on the car break-in because he wanted to protect coach Jim Tressel and his brother Dick, an assistant coach, who had arranged for him to "borrow" cars from local dealers. The truth, Maurice said, was that the school had promised him passing grades to stay eligible, professors easy on ballplayers, do-nothing independent-study courses, a tutor to do his homework (Bob Eckhart, who'd helped other players), a car-of-the-month, a no-work job, and bonuses for reading stories to boosters' kids, the amount of the bonus determined by how well he'd played the previous Saturday. After OSU beat Michigan in November 2002, a game in which Maurice ran more than a hundred yards and a touchdown, a booster paid him more than $6,000.

According to Maurice, Tressel's staff arranged for him and at least twenty other players to receive special treatment, including allowing them to live off campus their freshman year though it was against university rules. (I can't say what is true and what isn't but this is what Maurice maintained in his interview with Tom Friend.) What had begun as my spin for a light-weight piece on prepping for the draft had suddenly exploded into a juicy exposé for Friend and ESPN. Partway through the process, Hai and his group started to balk. Either they realized this wasn't such a good idea or they decided that if they went ahead with it, they wanted to be guaranteed the cover of the magazine. Friend couldn't promise the cover. But the story had been told.

I did my best to run interference, almost always working through Hai, rarely directly contacting Maurice. They wanted to kill the article. And they weren't the only ones. I learned the Ohio State University Athletic Director, Andy Geiger, had flown to New York for what turned out to be a contentious meeting with the bigwigs at *ESPN the Magazine*, trying to bury the story. It was too late. Friend wrote it, *ESPN* ran everything they could corroborate, and it caused a furor, albeit short-lived. There was a burst of outrage . . . and then nothing. Ohio State adamantly denied everything. They attacked Maurice's credibility—not hard to do. Friend got hate mail, even death threats from Ohio State fans. The NCAA took no more than a cursory look. Why didn't they launch a big investigation, with all these alleged rules violations? Simple: they didn't want to know. Or maybe they realized they lacked the authority to find out since Maurice was no longer a student-athlete and didn't have to answer their questions. Of course, later, the NCAA would turn the heat up, largely due to public pressure, and the whole ugly matter would be exposed (much more about this later).

By this time, my role with Steve had evolved into being the specialist on the draft and the rookie process. I was the blunt force, telling Maurice how he was being perceived in the draft process, what his deficiencies were, and how to fill the holes to get drafted as high as possible. But Maurice had an urge to constantly do what was bad for him, as anyone could see by taking one look at his living situation and entourage. Steve and I used to joke, if you put a pile of shit and a pile of money on the table, Maurice would reach for the pile of shit. He was probably the first player I worked with who I didn't like personally. We had moments of clarity in which I'd find him to be a sympathetic character, but they wouldn't last and he'd revert to prima donna. Thankfully, Steve had a higher tolerance level for his behavior. Ultimately Maurice signed with us, but it was clear that this would be our one rep agreement with only Steve Feldman's name on it.

Still, the shit had hit the fan from the *ESPN* article and it was up to both of us to clean it up. This was January 2005, time to focus on the Combine, training, and then the draft. After we had signed our other players and set them up in apartments in Long Beach, we got them started with our trainer, Chuckie Miller, out of his private gym, on the field at Long Beach City College and up and down the sand dunes at the beach. Chuckie had played for many years and had trained a lot of great players. Hai would often brag to us that Maurice's training was so far superior to what anyone else was doing, saying that he'd run circles around the other guys at the Combine. But when I heard about his regimen, there was one thing missing: running. Not to state the obvious, but Maurice was a running back. And we were never allowed to see him actually training. Except once when he was working with the USC Olympic sprinter Quincy Watts, before he started to work with Poliquin. Even then, even working with an Olympic sprinter, Maurice wouldn't run; he just jogged around the track. We wanted Maurice to work out with Chuckie Miller on the sand dunes, so Steve and I went to Hai's house and got Maurice to follow us out to Long Beach. When we arrived at the dunes, Maurice was in his car on the cell phone and wouldn't get off. Finally, he finished his conversation and said he doesn't run on the sand. We told him, "It offers great resistance and strengthens all the muscles in your lower body. It helps with explosiveness. If you can run shuttle drills and three-cone combine drills in the sand, it's much easier to do it on a flat surface, when you get timed." He just said, "No." Oh shit, we thought, we're in for trouble at the Combine.

In February, Steve and I told our concerns to Hai and David Kenner (whose whole rap history mesmerized Maurice), hoping they could influence Maurice. I wasn't just a little worried; I was going berserk over what could happen at the Combine in Indianapolis. We reiterated that Maurice had to show up at the Combine at the same weight or less than what he'd been a year earlier, because he sure looked too heavy. Maurice also had to nail the interview process and give the answers the NFL people wanted to hear to every question, showing that he'd matured, especially in light of the *ESPN* story. We told Hai and David that he had to do better on the Wonderlic than last time. It seemed as if they were listening, especially Hai, who, after all, was paying the bills on everything. He knew Maurice was his investment, boom or bust. We started working with Maurice right away on the interview and the Wonderlic, but his weight was not looking good. He refused to get on a scale.

We got to the Combine, checked into the hotel, and still didn't know what he weighed. Maurice was set to be officially weighed the next morning, then run through the whole process. This was the first time the Combine was televised, and Steve set up a live interview with Rich Eisen and Terrell Davis on the NFL Network to be held after Maurice's performance at the Combine. That night Maurice was dressed in layers and layers of clothing, and he worked on the treadmill and elliptical at the hotel for hours, pouring sweat, trying to lose water weight before the weigh-in, like a boxer.

The next morning, Maurice weighed in a couple of pounds lighter than he had the year before, and the buzz was great. "Wow, Maurice is in shape." Nobody knew how he got there. And he managed to do well with the bench press, lifting 225 pounds twenty times. Then came the press conferences. We had prepped him very well and he's a good speaker. This was the new Maurice Clarett, new attitude, new maturity, a new man, just what the teams want to hear. So far, it was going great. Next was the Cybex test, a part of the physical that we had told him *not* to take. In fact, I've told lots of players not to take it. For the Cybex, they strap one leg down and have you do leg extensions until your leg is completely exhausted, so the next few days you have dead legs when it comes time to run the forty-yard dash. If they really pressed a player to do it, we always told them to do it after the forty, which pisses off the people running things but there's not much they can do and they'll never actually reschedule it. Amazingly, Maurice did what we said and skipped the Cybex.

Instead, we worked on more prep for the Wonderlic. The next day it was time for the forty-yard dash and the other field work. Gil Brandt, an NFL legend who runs the Combine and happened to be supportive of Maurice, broke precedent and let me and Steve into the media green room, with all the writers, to watch the monitor while Maurice ran. Most of the beat writers had no idea his agents were floating among them so they were openly rooting against Maurice. He got ready to run and it was as if everything was in slow motion. Not because that's how I imagined it, or because it was important to me—this was because Maurice was literally running in slow motion. No burst, no explosion, just flat. He finished the forty in 4.7-plus seconds, a good two tenths of a second slower than the 4.5 he needed. Disaster.

There was laughter and howling in the media room, pretty cold delight. Now Maurice was supposed to run routes and running back drills. The only thing he could do worse than his forty time would be to just quit. And that's exactly what he did. He walked off the field. He knew he was fucked so he walked. But instead of going to his hotel room, he went into his interview with Terrell Davis and Rich Eisen to discuss the most anticipated but worst Combine performance in NFL history. Somehow he stumbled through it. When they asked him why he'd walked off, he said he just wasn't feeling it and besides, he was going to work out at Ohio State's Pro Day the next week and scouts could see him there. That sounded like a reasonable answer but it opened up a can of worms. First, we couldn't get him fixed up in a week. Second, we had no idea if Ohio State, having thrown him out of school and then read about him ripping Jim Tressel apart in *ESPN the Magazine*, would let him work out there.

We just tried to hustle him out of the hotel—Steve, David Kenner, and me—and out of town, past the fans yelling at him, stuff like, "I can drink a forty faster than you can run one," and him just staring at the ground. Once on the plane, he started downing miniatures of Grey Goose, one after another, never showing any sign of being drunk. Steve and I were hit with another rude awakening. Maybe he was an alcoholic too. Maybe that, plus being out of shape, was the thing slowing him down.

We followed up the trip with a "Come to Jesus" meeting—it was time to train, according to our rules, or we were dropping him as a client. And if Steve Feldman, who'd made a name for himself dealing with misfits, walks away from you, that's a curse the scouts won't miss. We recommended, and Hai and David agreed, to have Maurice train with Todd Durkin, a phenomenal trainer who'd worked with LaDanian Tomlinson, which ought to be as impressive as Poliquin working with David Boston.

While Maurice was doing that, I had to deal with the Ohio State Pro Day problem. No way would Maurice be ready in a week, and we couldn't have him pull out of Pro Day on his own; it would just confirm him as a quitter. So the only way out was to hope Ohio State would kill it. That was our bet. I sent a formal request for Maurice to participate, crossed my fingers, and luckily they sent us a formal rejection. Then I leaked that story to John Clayton of ESPN—Maurice wanted to do Pro Day at Ohio State but the school wouldn't let him—and, as I expected, it went viral. Now all we had to figure out was where scouts would see him and when he could actually be ready. The NFL rule was that teams can only attend a player's workout where he played college or high school ball or at a "conjoining metropolitan area," meaning pretty close to either of those. It turned out Charlie Frye, the quarterback prospect out of University of Akron, was going to do

his Pro Day in Akron in early April, one of the last scheduled "pro days" of the cycle. If we could piggyback with him,
that would buy us an extra eight weeks. Akron isn't that
close to OSU, which is in Columbus, but after some back
and forth with the league, they agreed to let Maurice work
out there.

But there will still problems. The athletic department at
Akron wouldn't agree, and most importantly, Charlie Frye
wouldn't agree. Everyone thought it would create a circus atmosphere and steal attention from Frye. All the while, Maurice was supposedly working out in San Diego but Durkin
reported that it had been a struggle to get him to workouts
each day. Finally Hai and Kenner got Maurice's cousin,
Vince Morrow, to live with him, like a babysitter, to make
sure he showed up every day for his drills. And I kept searching the state of Ohio for a place to do a Pro Day. Maurice
wanted to do it at Warren G. Harding High School, in Warren,
Ohio, because it's where he played and they have a hard Tar-
tan track. And he knew it was the same surface that fellow
college exile and NFL hopeful Mike Williams of USC had
run on. On this kind of track, you can't wear track spikes and
instead have to wear flat-bottom sneakers, but it lends itself
to fast forties. Of course, scouts know this and adjust for it,
but each scout adjusts differently so maybe it was worth it . . .
unless it rained, and the track got slick and the grass field
turned to mud and craters. Then I'd have to find a place for
Maurice to run indoors. I gave myself an instant Ohio geography lesson and came across a place called Farmer Jim's Indoor Soccer Complex in the town of Cortland, just close
enough to Warren to meet the NFL rules. And Farmer Jim's

indoor surface is the original Astroturf over concrete—hard as rock, literally, and fast. Maurice didn't want to do it there so the plan was to go to the high school and if it rained, we'd call an audible and send the scouts to Farmer Jim's. At this point, I was figuring whatever could go bad, would.

And even on the trip out from L.A. to Ohio, it turned out that way. Steve and I were in the Phoenix airport for a connection, and I was on the phone with John Clayton of ESPN, and suddenly there was a scene with a police officer escorting a prisoner who somehow must've convinced the cop to take off his cuffs so he could take a leak or something, and the prisoner started beating the hell out of the cop, right in front of us. I ran over to the fray and asked the cop if he needed help. He said yes, so I grabbed the convict, threw him down, and pounced on top of him while Steve kicked him a few times for good measure. The cop picked himself up and took control again. John Clayton ended up writing a feature entitled, "Clarett's Agents to the Rescue." Steve and I concluded that everything to do with Maurice Clarett is trouble, even a walk through an airport. It's funny but too true.

Of course, when we got to Warren, Ohio, it poured rain. We gave ourselves a head start and told everybody to reroute with directions to the location twenty minutes away, so we could get to Farmer Jim's ahead of the pack.

Typically the order of the workout is they take height and weight, then bench press, vertical jump, broad jump, then the forty, shuttle drills, and position work. We had about an hour and a half until the workout started and we figured Maurice was still a little heavy so the first thing we did was crank up the heat until it was like a sauna. Then we hid the scale in a locked closet so we could say, "Who'd have thought they wouldn't have a scale?" Even if they came up with a scale later on, we'd have ninety minutes for him to sweat off another couple of pounds. Then Steve and I took a measuring tape to recheck the distance for the forty because Maurice couldn't afford the time of a fraction of an extra step. The workout started and there was more media than scouts—about four or five teams, including the locals, the Browns and Bengals. After warmups, Maurice was ready and the scouts started bitching about wanting a scale. We said we'd scheduled the run for one o'clock and we were ready. We videoed the whole thing for the teams that weren't there and we were planning to do the entire workout first (the parts that would make him sweat), and the measurements afterward. If Maurice got weighed later, we could edit the tape to put the weigh-in at the beginning of the workout. Every little bit that might help. Embellishment. Finally . . . he ran: 4.68. Not the 4.5 we wanted but more than a tenth of a second faster than his 4.7+ last time. We called John Clayton at ESPN and on *Sports Center* they reported, "Maurice Clarett had his workout today and though he was two pounds heavier than at the Combine, he ran faster." All they focused on was the improvement. In reality, it was the surface he ran on, but sometimes perception is better than reality.

It had been a roller-coaster ride since the Combine. Before it started, there were people saying Maurice might not get drafted at all. Then after his interviews, some said he could go as high as the second round. Then he worked out and went into free-fall. Now, three and a half weeks before the draft, we'd had his Pro Day and the positive chatter was picking up. We thought we were doing great, a minor miracle in fact.

But it wasn't okay with Maurice and his handlers. Kenner, Hai, Maurice, and his mom, Michelle, seemed to think I was getting quoted too much in the press. Plus Hai and Kenner had the idea of building their own athlete management business, with Maurice as the centerpiece. To them, my media attention was stealing thunder from their new business plan. To me, I was managing the media blitz the way I'd observed Wichard doing it for years, and it was working. They weren't happy and they summoned Steve to a private meeting—very ominous. I was in Palm Springs for a couple of days off with my family. Steve was very uncomfortable given all we knew, had heard, and read on the Internet about these guys. Who knew what they might do? Steve even called Tom Friend to let him know the meeting was happening so somebody in the media would know where he was that day in case he disappeared. He got to the meeting and they really unloaded on him, saying how dissatisfied they were, how much they disagreed with what I was doing and how I was doing it. They didn't threaten Steve but even so, these are not people you want to have mad at you.

We just kept doing our job. Our goal wasn't just to keep Maurice or ourselves in the headlines; it was to get some meaningful buzz—draft news—out there about him, something with some shred of truth that we could leak to the press. And we got it. One morning, Steve was on his treadmill and he got a call from Bill Parcells, then the head coach of the Cowboys, giving him the third degree about Maurice. Was he really ready to play? Was he getting in better shape? What was his attitude like? And he indicated, if the answers were good, the Cowboys were interested in taking Maurice at some point in the draft. We embellished that conversation in the retelling to suggest Parcells had targeted Maurice for the fourth round. It was not exactly what he'd said but, to coin a phrase, it was "leakable" and the morning of the draft, it "somehow" got out. The Internet is amazing. Click: the bloggers get it, couple it with a quote or two from Parcells about interest in a "big back," then the sports sites pick it up, then the national media run it, and the more it runs, the more real it gets. Once it was out, we figured the fourth round was the floor, the latest we projected he'd go in the draft, and if another team was interested, they'd think they would have to draft him ahead of the Cowboys.

We knew that Mike Shanahan and the Broncos had an interest in Maurice because, even though they weren't at his Pro Day, they'd asked for a tape of it. We knew the Broncos had a nontradable compensatory pick (a selection the league gives based on free agents lost the previous season), the last pick in the third round, but didn't have a pick in the fourth. We figured they didn't want to take the chance the Cowboys would take him in the fourth, as we had spread the word they planned to. It was a long shot—the Broncos had only rumors to gauge Dallas's interest—but, to our amazement, it worked. Maurice Clarett, the magnet for trouble, was picked on the first day of the draft. He didn't fall out of the draft like some people predicted. He didn't even go late. He went to Denver, a team that had a history of a great running game, and he went to Mike Shanahan, who everybody thought was a genius with running backs—the guy who'd drafted Terrell Davis.

Finally, Hai Waknine and David Kenner were happy. So were Maurice and even his mother.

It really was a miracle. Maurice had been consistently lazy, constantly in or flirting with trouble, and had been away from football for a long time. He wanted to be a pro running back, whose job was to be fit and fast, but he'd run slow times twice and was overweight. He'd been suspended, banned, and arrested—and he didn't even look like he was trying hard to come back. Yet somehow, he was drafted ahead of one hundred fifty other guys. If ever I'd earned my money as an agent, it was while representing Maurice Clarett. So, how did he repay us?

The next step was mini-camps, immediately after the draft. Rookie mini-camp is three to four days for the teams to see the players they've drafted. Right away, Maurice had a run-in with the strength and conditioning coach and went to Denver's GM Ted Sundquist, and demanded that the coach be fired. Here was a third-round pick demanding the ten-year strength coach get canned . . . and we hadn't even negotiated his contract yet. Then his drinking problem resurfaced. We got a call from the Broncos one day informing us that Maurice was frantic that he had left a bag in the back of the limo he had taken from camp to the airport. We started calling to track down the bag and the driver said Maurice hadn't left anything in the car except a Gatorade sports bottle, which he took to Maurice, who snatched it from him as if it were more than a plastic bottle. We came to find out Maurice had his bottle with him at practice, on the sidelines. He took a swig and allegedly told Rod Smith—Mr. Bronco—his All-Pro wide receiver teammate, that he's "gotta get his Goose on."

Yup; his water bottle was evidently full of Grey Goose vodka. The more the team saw him in action, the more they saw that the wiser, more mature Maurice Clarett was fiction.

Still, Steve and I managed to come out with a good contract in our dealings with the same Ted Sundquist that Maurice had asked to fire the strength coach. We worked out the structure of a guaranteed $410,000 signing bonus, plus his salary. Just keeping Denver interested was no small feat in itself. Fortunately ego sometimes overcomes logic: *If we picked him, we can make him a star.* The Broncos seemed to believe the franchise history showed they worked magic with running backs and could do it again, and they had the magician in Mike Shanahan. Magic or not, this would be some trick. We then went to David Kenner's office in Encino and got Sundquist on the phone to review the details. But Kenner said he'd already discussed it with Maurice and it was unacceptable. They didn't want a piddling four hundred grand up front. Maurice Clarett was going to be a superstar and he wanted a deal built on incentives that would reward him like the first-round pick he should have been. Kenner told us to work out the details and walked out of the room.

What they wanted was basically a suicide deal, especially for a player as volatile as Maurice. A little bit of contract negotiating background here: the NFL instituted a salary cap in 1994, permitting teams only so much money they can spend per year. (The actual figure is complicated to arrive at, and varies based on a lot of factors.) If they give a player a big bonus, they pay it out up front, but for bookkeeping and salary cap calculations, it gets amortized over the term of the deal. However, if the team lets the player go early, they have to accelerate the bookkeeping, paying out all the guaranteed money, including the bonus, immediately. That, in turn, means it eats into their total team salary cap number immediately. Sometimes a team's inducement to give a player a second or third chance is to prevent taking the salary cap hit all at once. We wanted those extra chances for Maurice.

Instead, because of David and Maurice, we were losing a good deal. And Steve and I looked like fools to the Broncos. Worst of all, it was bad for Maurice. Fortunately Sundquist was a decent guy and was open to keep talking. At one point in the negotiations, Steve and I went for a walk in Beverly Hills to get something to eat and I said, "You know, the whole thing is a shame because I'll bet you a dollar Maurice Clarett never plays a down in the NFL." He took the bet, I think just because it would be too pessimistic not to. We finally worked a deal in which Maurice got heavy incentives on the back end, despite the front office saying they couldn't do it because it would be changing team policy, and even the players' union saying it was too far out of the ordinary. We explained that our client was insisting on it even if it wasn't good for him.

We put the best spin on it we could. We told the media that Maurice was saying, don't just pay me for showing up, pay me for what I earn, for the way I actually perform. The talking heads on ESPN picked it up and reported that Maurice was showing a mature attitude. Just because he'd been drafted in the third round, and was getting third-round money, he was willing to give it up and show people how hard he'd work. He would prove his value. It made a good story. The question was, would it turn out to be true?

What we did get into the deal was a set of off-season bonuses. All Maurice had to do was show up for off-season workouts and he'd collect the equivalent of the rejected signing bonus. That way the team got some assurance, or at least hope, that he'd overcome his bad work ethic to get his money. As it turned out, Maurice, not being in the shape he should've been in, strained his hamstring in training camp and nursed the injury for most of the preseason, saying he wanted to be completely healthy for the regular season. We tried to explain to him that with other running backs showing their stuff in the preseason, if Maurice didn't win a spot on the roster, for him there wouldn't be a regular season. For the last preseason game, the Broncos reported that Maurice wasn't hurt so technically he could play, but as Steve and I had predicted to Kenner, they didn't play him. The decision had been made. If they had played him, and he'd gotten hurt, they couldn't have cut him without an injury settlement. They kept him out of the game and then they cut him. Maurice never took a preseason snap, never played a down as a Bronco, and other than preseason pay, never got a salary or bonus.

We had a couple of phone calls from him after that in which he asked, "Now what?" First, he had to clear waivers, that is, give another team a chance to pick him and pick up the terms of his contract. But that would've meant paying him those big back-end workout bonuses, which wasn't going to happen. Maurice cleared waivers in twenty-four hours. Every NFL team had the chance to sign him, and nobody picked him up. No one wanted to touch him.

It was about that time that David Kenner and Hai Waknine started to think maybe they'd bet on the wrong horse.

Maurice was headed to the CFL or NFL Europe at best. (In fact, a year later, he was arrested for armed robbery and was convicted. In 2010, he played for the Omaha Nighthawks of the UFL.)

The whole fiasco was sad. We did our best to save Maurice from himself. And we almost did it. In the end, it didn't hurt our reputation. It probably helped it. It was almost as if prospects looked at us and thought, "Hey, if they can candy-coat a turd and get him drafted in the first day, imagine what they can do with me and with talent instead of drama."

Unfortunately, I did win that one-dollar bet with Steve (the only dollar I made in working with Maurice Clarett).

Sports Biz Meets Show Biz

The biggest news in the industry in 2006 was Tom Condon's move from IMG to CAA. Condon, who represented some of the biggest names in the game—Marvin Harrison, LaDainian Tomlinson, both Peyton and Eli Manning—said, "Two years ago, I told IMG that the sports agent of the future needed to have ties with other entertainers. These athletes are celebrities and entertainers just like movie stars and rock stars. But IMG wasn't interested." So he made a deal with CAA, Hollywood's powerhouse talent agency. Condon would remain in his home base of Kansas City, but he'd have the glitz and glamour of CAA to offer his clients. Going Hollywood was the new game in town.

Almost simultaneously, Steve Feldman had been in quiet talks with the Gersh Agency, a talent agency with a reputation for building strong personal relationships with talent and a distinguished client list that included timeless icons like Humphrey Bogart and Richard Burton, and recent TV stars like Debra Messing of *Will and Grace* and David Schwimmer of *Friends*. As we started recruiting in late 2005 for the 2006 season, the talks heated up. Steve was talking with Hugh Dodson, COO of Gersh, and with Toi Cook, who they'd brought in to be Director of Player Development. Toi had been a defensive back, out of Stanford, who played with the Saints and the Super Bowl champion 49ers, a very sharp guy and Stanford alum. With Feldman and me, they'd have a sports agent base.

We worked out the details in late '05 and early '06 and announced it in the spring. Gersh represented all kinds of major writers and directors, which should theoretically provide opportunities for ball players in entertainment, plus access to red-carpet events, hobnobbing with stars, going to premieres, a really glitzy package. This was big news. Everybody who heard about Condon and CAA could nod their heads and get it. But Feldman and Luchs? That was a coup. One year together, no first-round draft picks, but a lot of PR, a lot of buzz. Gersh was betting on our momentum.

We had to get clients to build our roster under their banner, not only Steve's NFL veterans or our handful of new guys, but clients for Gersh—with Hollywood potential—and demonstrate real synergy. It was a chance for me to show my value as part of the new venture.

The deal was, we would essentially turn over all of our income to the agency and take it back in the form of salary, but suddenly I was getting health benefits, a beautiful office in Beverly Hills, a support staff, and a great product to sell. I signed a three-year employment contract and collected a paycheck and that, in itself, was an improvement in my cash flow. When you represent athletes, you don't automatically get paid or have your piece deducted from their paycheck before it gets to you. You have to go collect it, and that's not always easy. You can get a little bit from the upfront signing bonus, something when the deal is done in August or September, but after that you don't get paid again until the regular season ends in December. Typically, you don't have money coming in again until the next crop of players' signing bonuses the following spring, unless you happen to pick up free agents at the end of the season. You have to manage your money to carry you through these long periods and you have to hope the player makes paying you a priority. But with this new arrangement, I was getting a paycheck every two weeks, plus a built-in bonus structure as a performance incentive. Prior to Gersh, any players Steve and I had together, we had split sixty for him, forty for me, because he picked up the expenses.

Leading up to the Gersh deal, we were out recruiting players. I'd been talking to Jon Alston, a linebacker from Stanford, who was friendly with David Bergeron, who we'd represented the year before. But at the end of the recruiting year, he did a one-eighty. We thought he was coming into L.A. to sign with us but his mother, who had evidently been an attorney, wanted him to go with Gary Uberstine because she thought he had a more substantial company with ties to the entertainment business. Alston just stopped returning our phone calls. Very classy. He'd had dinner with me and my wife. I'd taken him to see guys training. We'd talked every week. Then, suddenly, nothing. No good-bye. I should've been used to it by then, but I wasn't. I left him a pretty harsh phone message, describing him with trash talk he'd relate to, and figured that was the end of it. But, of course, it wasn't.

That same year, we had a couple of players in the Senior Bowl: Mike Bell, an Arizona running back (who we signed with the Broncos and coincidentally was assigned number 20, the number that would've been Maurice's), and Daniel Bullocks, Josh Bullocks's twin brother. We went down to Mobile to the game and I was visiting with Bell in his room. I walked down the hall and there was Jon Alston. We kind of stared at each other for a minute, and eventually I waved him off and walked away. He called after me, "No, no, hold on." I had already told Mike Bell how disappointed I'd been in Alston, which Mike must've shared with Jon. In the meantime, though it wasn't official yet, we'd made our deal with Gersh. And Alston was a drama major at Stanford, so our working with a Hollywood agency would mean something to him. He begged me to talk and, of course, I did. This was my chance to tell him how disrespectful he'd been and how he should have manned up and called me. He was very apologetic and he wanted to know what was happening with our business, with me, Feldman, my wife and kids, and most of all, the Gersh Agency. His apology was obviously straight from the heart . . . of his ambitions. We left the conversation saying if he wanted to come see us in L.A. to let me know. He'd already signed with Gary Uberstine, who had already paid for Alston's training at API (Athletes Performance Institute), a very expensive facility, laid out expense money, and flown his mother all over the place, but Jon was as willing to screw Gary as he had been to screw me. And even though he'd already burned me once, all I saw was another high draft choice.

Sure enough, back in L.A., he came to see me and Steve and meet with Dodson, Toi Cook, and Bob and David Gersh. We paraded him around the office, meeting one talent agent after another, this one who handles big-name comedians, this one who has directors, and writers, and so on. We talked about screenings and premieres, and how we could set up auditions for him, and he was eating it up. On the spot, he decided to sign a termination letter firing Gary Uberstine. There's supposed to be a five-day waiting period between when a client fires an agent and hires another, but most agents get around it by post-dating the representation agreements. There was just one more thing, Alston said. Would we mind flying his parents out from Louisiana? It was just as a formality, but he was very close to his mom and he wanted her blessing.

No problem. We put Alston's parents up in a boutique hotel in Beverly Hills and gave them the same tour of the office. But his mother gave off a really bad vibe. She was curt, almost rude, hard as nails. When she met with Dodson, she laid out her own plan for the agency to set up a branch in Louisiana where she'd help us recruit players. Ballsy. And a really bad idea. Then we were sitting in Bob Gersh's office, running through Steve's track record, the great players he's represented, from Lee Roy Selmon to Andre Rison to Junior Seau. She was not impressed and said something like if a rock sits by the side of the road long enough, eventually it grows moss . . . or some such analogy. Steve politely excused himself, which took all the self-control he could muster, and I was stuck taking them out to lunch, where the insult continued. She didn't even attempt to make small talk. She took out a book and began reading at the table. We got them back on a plane, ducked the idea of her "branch office," and proceeded with the paperwork with Alston. We didn't discuss Jon's momma's drama with him—why embarrass him? Our goal was to keep him happy and sign him. And we did. *Variety* did a story on it, featuring Jon Alston, drama major from Stanford, the first player to sign with us at the Gersh Agency, attracted by the Hollywood connection.

We were in contact with Michael Hoffman, a young agent who worked with Uberstine, and they were plenty pissed at us. We assured them, and Jon, that all the costs they had laid out on behalf of Alston—training at API, per diem living, whatever—would be reimbursed. Jon was obligated to repay the money, so we were just promising that we'd make good, out of our pockets, on his promise. They sent us a breakdown of expenses and we disagreed with some items, such as travel to Las Vegas for him and his family, a laptop computer, entertainment costs, some things not directly related to training. We cut a check for what we thought was right but Jon was worried they'd file a grievance against him, which they did. He paid some of the costs that were in dispute. Part of the deal with API, the training facility, was that they'd get a bonus if Jon was drafted in the first, second, or third round, a different amount for each round. He was the thirteenth player taken in the third round by the Rams that year so they got an additional $1,500, which we thought was excessive; but we paid it.

NFL Economics: Short Course

Jon Alston's was a typical NFL deal, not as lucrative as most people think—not for him, and not for his agents. Take a look at the economics: We got him a signing bonus of $550,000, plus his first-year base salary of $275,000, for a total of $825,000. As his agents, we received 3 percent, which was $24,750. But between Uberstine and API we paid back almost $25,000, so we were essentially at breakeven, or worse if we factored in the nonrecoupable expenses of recruiting him. His salary went up in year two to $360,000, so if all went well, we'd get 3 percent, or $10,800. There may be glamour in the business, but except for the superstars, the money is less and you can't spend glamour. It takes a lot of deals with a lot of players to add up to a real business.

Meanwhile, we were out beating the bushes for clients. Alston had been a good get, but we still needed more that year. So, to bring us to the attention of players, at the Super Bowl, Gersh sponsored the Hawaiian Tropic Model Search. The event featured beautiful girls in bikinis showing off their tans for the judges who just happened to be our clients ... and yes, it brought players and their friends, some of whom became new clients. And, at the Senior Bowl, I'd connected with a financial advisor to some of the players and asked him if any of them might be lured by the Hollywood connection.

He told us about Marcus Spears, first-round pick out of LSU drafted by the Cowboys, a client of Jimmy Sexton. Spears was a charming, good-looking guy with a big personality, and we set up a conversation. I started pitching him about how Gersh represents these big-name comics, Jamie Foxx, Chris Tucker, Dave Chappelle, and Monique. Marcus loved Monique, who was going to do a concert in Dallas, and we got him VIP tickets. He was trying to decide whether to come out to L.A. to meet with us, and if he did, he wanted to bring his sister. I had him on the phone and I held the phone up to the window, to the outside traffic, and I said, "Marcus, do you hear that? Do you? You know what that is? That's Hollywood calling, baby. Are you gonna answer the call?" He laughed, eating it up, and he and his sister flew out to see us. Besides Hollywood, I had a connection with Jim Rome and his syndicated sports radio show. I'd known him for years, including in our childbirth classes and from trick-or-treating with the kids, and our wives had become close friends. I called and asked if he wanted to have Marcus on his show, and he jumped at it. (Cowboys training camp that year was all over the news, because they'd recently signed superstar receiver and one-man circus Terrell Owens.) We had Marcus picked up in a limo and taken to the studio and he hadn't done much national media so his head was spinning from the attention. By the end of the trip, we had him. Even though he and his coach, Bill Parcells, were both represented by Jimmy Sexton, Marcus fired Sexton and hired us.

Next up was Mike Patterson, a defensive tackle from USC, picked by the Eagles in the first round in 2005. Now, in 2006, we obviously weren't going to get a commission on his current contract, but he was still a talented young player, and we thought he had potential to earn us some money and some cred with Gersh.

We'd actually gone after Patterson the year before, ahead of the draft, but not signed him. Funny story, actually: Steve and I had pursued him in his last year at Southern Cal, met with his family, since he was a local kid, and finally, thanks to an undrafted player named Johnny Walker, were able to get a formal meeting with Patterson in December 2004. We were at his apartment in a complex filled with other USC players, like Lawrence Jackson, who was going to be a first-rounder the next year. Patterson told us he was about to sign with Gary Uberstine, who was also the agent for Pete Carroll, Patterson's own coach at USC. But we told him about how some of Uberstine's players had fallen in the draft but we could maximize where he got picked (the old Gary Wichard pitch). We showed him our client list, went through our Playbook presentation, and created good chemistry. The meeting went well and Patterson said that, instead of signing with Uberstine as he'd planned, he was going to hold off, wait for the Senior Bowl, and think about it. Patterson walked us to our car and Steve, in his usual surfer shorts and T-shirt outfit, broke into an impromptu tap dance in the parking lot, stomped his feet, stopped, and said, "Can Gary Uberstine do this?" Patterson was laughing and we clearly had made a lasting impression.

Then something unusual happened. We went to the Senior Bowl to spend some time with our players and keep up contact with Mike Patterson. Pete Carroll, who was supposedly in Hawaii on vacation with his family, suddenly showed

up in Mobile, Alabama, on the practice field. We talked to
Patterson after practice and he told us that Coach Carroll had
talked to him about Uberstine. Evidently Uberstine knew
we were all over Patterson and he was about to lose out so he
called in his big gun, his client Pete Carroll, to save the day.
And that's just what he did for Uberstine. Patterson didn't
want to go against his coach's wishes so he stuck with Uberstine and walked from us.

So, could that make Pete Carroll a runner for Gary Uberstine? I guess it depends on how you define "runner." A runner,
by my definition, is *any* unofficial, unsanctioned, unlicensed
go-between who gets paid, or stands to gain in some other
way, by helping to recruit a player for an agent, typically
frowned upon by the NFLPA, and using a runner is improper
without full disclosure.

Fast forward to 2006, when Patterson had just completed
his rookie year and Steve and I had joined Gersh. Patterson's
financial planner happened to be the financial planner for Jon
Alston, who we'd just signed. The planner said, "Mike, do
you know Steve Feldman and Josh Luchs at Gersh?" And he
said, "Yeah, I almost went with those guys." So we brought
Patterson to our new offices and talked with him about all the
opportunities Gersh offered outside of football. He already
knew our track record, and he explained to us why he had
signed with Uberstine in the first place, why he now regret-
ted it. He said he had now decided to make the switch. He
got a letter together to fire Uberstine, sent it, and started to
wait out the NFLPA's mandatory five-day waiting period
to make it official. As soon as he sent the termination letter,
his phone started ringing. First it was Pete Carroll, whom
Patterson hadn't heard from probably since the Senior Bowl,

insisting that firing Gary was a mistake. Then Mike heard from Derrick Deese, another USC player, another Uberstine client, now with the 49ers, saying virtually the same thing. We'd gotten Patterson an invitation to a party at the Playboy Mansion by way of Toi Cook at Gersh, also an ex-49er. Derrick Deese was at the party too and he was all over Patterson to withdraw the termination letter to Uberstine. But this time Mike had made up his mind and stood by his decision to come with us.

We always knew Pete Carroll was tight with Gary Uberstine, dating from when we'd tried to recruit at USC and Carroll's rules kept us away from the field or the locker room, but allowed Gary in with access to players under the guise of being Pete's agent. During the Carroll era, the list of USC players signed by Uberstine was impressive—nine players from one school—and would seem more than coincidental.

But Uberstine didn't sign all the best USC players during Carroll's tenure. In 2003, agent David Dunn promised Pat Kirwan, perhaps Carroll's closest friend, $100,000 for helping to deliver the USC quarterback and Heisman Trophy winner Carson Palmer to his agency, Athletes First. (Kirwan and Carroll's friendship goes back to when they both worked for the Jets, continuing through Carroll becoming head coach of the Seattle Seahawks and Kirwan's name even being bandied about as a GM candidate.) The Dunn-Kirwan arrangement was controversial since, at the time, Kirwan was a commentator for NFL.com, a job one might assume required independence and objectivity, not simultaneous employment by a sports agency . . . aka "runner." Once in the door, having represented the number-one draft pick in the country, Dunn signed ten USC players during the Carroll years.

Compare Uberstine's or Dunn's results with Tom Condon of CAA, acknowledged to be one of the top agents in the game, who signed only four players. Or Drew Rosenhaus, supposed powerhouse agent who only signed two USC players. I signed three—one with Wichard, two with Feldman.

Thanks to our record, plus the Hollywood wild card, Steve and I were meeting with almost any player we wanted, not always signing them, but always in the hunt. Between the players we already had, the defections to us, and the rookies, we were off to a great start at Gersh, and I was finally making a pretty good living—in six figures with bonuses and benefits.

After signing Josh Bullocks in 2005, we got his twin brother, Daniel, in 2006. We had advised the brothers, and their mother, Peaches, to avoid coming out the same year and competing against each other in the draft (they were both safeties, and both played for the same school, Nebraska). The odd thing was, a year apart, both were drafted number forty overall, eighth in the second round, Josh to the Saints, Daniel to the Lions. The same year, 2006, we had Richard Marshall, defensive back from Fresno State, picked in the second round by the Panthers.

We went to Columbus, Ohio, to make a run at stars Troy Smith and Santonio Holmes. Our intro came by way of Steve's former client, Greg Bell, a former first-round draft pick out of Notre Dame who in 1988 had led the NFL in rushing TDs, played for the Rams and Bills, and was now a financial advisor with ties to players at Ohio State. Troy Smith, it turned out, wasn't going to come out until the next year, 2007, when he'd go on to win the Heisman Trophy but free-fall in the draft after a big loss to Florida in the BCS Championship. But Santonio was still available. We met him as he was coming out of the football building. As I recall, when he saw us, he must've immediately thought, these guys are here to offer me money, because early in the conversation, he said to us, "Listen, I want to save you the time. We don't need to meet. I've been taking money from Joel Segal the last couple years, and he's been taking care of my family too." Clearly, while I had stopped paying players, the practice hadn't died. Segal was a prominent agent who had gotten busted by the NFLPA for improper benefits but had been reinstated, and had signed Reggie Bush and become an NFLPA "favored" agent. He signed Santonio, who was taken in the first round by the Steelers. Santonio later denied having said Segal paid him, but I heard him say it and so did my partner, Steve Feldman.

"Favored Agents"

I know firsthand that the NFLPA has favored agents because of a conversation I had with a former client and friend. Nolan Harrison and I were as close as a player and agent could be. In fact, when the Rodney King verdict was read in 1992 and riots broke out, Nolan was with me at my parents' house and my mother wouldn't let him leave the house for a few days fearing for his safety. Never mind that Nolan was a six-foot seven-inch, three-hundred-plus-pound defensive tackle for the L.A. Raiders who could take care of himself. To my mom, he was just a twentysomething kid who needed someone to look out for him. I was honored when Nolan asked me to be a groomsman in his wedding. And Nolan was the only client I had who'd attended both of my parents' funerals, signing a deal Doc and I had completed with the Pittsburgh Steelers in my parents' driveway while we were sitting shiva for my mother.

Nolan became the team's Players' Union representative and had gotten close with the powers at the NFLPA office in Washington. As the last active client I had recruited with Doc, it came as a shock when he fired us without any explanation. I was stung by it for years. After Nolan was long retired, and I had become the VP of football at Gersh, one day he came to see me and explained what had happened. Apparently, some of the honchos at the NFLPA had questioned how he could be represented by agents like me and Doc. They listed agents they preferred, not just hinting but naming names, and it's safe to say that neither Doc nor I was among the names they listed. So he hired an agent from the NFLPA "favored" agent list, Ralph Cindrich.

A good gauge of how you're doing as an agent isn't just who you sign, it's who you meet with, who feels they need to meet with you. Feldman-Luchs-Gersh was getting to be a must-meet for some of the top-tier players. It was like having a list of who you had dated on your résumé. For the 2007 draft, we had good talks with Steve Smith, the wide receiver who played at USC and was drafted by the Giants in the first round. He signed with Eddie DeBartolo, who'd been an owner of the San Francisco 49ers but was barred from active control of the team for a year, and fined $1 million, for failing to report a felony. DeBartolo later lost control of the team altogether and opened a sports firm. To recruit Smith, he called in the biggest of big guns and got All-Everything receiver Jerry Rice to put the heat on Smith to sign. Even so, I kept on top of Smith, figuring maybe he'd defect at some point.

(All photos courtesy of Josh Luchs unless otherwise noted.)

Various money orders payable to prized draft prospect quarterback Ryan Leaf, documenting some of the money given/loaned to him, by me, during his years at Washington State.

One-Liner by School Name / High Grade
Class Year 2004
Report Dates From 1/1/03 To 6/30/03

School	CP	PP	Area	Jsy	Player	Report Date	HAW SPD HWS FACTORS	Height	Weight	Speed			Scout	1st Pos Grade	High Grade
TOLEDO	DE	DE	7	99	OFILI, FRANK	3/4/2003	4.0 7.0 5.5 6022	V 262	V 4.83	4.79	4.80	V RI1 Smith	1 29 23	4.40	4.40
TROY ST	OT	OT	4	76	HALL, BRANDON	4/23/2003	6.0 2.0 4.0 6031	V 327	V 5.60	5.45		V GO1 Turner	1 27 17	5.20	5.20
TULANE	QB	QB	5	7	LOSMAN, JONATHAN	4/17/2003	5.0 8.0 6.5 6024	V 212	V 4.80	W 4.80 A		V FO1 Weidl	1 22 14	7.20	7.20
	OH	OH	5	26	MOORE, MEWELDE	4/17/2003	5.0 8.0 5.0 5102	V 206	V 4.60	W 4.63 A		V FO1 Weidl	1 24 16	5.50	5.50
	WO	WO	5	8	NARCISSE, NICK	4/17/2003	3.0 6.0 4.5 5107	V 176	V 4.47	W 4.49 A		V FO1 Weidl	1 34 25	4.80	4.80
TULSA	WO	WO	9	82	BRYANT, ROMBY	4/4/2003	6.0 8.0 7.0 6012	V 181	V 4.38	W 4.46 A		V FO1 Bonaven	1 33 30	5.30	5.30
TUSCULUM	DC	DC	5	23	COLCLOUGH, RICARDO	3/26/2003	6.0 6.0 6.0 5108	V 185	V 4.49	4.50		V FI1 Weidl	1 31 13	5.70	5.70
TUSKEGEE	OH	OH	4	3	FLORENCE, CORTLANDT	4/30/2003	5.0 3.0 4.0 6001	V 190	V 4.71	4.78	4.72	V GO1 Turner	1 22 13	4.10	4.10
UCLA	DT	DT	10	77	LEISLE, RODNEY	4/18/2003	5.0 4.0 4.5 6030	C 288	C 5.10			E RO1 DiMarzo	1 28 15	6.00	6.00
	WO	WO	10	1	PERRY, TAB	4/18/2003	9.0 4.0 6.5 6021	C 219	C 4.61	4.65		C RO1 DiMarzo	1 30 19	5.00	5.00
	DT	DT	10	75	BOSCHETTI, RYAN	4/18/2003	7.0 3.0 5.0 6040	C 293	C 5.14	5.18		C RO1 DiMarzo	1 46 34	4.90	4.90
	DE	DE	10	43	BALL, DAVE	4/18/2003	6.0 1.0 4.5 6052	C 272	C 5.07	5.08		C RO1 DiMarzo	1 39 20	4.40	4.40
	OB	OB	10	11	CHILLAR, BRANDON	4/18/2003	6.0 3.0 4.5 6030	C 234	C 4.85			E RO1 DiMarzo	1 40 18	4.40	4.40
	DE	DE	10	49	BALL, MATT	4/18/2003	6.0 4.0 6.0 6050	C 276	C 4.90	4.99		C RO1 DiMarzo	1 39 28	4.00	4.00
UNLV	DT	DT	10	91	CANTERBERRY, DIETRICH	4/23/2003	8.0 1.0 4.5 6034	C 304	C 5.32	5.30		C GO1 DiMarzo	1 33 19	5.40	5.40
	OH	OH	10	1	CROOM, LARRY	4/23/2003	4.0 5.0 4.5 5095	C 200	C 4.80			E GO1 DiMarzo	1 22 13	4.90	4.90
UTAH	DE	DE	10	86	KAUFUSI, JASON	3/10/2003	2.0 9.0 5.5 6022	V 242	V 4.65			E AI1 DiMarzo	1 43 12	5.40	5.40
	DC	DC	10	17	PARKER, ARNOLD	3/10/2003	9.0 7.0 8.0 6016	V 211	V 4.44	4.43		V AI1 DiMarzo	2 29 18	5.40	5.40
UTAH ST	TE	TE	10	89	COOLEY, CHRIS	5/2/2003	5.0 5.0 5.0 6032	C 252	C 4.87	4.91		C AI1 DiMarzo		5.20	5.20

28-May-03 10:10 AM

National Scouting Combine spring grades, including three Pro Tect clients: Tulane quarterback J. P. Losman, UCLA defensive tackle Rodney Leisle, and Utah State tight end Chris Cooley. We obtained the reports from confidential sources, then altered key data, photocopying pages to cover any imperfections. Losman's grade was altered slightly downward so that when he went in the first round, we could take the credit for improving his outcome; Leisle's grade was moved down so it would not appear that he dropped in the draft but was expected to go when he did; and Cooley was not altered because he went higher than projected, again a chance for us to take credit.

School	Ch	PP	Area	Jsv	Player	Report Date / FACTORS	HW SPD HWE	Height	Weight	Shred	Scout	1st Pos High Class Grade
TOLEDO	DC	DE	7	99	ORILI, FRANK	1/4/2003 4.0 7.0 5.5 6022	V	262	V 4.88	4.79 4.80	V RI1 Smith	1 29 21 4.40 4.40
TROY ST	OT	OT	4	76	HALL, BRANDON	4/23/2003 6.0 2.0 4.0 6031	V	327	V 5.60	5.45	V GO1 Turner	1 27 17 5.20 5.20
TULANE	QB	QB	5	7	LOSMAN, JONATHAN	4/17/2003 5.0 8.0 6.5 6024	V	212	V 4.80	W 4.80 A	V FO1 Weidl	1 22 14 5.70 5.70
	OH	OH	5	26	MOORE, MEWELDE	4/17/2003 5.0 5.0 5.0 5102	V	206	V 4.60	W 4.63 A	V FO1 Weidl	1 24 16 5.50 5.50
	WO	WO	5	8	NARCISSE, NICK	4/17/2003 3.0 6.0 4.5 5107	V	178	V 4.47	W 4.49 A	V FO1 Weidl	1 34 25 4.60 4.80
TULSA	WO	WO	9	82	BRYANT, ROMBY	4/4/2003 6.0 8.0 7.0 6012	V	181	V 4.38	W 4.46 A	V FO1 Bonavzo	1 33 36 5.30 5.30
TUSCULUM	DC	DC	5	23	COLCLOUGH, RICARDO	3/26/2003 6.0 8.0 9.0 5106	V	188	V 4.49	4.50	V FI1 Weidl	1 31 11 5.70 5.70
TUSKEGEE	OH	OH	4	3	FLORENCE, CORTLANDT	4/30/2003 5.0 3.0 4.0 6001	V	190	V 4.71	4.78 4.72	V GO1 Turner	1 32 13 4.10 4.10
UCLA	DT	DT	10	77	LEISLE, RODNEY	4/18/2003 5.0 4.0 4.5 6030	C	288	C 5.10		E RO1 DiMarzo	1 29 15 4.90 4.90
	WO	WO	10	1	PERRY, TAB	4/18/2003 9.0 4.0 6.5 6021	C	219	C 4.61	4.65	C RO1 DiMarzo	1 40 19 5.00 5.00
	DT	DT	10	75	BOSCHETTI, RYAN	4/18/2003 7.0 3.0 5.0 6040	C	283	C 5.14	5.18	C RO1 DiMarzo	1 46 34 4.40 4.40
	DE	DE	10	43	BALL, DAVE	4/18/2003 8.0 1.0 4.5 6052	C	272	C 5.07	5.08	C RO1 DiMarzo	1 39 20 6.00 8.00
	OB	OB	10	11	CHILLAR, BRANDON	4/18/2003 6.0 3.0 4.5 6030	C	234	C 4.85		E RO1 DiMarzo	1 40 18 4.40 4.40
	DE	DE	10	49	BALL, MATT	4/18/2003 8.0 4.0 6.0 6050	C	276	C 4.90	4.90	C RO1 DiMarzo	1 39 28 4.00 4.00
UNLV	DT	DT	10	91	CANTERBERRY, DIETRICH	4/23/2003 8.0 1.0 4.5 6034	C	304	C 5.32	5.30	C CO1 DiMarzo	1 33 19 5.40 5.40
	OH	OH	10	1	CROOM, LARRY	4/23/2003 4.0 5.0 4.5 5095	C	200	C 4.80		E GO1 DiMarzo	1 72 14 4.90 4.90
UTAH	DE	DE	10	86	KAUFUSI, JASON	3/10/2003 2.0 3.0 5.5 6022	V	242	V 4.55		E AI1 DiMarzo	1 43 12 5.40 5.40
	DC	DC	10	17	PARKER, ARNOLD	3/10/2003 9.0 7.0 8.0 6016	V	211	V 4.44	4.43	V AI1 DiMarzo	2 29 16 5.40 5.40
UTAH ST	TE	TE	10	89	COOLEY, CHRIS	5/2/2003 5.0 5.0 5.0 6032	C	252	C 4.87	4.91	C AI1 DiMarzo	5.20 5.20

PRO TECT CORP
MANAGEMENT
LOS ANGELES • NEW YORK

TERRELL SUGGS
NFL GAMEPLAN

Suggs

17383 Sunset Boulevard, Suite 250 • Pacific Palisades, California 90272 • (310) 230-2121 • FAX (310) 230-2126

Pro Tect Management's customized, bound Game Plan to pitch, and ultimately sign, Arizona State linebacker Terrell Suggs.

Me and my buddy Ryan Leaf, clowning around prior to our Las Vegas road trip, during which I wouldn't pick up the tab for his back-up quarterback pals, and after which our relationship was never the same.

My larger-than-life mentor, confidant, and partner, Harold "Doc" Daniels, now wracked with illness, but nevertheless by my side at my wedding.

Doc Daniels and I meeting up with a client, Michigan State quarterback Tony Banks, at the St. Louis airport to receive his rookie signing bonus from Rams executive Jay Zygmunt.

Young Josh Luchs, sixteen-year-old ball boy, in official, team-issue short-shorts at Raiders training camp—my first job in football.

Stanford star defensive end Willie Howard introducing my daughter Sophie to "bling."

Agent duties: Client Terrell Suggs and I at the 2003 NFL Rookie Premiere photo shoot for trading card companies.

Los Angeles Raiders defensive end Greg Townsend—my first client—and me at the Pro Bowl.

Corey Dillon's first annual golf tournament to benefit Boys & Girls Clubs: Steve Feldman, defensive tackle Mike Patterson, running back Corey Dillon, and me (right to left).

Sports Illustrated

OCTOBER 18, 2010 | SI.COM

"I WILL NEVER FORGET THE FIRST TIME I PAID A PLAYER..."

(By JOSH LUCHS)

CONFESSIONS OF AN AGENT

As Told to
GEORGE DOHRMANN

The *Sports Illustrated* cover story—October 12, 2010. I told the truth and began a new life. (*Sports Illustrated*/Getty Images)

We also met with JaMarcus Russell, the quarterback out of LSU who would be the number-one draft pick of 2007 by the Raiders. We got to him by way of Marcus Spears, who had been his roommate; we even met with his mother at their home in Mobile, Alabama. To get his attention, we bought a not-very-subtle billboard ad close to JaMarcus's apartment that he had to drive past every day on the way to practice. It featured huge photos of his good friend Marcus Spears both as National Champion at LSU and as a Dallas Cowboy and was signed "Gersh Sports" so the connection between college success and NFL success was crystal clear: us. We met with Joe Thomas's dad about Joe, an offensive tackle from Wisconsin and a 2007 first-round pick by the Browns. Plus we were in the running for Marshawn Lynch, a Cal running back drafted in the first round by the Bills, and Adam Carriker, a Nebraska defensive end, drafted in the first round by the Rams (a bad fit for the Hollywood pitch).

We were even getting meetings with players from teams we'd never previously gotten around to recruiting. Just before the 2007 Rose Bowl in Pasadena, we had somebody who was tight with a lot of Michigan players hook us up with LaMarr Woodley, a linebacker and second-round pick by the Steelers. We were late on these guys and had never flown to Ann Arbor to meet with them, but LaMarr came to the office at Gersh along with his teammate Alan Branch, a defensive tackle and second-round pick by the Cardinals.

We did sign Chris Henry, a running back from Arizona, ultimately a second-round pick by the Titans in 2007. We'd gotten him a part in a TV pilot for MTV, "24 Before," a docu-drama in which people were followed for twenty-four hours before a major life-altering event, in his case the NFL draft. They were going to intercut between Chris and a young female soldier being shipped out to Iraq but Chris's dad, who was a corrections officer, vetoed the idea of cameras in his house. Even though Steve Smith had signed with DeBartolo, we put him in the show and he had MTV cameras with him on draft day, something Eddie DeBartolo couldn't do. We thought it might pay off for us down the road. In the end Chris Henry was the eighteenth pick and Smith was nineteenth, back-to-back in the second round.

We were also chasing Kenny Irons, the Auburn running back. He and his brother, David Jr., a cornerback at Auburn, both NFL prospects, came from a big football family. Two uncles and three cousins played college and/or pro ball. Kenny and David's father, David Sr., made it clear that the selection of an agent went through him, or rather through his garage. To paraphrase, his blunt terms were, "Whoever is going to represent my boys is going to make a lot of money and whoever that's going to be is up to me. Their agent is going to buy me an S-class Mercedes." That was the price of representation. Plus, he had his own gym and said whatever an agent might have paid for a facility to train his boys before the Combine, would be paid to him. The Irons brothers didn't sign with us but it was because we backed out early due to the "terms" dictated. They eventually went with Fletcher Smith. Whether he ponied up the price of entry, who knows. Kenny got hurt, was drafted in the second round by the Bengals, got hurt again, and only played two years. David was a sixth-round pick by the Falcons. Did the father get his Mercedes? I don't know that either. If it was after the season, it wouldn't have been illegal to give him a car unless the promise of the car came during the season, in which case, it's an illegal inducement to sign. In any case, based on the Irons's careers it would have been a bad investment. And it would have been sleazy, not that that's anything new.

Solo, I made my first trip to Florida State to meet with linebacker Buster Davis, short, squat, and undersized, and running back Lorenzo Booker, also undersized but not in ego. I really hit it off with Davis; I flew to Daytona to meet his family at his request, and then he called us the night before the Orange Bowl to say when he came out to Los Angeles, he wanted us to have arranged for a Mercedes for him, with his specific list of options. I ran around to dealers to find somebody who would do all the paperwork, have a car ready for him to buy, with the options he wanted, just waiting for his signature, and then he vanished. Somewhere in the Valley, a Mercedes was sitting on a lot that never got picked up and a car salesman was pissed off at me. I never heard from Buster again. He signed with another agent, Todd France, and again, I have no idea if he ever got his Benz. As for Lorenzo Booker, he was good-looking, charismatic, with stars in his eyes. In fact, he told me that when he had the ball and was headed for the sideline, he just let himself run on out of bounds, rather than fight for an extra yard and run the risk of hurting his body. He was saving it for a longer career. Lorenzo had a cousin, a wanna-be agent, who got himself inserted into the process, came to visit us a couple of times, and eventually got himself a cut of whatever deal they'd make. They went with an agent named Ryan Slayton who I'd never heard of. Lorenzo has had an inconsistent career in football and no career in Hollywood, so we dodged a bullet.

In 2007, Troy Smith ended up going with Eddie DeBartolo

Jr., the NFL owner–turned felon–turned agency owner, who
had also talked to Toi Cook about joining us at Gersh. Big-time
sports can be a small, sordid world. And the rules can be, shall
we say, fluid. You can't own a team if you commit a crime, but
you can own a company that represents players. Agents can't
lend money to players but coaches can steer players to agents.
Players can't take money while in college but if the fact that
they had taken money comes out once they turn pro, there
are no consequences to them individually. And it's incestu-
ous: the agent who was your enemy on one deal is your ally
on the next. That is, the fucker becomes the fuckee and vice
versa.

And I was about to become the fuckee.

I was recruiting for the 2008 draft, going after Keenan
Burton, a wide receiver from Kentucky, drafted by the
Rams; Eddie Royal, a Virginia Tech wide receiver drafted by
the Broncos; and Dustin Keller, a tight end from Purdue,
first-round draft pick by the Jets. Keller was so taken with us
and the Hollywood world that he flew his brothers out to
L.A. on his own dime and went to Venice Beach and bought
his one brother, a big reggae fan, a painting of Bob Marley.
And then I had my world turned upside down.

CHAPTER 8

Luchs vs. Wichard

This is a recap of the legal battle that ensued between me and Gary Wichard. I recount it not to bury you in legalese, not to be overly defensive on my own behalf, but to shed more light on the justice, or injustice, of big-time football. To borrow a phrase, you be the judge.

Instant replay. In 2004 I left Gary Wichard for Steve Feldman but I fully expected to continue to collect commissions on the players Gary and I had signed together. That's the way our agreement was structured. But after I resigned, I wasn't getting payments. I called the Pro Tect office; I spoke to Gary's assistant, Beth, who was very uncomfortable with my questions; and month after month, well after I knew the players had paid Gary, I still got no payments. Later I found out the trigger for not paying me may have been the conversation Chuck Price had had with Gary when he was competitively shopping Matt Leinart with us, Gary, and who knows who else. Price had repeated Manuel White Jr.'s comment that I had claimed to represent Terrell Suggs, which led to Gary calling and ranting and me trying to explain I never had said that, only that I'd helped recruit players like Suggs—but Gary had been too busy ripping me a new one over the phone to hear me.

I kept calling, kept trying to collect, and I was worried about any statute of limitations. I assumed that if I didn't file a suit demanding to be paid before the year expired, I might lose my right to collect my money. My brother-in-law hooked me up with an attorney. We sent a demand letter, then filed a breach of contract suit in January 2005. They responded with a letter saying Gary wasn't paying me because I had opted to compete in the industry, and they filed a counter-suit on that basis. That suit was thrown out of court, because Gary's corporation technically no longer existed (and besides, the precedent in California courts is that noncompete clauses are essentially unenforceable). The whole David Dunn–Leigh Steinberg case had hinged on a noncompete clause that didn't hold up. And we didn't even have a noncompete clause in our deal, only something that said I couldn't raid Pro Tect clients while working elsewhere—an obligation I had honored.

Throughout the whole process, I was convinced that Gary was stalling so I'd accept a settlement for less than he owed. He had a history of doing that with other young guys who worked for him. For that reason, I didn't want to work with an attorney on a contingency, a percentage of money collected. I figured this matter was cut and dried, and I was going to get most, if not all, of what I was owed. So I decided to hire a lawyer by the hour and be done with it.

Meantime, Keenan Howry, who had fired Gary and hired me in 2005, received a bill from Pro Tect for more than $9,000, which he didn't think was right, so he called me. I helped him refigure it, and it was only about $5,300 he actually owed for commissions. My best guess is the error in the bill was due to a human miscalculation. Howry asked me how to make the check out and I said, to Pro Tect. In light of the fact that I was suing Gary for back commissions, the appropriate thing to do, I thought, was to give the check to my lawyer. I explained this all to Keenan and turned the check over to my attorney. The lawyer and I were on a lot of calls together, but it seemed like he was churning hours, and we're not getting anywhere . . . at $400 an hour.

So I called another lawyer I knew, my old friend Mike Trope. He was working at a law firm in Brentwood and we had lunch, during which I showed him the complaint. As it turned out, my attorney had referred some past cases to Mike, so he didn't want to jeopardize that relationship by poaching a client. Instead, he referred me to a female attorney he had sometimes used to do preliminary work, who agreed to work at a discounted rate. She reviewed the complaint and concluded it was drafted incorrectly because Gary's corporation had been dissolved and could leave me with a judgment against a nonexistent company. I switched over to this woman with the understanding that she would handle the basic pretrial work, and Mike Trope would do the depositions and trial because of his familiarity with the inner workings of the NFL and the agent business. He's a brilliant lawyer and had represented some high-profile sports characters—such as Lloyd Bloom and Norby Walters, two notorious agents who had been accused of giving gifts to college athletes—so if we went to trial I knew I'd have a big gun.

Now, here's where the details get a little complicated: 1) I told Trope about the check from Keenan Howry and Trope asked if my first attorney was holding the check or the proceeds from the check. I didn't know. Trope said, "He must be holding the check itself, because he couldn't have put it in his trust account." I had no idea how lawyers' trust accounts worked, so I figured Mike was right. 2) I left the first attorney but he wanted his final payment of about $6,000 or he would sue me. I told my new attorney and she reached a settlement with the first one, part of which stated that he would forward the Howry commissions he was holding. I later discovered that he had endorsed the check and put it into his own trust account, despite what Trope had originally thought. 3) When he sent a check to my new attorney, she returned it with "Rejected" written on it because she concluded that possession of it would look like improper behavior on her part. She protected herself but breached her fiduciary duty to me as her client by not telling me about the whole incident. 4) I thought the issue with the check had been resolved and that it had eventually gone to Gary Wichard's attorney. I thought wrong.

In fact, when I was deposed by Gary's attorney and asked about any checks I had received from players I shared with Pro Tect, I said I had forwarded them to Wichard's office. Then, in a second deposition, I was asked the same question repeatedly, thought hard about it, and said there was this commission check from Keenan Howry that had been given to my attorney. I didn't think it would matter because it was in the hands of counsel, and I presumed it would be forwarded to Wichard, but I couldn't have been more wrong. Once I acknowledged the Howry check in the second deposition, it was interpreted as a contradiction of what I'd said earlier and called into question everything from the first deposition, and Gary even filed a police report on Christmas Eve that the check was "stolen" (at least the DA recognized it was a civil matter and disregarded it). To use a legal term of art, it started a shit storm.

It was an expensive shit storm. The legal bills kept coming like a tidal wave—$6,000, $7,000—to the point where I had to take out a second mortgage. Fortunately, my wife and my in-laws were 100 percent behind me, telling me to get what I was owed. And Steve Feldman agreed with my position that there was no basis for Gary not paying except to try to wear me down to a lower settlement.

The lawsuit drama dragged on from 2005 to early 2008, until we were a couple of months from the trial I'd thought would never happen. I did get a settlement offer from Gary but it was more like attempted blackmail in an extortion letter. He said I should take about $50,000 or he'd go to the NFLPA with a complaint that I'd withheld a player's commission money from him. I was comparing that "offer" (or threat) to $170,000 owed in commissions to date, plus future commissions for players we shared, including a new deal for Terrell Suggs that had the potential to earn me as much as $700,000 if Suggs played out his contract. All together, it was over $1,000,000 owed vs. $50,000 offered. Gary's specific threat was that he would file a grievance with the NFLPA against Keenan Howry for nonpayment of the $5,300 fee (even though he'd billed Howry for more than $9,000), which would theoretically trigger a breach of fiduciary duty action by the union against me. My lawyers thought it was a ridiculous threat. It was transparent that Gary knew the money was sitting in trust; and furthermore, they argued the NFLPA would not get involved in a dispute between agents that did not impact any players. Gary just wanted to use the union rules to gain an advantage in the civil proceeding, not really follow through with an NFLPA action against Howry. I didn't accept his offer and he filed the grievance.

In the end, the case that we never thought would go to trial, went to trial. And in a matter that was supposed to be cut and dried in my favor, the jury ruled against me and found no breach of contract. Plus, whoever lost at trial had to pay the other's attorney's fees. Bottom-line: In large part due to the attorney's mishandling of the $5,300 Howry check, instead of getting $1,000,000 and more in commissions, with the cost of appeal and interest, I now owed $650,000 to Wichard's lawyers. I ended up suing my attorney for malpractice (Trope had bowed out). The lawyer's insurance company offered a settlement to pay Wichard and the new lawyer's contingency. I won, if you can call it that, but it was hardly the end of the bad news. I still had the NFLPA complaint to face.

Suge Knight's "Stepson": The Last Player We Recruited Together

The legal mess with Gary Wichard was a major distraction, but I still had a business to run—in fact, with the prospect of losing money, I needed to be more effective than ever. So I kept on recruiting. As it turns out, the last player Steve and I would recruit together was Chauncey Washington from USC. (In fact, by the time Chauncey was ready to officially sign with us, the NFLPA had already dropped its final hammer on my head.) Steve called and asked me to meet Chauncey at a rental car place in Los Angeles. I was thinking Budget or Avis for a nice midsize to get him back and forth to workouts. Instead, I met Chauncey at Black and White Rental Cars in Beverly Hills, an outfit that specializes in luxury vehicles. Chauncey explained that his "step-dad" wanted him to "roll in style" but due to his step-dad's "current situation," they needed me to put it on my credit card.

Chauncey promised me that we'd go right over to the Peninsula Hotel in Beverly Hills, where his step-dad would give me the cash to cover a one-week rental. This plan had all the makings of a disaster, and I felt a sense of déjà disaster: I'd lived this b.s. before. At least I had the good sense to increase the insurance limits on my American Express card before Chauncey got behind the wheel of his $100,000 Mercedes. He drove me over to the hotel, where we met the step-dad he kept talking about, a man who turned out to be none other than the notorious rap mogul (and ex-convict) Marion "Suge" Knight.

Ensconced in a massive hotel suite, the infamous rap impresario Suge came to the door wrapped in a white terry-cloth robe, then perched on a chair in the middle of the room, flanked by Asian girls performing manicures and pedicures on his digits. My déjà disaster alarms were going nonstop. I jokingly asked if he'd mind closing the French doors to his balcony, a reference to the crazy story of Suge hanging rapper Vanilla Ice off a balcony over the rights to the hit song "Ice

Ice Baby." Suge laughed and then we traded a few old war stories; Doc Daniels had actually represented Suge when he was a replacement player for the Rams during the 1987 strike. He even remembered that I was Doc's "Jew-boy."

The whole time I was waiting for Chauncey to bring up the cash for the rental car, but it wasn't happening. Suge said he was heading to Las Vegas for the weekend and I should go along for some fun. Maybe when I was single and fifteen years younger and dumber, I would've gone, but not now with a wife and two daughters. I could just imagine that call to my wife: "Jen, honey, I'm gonna skip dinner tonight and in fact I'll be gone all weekend so could you do me a favor and fill in for me as a coach for our daughter's soccer team cuz I'm gonna hop a private jet to Vegas and whoop it up with Suge Knight? Okay, honey?" Not okay. Chauncey never did ask his step-dad for the money, and I sure as hell wasn't going to ask Suge for it. I left empty-handed and financially responsible for a $2,500-per-week rental car. Sunday morning, I read in the paper that Suge had been arrested that weekend in Vegas on a domestic violence charge. At least I'd made one good call.

An entire week went by and as I'd feared, Chauncey didn't return the car. I started fielding daily calls from Black and White Rental Car. Then another week, and another $2,500 on my AmEx card, went by. (Hey, at least I was earning a lot of reward points.) The next week Chauncey was leaving for the Combine in Indianapolis so I figured/hoped he would return the car at that time. Chauncey did leave for the Combine, but he drove himself to the airport and parked the car at some obscure lot while he was in Indianapolis for the week. Another $2,500 in rewards points. All told, Chauncey burned around $20,000 on the rental car, all on my card.

Lucky for us he earned almost twice that in rookie football card deals with Topps, Upper Deck, and others, so he'd have little trouble paying it back . . . if I could get him to sign the deals before the predraft deadline, which I did but it was no small task.

We got out without too much personal damage. Chauncey was a seventh-round pick of the Jacksonville Jaguars and received a modest signing bonus. But dealing with Chauncey was yet another reminder of how ugly the business can be—an unfortunate end to my work with Steve Feldman.

Justice NFLPA-style

Just before the trial, I received a letter from the NFLPA informing me that they had begun their own inquiry for breach of fiduciary duty—Gary's wild threat—citing my having made inaccurate statements in my depositions. I hired another lawyer, this time David Cornwell, one of the nation's leading sports attorneys (along with his associate, Brandon Witkow), as Cornwell had represented NFL athletes, agents, and even the league itself. Cornwell contended that the fiduciary duty breach claim would normally come from the one owed the duty, which would've meant Keenan Howry. But the union, by way of an organization called CARD (Committee on Agent Representation and Discipline), took the position that they were acting on behalf of all players in the union, that the damage was to their overall membership and marketplace. I never spoke to CARD and nobody from the NFLPA ever contacted me or Keenan Howry. But they were supposedly weighing the facts of the case.

Meantime, Hugh Dodson, COO of the Gersh Agency, who

had become licensed as an agent, was at the NFLPA meeting in northern California. On a huge screen, in front of a large group of other agents, the union officials projected a notice that I had been suspended for twelve months and fined $25,000 for misappropriating funds and lying in depositions. They posted it before I'd even responded to their letter and before informing me of their decision. A mad agent scramble for the phones ensued, people trying to pick off my clients. The body wasn't even cold and already the vultures were circling. Within minutes I was getting calls from my clients, who'd been getting calls from agents. Eventually I received a letter notifying me of what everyone else already knew. That's the due process of the NFLPA. You can appeal, but you're neutered in terms of recruitment while you're appealing. No one wants to sign with a guy who might be suspended.

Naturally, we exercised my right for an appeal. Cornwell made my case to the arbitrator, Roger Kaplan, who'd handled almost every case for the NFLPA for the past twenty-five years. Kaplan was hired by the union and paid by the union and, not surprisingly, he rarely disagreed with the union. He extended the hearing from one day to two because he said he had a hot date lined up while he was in town. The first hearing was in L.A., the second at his office outside of Washington, D.C., which cost me about $10,000 in additional legal fees and travel. A few months later he rendered his decision. No shock: He upheld the suspension, and even the full amount of the fine. So now I owed a $25,000 fine; I'd lost my job at Gersh; and I had almost no clients. It hurt Steve, too. He lost most of the clients he had with me; he hung on to his older ones, but a lot of those were close to retirement. I paid $12,500 to the Players' Trust and the other $12,500 to another NFLPA charity. I was broke, with no college degree, and I had a wife and two little kids, ages four and six. Besides the death of my parents, it was the lowest moment of my life.

Here I was, a guy who had done all kinds of things wrong in the football agent business. I'd paid college players, given them loans they'd never repay, paid money to runners to get me to players; I'd cooked up information for Game Plan and Playbook sales materials, I'd gotten questions and answers to Wonderlic tests, I'd picked up the tab on debauched trips to Las Vegas. All that and I wound up getting suspended for giving a small check to my attorney to hold—not for cashing it or spending it, just for having him hold it! The string of lawyers I'd hired made *My Cousin Vinny* look like Clarence Darrow. One bumble after another, and finally a kangaroo court controlled by the NFLPA. It was a travesty of justice. Or . . . it was my comeuppance. I didn't get nailed for what I had done. I got nailed for something else. In the symmetry of life, maybe I got what I deserved.

I was suspended for twelve months but it might as well have been a career death sentence. Twelve months of not being able to recruit players or negotiate on behalf of current players is a lifetime. Other agents recruiting against me in the future would've used the arbitrator's decision as a reason players shouldn't sign with me. *That guy stole a player's check— ask the NFLPA.* I was done at Gersh; and I was done with Steve Feldman, despite his personal loyalty. The day I received the decision on my appeal—an unequivocal "no"—my wife walked into our den and said to me, "Josh, there's a career open house at Marcus and Millichap, the commercial real estate company, right down the street from us. You should go check it out. You like real estate, you like people, you know how to sell." Despite all I'd been through, at my lowest moment, my wife, my partner, my moral compass had total faith in me. She didn't need to read the NFLPA decision. She said she didn't want to waste another minute of our lives on it. I followed her gentle nudge. That same day I walked into the real estate office, signed up for training, and started over—clean. End of my life as a football agent, start of my new life as a commercial real estate agent.

Postscript: Twelve months later, having paid my fines, I was reinstated as an NFLPA agent and had to decide if I'd stick with selling commercial properties or dive back into the cesspool. For once, I stayed on the shore.

CHAPTER 9

Coming Clean

About nine months after I'd been suspended, and after nearly twenty years as a sports agent, I thought long and hard and decided it was time to come clean about the whole business, the way I had done it and the way other agents do it. George Dohrmann, Pulitizer Prize–winning sports writer, had spent months trying to convince me to go on the record about my experiences. Eventually, he persuaded me, and it became a cover story in *Sports Illustrated*, entitled "Confessions of an Agent." I named thirty former college players who took money or accepted improper benefits from me. At the end of the story, the magazine included responses from those mentioned, reprinted below:

CONFESSIONS OF AN AGENT—RESPONSES

- When informed of the allegation that he had accepted money from Luchs, Kanavis McGhee asked *SI* to call back the next day. He did not return subsequent phone and e-mail messages from *SI*.
- Greg Townsend confirmed the details of his relationship with Luchs.
- Chuck Webb could not be reached for comment (*SI* left messages for Webb through his family).
- Mel Agee, Harold (Doc) Daniels, Chris Mims, Travis Claridge and Leon Bender are deceased.
- Carl Greenwood, Othello Henderson, Matt Soenksen, Chris Alexander, Bruce Walker, Jonathan Ogden and Singor Mobley confirmed receiving money or extra benefits from Luchs.
- Jamir Miller, Tony Banks and John Rushing declined to comment.
- Ryan Fien, Joel Steed and Torey Hunter said they did not receive money from Luchs.
- Vaughn Parker said he knew Luchs but had no comment as to whether he took money from Luchs.
- Greg Thomas, Delon Washington and Darick Holmes did not respond to phone messages.
- Phalen Pounds said Luchs was "a good guy" but declined to comment as to whether he took money.
- Rob Waldrop denied that Luchs paid him. He recalled that he had lunch with Luchs and that Luchs

offered to pay a friend in an effort to get to Waldrop, but he said that he did not accept any money.

- Ryan Leaf declined to comment on specific allegations. "I remember Josh," Leaf said in a statement. "As I recall, he was an old hometown friend of one or two of my teammates and we all hung out a bit. I don't remember him aspiring to be an agent. We were all about the same age and we were interested in having a good time more than anything else."

- R. Jay Soward confirmed receiving money from Luchs.

- Gary Wichard's lawyer, Howard Silber, said his client declined to comment.

- Mel Kiper denied that it was prearranged for him to call during the Willie Howard meeting or any other. "I would never have called Gary, but Gary and other agents often call me and ask me to speak to players," said Kiper. "Gary is my friend, but I do that all the time for many different agents. I give players my opinion of them as football players. But I would never promote Gary or any other agent to a player." As for the belief among some agents that he favors Wichard's clients, Kiper said, "My player ratings are not related to my relationship with Gary or any other agent. There are many examples of players Gary represented who I have not ranked highly." (Howard confirmed to SI Luchs's account of Kiper's calling during Howard's meeting with Luchs and Wichard.)

- John Blake's lawyer, William H. Beaver II, said his client declined to comment.

- Kenyon Coleman declined to comment.

- Jeremy Shockey did not respond to messages left through the Saints or his agent, Drew Rosenhaus.
- Through a New York Jets spokesperson, Santonio Holmes denied taking money from any agent while in college or telling Luchs and Steve Feldman that he had taken money. Feldman confirmed to *SI* that Holmes told him and Luchs that an agent was paying him.

I was interviewed by Bernard Goldberg on HBO's *Real Sports with Bryant Gumbel*. And shortly after, I started writing this book. It was time to tell the truth. After the *Sports Illustrated* story ran, the NFLPA called an emergency meeting of CARD and, citing that, among other things, I'd urinated for a player when I was sixteen years old, permanently revoked my certification. It was like wasting a bullet on a dead horse. Emergency meeting? For a guy who'd just walked away from the business? No need for future appeals. That's okay. I was done.

Since I went public with how the sports business really works, I've gone from being just another agent doing what agents do to a whistle-blower, double agent (pun-intended), reformer, crusader, and expert on the dark side. I've been on countless radio and TV shows, have been interviewed by magazines inside and outside of sports, and ironically, as a rule-breaker have been asked to serve on or speak at numerous sports law conferences, interestingly on the subject of ethics.

Shortly after my story was published, I was invited by the

NCAA to speak at their so-called compliance meetings, to help educate the very body whose rules and values agents like me were—and still are—flouting. I assisted in some high-profile investigations. ESPN.com ran an Associated Press story on October 27, 2010, excerpted below.

NCAA SEEKS INSIGHT ON ROGUE AGENTS

INDIANAPOLIS—The NCAA is taking a new approach to weeding out rogue agents . . . Spokeswoman Stacey Osburn confirmed in an e-mail to The Associated Press that the governing body had also been gathering information from former agent Josh Luchs.

The goal is to dissuade agents from providing improper benefits to college players—and players from taking benefits and running to the NFL. The panel seeking solutions is looking at a wide range of possibilities.

. . . The union [NFLPA], league, NCAA and other entities are discussing ways to halt the problem of agents, and college players, who break the rules. A series of high-profile cases are currently under investigation by the NCAA.

From then on, it's been a flood. In January 2011, I spoke at the University of Oregon School of Law in Eugene, Oregon. I was nervous about how law students would respond to someone like me. They're there to learn the "ideal," the law, and the way things are supposed to be. What I was talking about was the opposite, the very "real" way things are, not how they should be. Right away, one thing struck me as odd. Despite the fact that the university was putting on the Sports and Entertainment Law Conference, there was no participation, nor were there even observers from, the University of Oregon Athletic Department. The way the Warsaw Sports Review, published by the University's Marketing Center, put it afterward was: "JOSH LUCHS JOINS UNIVERSITY COMPLI-ANCE OFFICERS AT UNIVERSITY OF OREGON LAW CONFER-ENCE ... Luchs, who has recently been in the spotlight for his tell-all . . . where he confessed to paying players, was stra-tegically placed between the Oregon State Associate AD and the Washington State Associate AD to add to the contro-versy of the panel." In a strange twist, I also recruited an-other ex-client of mine to speak on the panel: former Oregon wide receiver Keenan Howry (of the infamous $5,300 check in the Luchs vs. Wichard case).

Amazingly, this was the first time I'd ever seen any uni-versity compliance people in my professional life, in spite of the fact that part of their job was to monitor people like me. I'd heard they existed, but like rare animals in the wild, I'd never seen one. During the panel the Washington State com-pliance person said, "We don't know what we don't know." I took that to mean a couple of things: First, they are protest-ing that there's so much to know, so much going on, they can't possibly stay on top of all of it. Second, if they don't know about something, they have less liability. It's not as if they knew about a violation but ignored it. What was clear was that as a body, a compliance department is in way over its head.

In March 2011, I shared the dais with another agent at the University of Texas Law School in Austin. This is how they promoted it:

Sports Agents Josh Luchs and Bob Boland to Speak at "The Role of Agents in Entertainment & Sports" Conference. Josh Luchs, a former National Football League agent who was recently featured in *Sports Illustrated* and on *Real Sports with Bryant Gumbel* regarding his admission of paying college football stars for nearly 20 years, will speak at The University of Texas School of Law's Texas Review of Entertainment & Sports Law second annual symposium on Thursday, March 24. Luchs will discuss his experience paying players in the hope of signing them as clients and violating NCAA ethics rules with several professors and agents, including Bob Boland, a professor at New York University and well-known sports agent. He has negotiated more than 100 player and endorsement deals in a variety of sports, including the NFL.

This was the first time I'd done a lecture rather than just field questions on a panel, so I was nervous. And to make it a little more intimidating, the event took place in a mock courtroom in front of the seal of the Great State of Texas. If I ever envisioned myself in a Texas courtroom, it would have been under very different circumstances, perhaps subpoenaed, but never as an invited guest, let alone as an expert. I didn't get to feel good about myself too long, though. The dean of the University of Texas Law School, Lawrence Sager, introduced the participants, including esteemed professors, and former Texas linebacker Brian Jones, now a CBS football analyst. Then he introduced me as a "former criminal." There was an audible gasp from the crowd, waiting for me to go after the dean for his defamatory remark. The large contingent of lawyers, and even I as a non-lawyer, knew there's supposed to be a presumption of innocence in America. And I'd never been convicted of any crime. Who'd have thought the dean of the law school would sound like a tabloid sound bite instead of a legal scholar? I held my tongue (an older and wiser me).

A couple of highlights from the conference: A current student asked my advice privately on an agent situation he was in the middle of. He was a former roommate of some University of Texas players now in the NFL, who he said had been paid by agents while in school. Having witnessed how the agent-player world works, he was now in a situation with two major sports agencies battling over UT prospects, both of whom had offered him a job as a runner to help deliver next year's players for meetings and as clients. He was asking me the best ways to protect himself and his interests, and how to parlay it into a job as an agent with one of the sports agencies. In other words, business was going on as usual— right there at the conference that was specifically designed to stop it.

One of the lecturers was well-respected Villanova law professor David Caudill, whose research and scholarly interest is focused on sports and entertainment law. During the question-and-answer portion, he said the perspective I was providing was invaluable to the coaches and athletic directors and that any school that did not take advantage of the opportunity for me to speak to their student athletes is foolish. Then he asked if he could be my booking agent . . . to much laughter from the crowd. Professor Maureen Weston of Pepperdine's School of Law, also on the panel, asked me to speak at her school in Malibu and I agreed.

Before the conference, Mike Powell from the Texas secretary of state's office and I discussed the proposed Texas law on agent conduct and his office's commitment to protecting the universities and athletes in Texas from agents and runners. I didn't hear any more from the dean. He ducked out shortly after the introductions and didn't return.

On April 1, I was on a panel at Fordham University's School of Law in New York City: Agents, Amateurism and Accountability: Legal and Ethical Questions Arising from the Relationships Between Lawyer/Agents and the Amateur Athletes Seeking Their Representation. The participants: Jean Afterman, Vice President, Assistant General Manager, New York Yankees; Jared Fox, NFL Agent, SportStars, Inc.; Richard Karcher, Professor of Law and Director, Center for Law and Sports, Florida Coastal School of Law; Josh Luchs, Former NFL Agent; Fernando Tamayo, Associate, Coffey Burlington and Former International Scouting Coordinator, Boston Red Sox.

During the conference, we were filmed for a segment of a documentary on sports agents being done by Morgan Spurlock, director-producer of *Super Size Me* (in which he eats nothing but McDonald's for thirty days) and *The Greatest Movie Ever Sold* (about product placement). His crew filmed some of the panel exchanges and then set up a one-on-one with me. The producer, Matthew Galkin, asked Jared Fox, the other agent on the panel, if he'd sign a release and be willing to be filmed, but Fox declined. Spurlock's take on the world of sports agents, *The Dotted Line*, premiered on ESPN in October 2011.

I continued to do sports and law panels, even speaking at Yeshiva University—coming full circle from paying a player with my bar mitzvah money. After that appearance, this ran on a multi–law school blog:

> **Josh Luchs at New York Law School!**
> Josh Luchs. Yes. THE Josh Luchs will be lecturing at New York Law School on April 28th . . . between 1–2pm. Do not miss out on a great opportunity to hear about the re- alities of the sports industry and how Mr. Luchs hopes to change it.

I am happy to say, I think I talked some of the students out of wasting a part of their lives on this business. My parents would've been proud.

It's been interesting, even enlightening, hearing about these rules from the side of the people who attempt to police them. In my career as an agent, I knew the rules as a complex lan- guage to be learned only in order to know how to circumvent them—almost a game in itself. As it turns out, behind the rules were people sincerely trying to enforce them, but by and large, they had no idea what I, or most other agents, had been up to.

I did another talk at the Philadephia Sports Law Confer- ence at Temple University. On the panel with me were Her- man Frazier, Senior Associate Athletic Director at Temple;

and Greg Sirb, Executive Director of the Pennsylvania State Athletic Commission, who is responsible for enforcing agent laws and getting agents registered. I told him and the audience I remembered receiving a letter from the Pennsylvania Athletic Commission office asking me to register and pay a fee, which I immediately threw in the trash. Greg confirmed there was nothing his office could do to mandate agent cooperation. The reason, he said, was it was the NCAA's problem. Its members make money from athletics and therefore have the financial resources, but not the motivation, to investigate; so, in general, they don't. On the other hand, his office, which is charged with investigation, is constrained by tight state budgets and overwhelming workloads. The organizer of the Temple event mentioned he'd asked Mark Levin of the NFLPA to participate in the panel but when Mark found out I would be there, he refused to participate and made some disparaging remarks about me. When I hear things like that, it affirms what I'm doing, opening up and telling the truth, making the powers that be uncomfortable.

While I was in Philadelphia, I did an interview on a local morning show, *Mike & Kerry*, on Fox. Kerry asked, "There are some people that say, okay, this guy, he crossed the line, why is he coming out now?" She went on, "Are these the ramblings of a man who's angry he never made it further being an agent than he did? I mean, you had one big client, Ryan Leaf." I had an impulse to get angry; where did she, a local TV talking head, get off telling me I was a failure? But instead, I clarified that I signed but did not end up representing Leaf. It feels good to tell the truth.

Next stop was New York Law, where I was to deliver a

lecture to a small group of law students. It happened to be the first day of the NFL draft. I took the train from Philadelphia to Penn Station and took a cab to my hotel, passing by Radio City Music Hall, where the draft was being held. I felt like an ex-addict having withdrawals. I should've been there. I wanted to know who was going to be picked. What teams would trade up or down. Which players would rise or fall. Who the surprises would be. I called my wife from the taxi to talk me down. I'd been hooked on the draft from the time I was a little kid, faking sickness so my mom would let me stay home from school. Any time I told her I wasn't feeling well, she'd ask, "Is it draft day?" Now it really was draft day and instead of being there, irony of ironies, I was on my way to lecture about the injustices of the system and my role in it.

Not long afterward, I came home to testify at the California Senate hearing in the L.A. Coliseum entitled "Protecting Student Athletes from Unscrupulous Athlete Agents." The hearing was to gather input and support for State Senator Kevin de León's proposed agent-athlete legislation, designed to regulate and punish improper behavior.

The first to testify was my old acquaintance, J. J. Stokes. J. J. was sworn in and claimed he had never been offered any money from agents or received any improper benefits. I reminded him I had offered him money and he said he did not remember. He acknowledged that he had known money was available if he wanted to get it but hadn't done so. Afterward, I brought up the Jamir Miller draft party he and other Bruins had attended and explained that since we had hosted it, by attending he'd have taken an improper benefit when he got a drink at the bar or food from the buffet. He said he paid for his own drinks. If so, he would have to have been the only person at the draft party to have done that—maybe the only person in the history of such parties.

I highlighted an area that I believe is a major chink in the armor supposedly protecting student-athletes. The staffs at university compliance departments are paid by those universities, not by the NCAA, so self-preservation plays a role. If they look too closely into where the player got the gold chain he's wearing it may lead to suspensions, sanctions, and possible forfeiture of games. The head coach would then call a press conference proclaiming they have the best compliance staff in the country. A little later, when the trouble is finally exposed, the compliance staff is likely to be the first to be fired and the head coach keeps his job and remains the highest-paid person at the university.

Senator de León asked USC Vice President of Compliance Dave Roberts why the civil remedies available to the university have not been pursued in, for instance, the case of Reggie Bush receiving payments from marketing agents. Other than the "promised" return of his Heisman Trophy, Bush received no punishment, while the school serves a two-year bowl suspension and national rankings free-fall (full story follows on page 214). Roberts's explanation was that such civil proceedings would open a Pandora's box of possible violations, which might lead to more sanctions, and that the NCAA does not offer immunity to its member institutions. Why would a school look into one set of violations that could uncover a whole new set of violations? I compared NCAA-style amateurism to 1920s Prohibition: "As long as you have Prohibition, you're going to have bootleggers." And I told De León, "Everybody is a potential runner, and that includes coaches and family members and players on the team."

Carmen Trutanich, City Attorney of Los Angeles, testified that currently agents have "absolutely no fear" of being prosecuted under state law but that they would if De León's agent-athlete bill were enacted. "If you're a sports agent," he said, "understand the cavalry has mounted." We'll see.

I was also invited to attend NCAA Regional Rules Meetings, the first of which was in Arizona. I found myself at the front of a room filled with more than a hundred compliance staff from schools, some of which I had visited, and many at which I had paid players. I was ready to be treated like the least popular girl at the dance. To my surprise most of them were appreciative that I was willing to be so candid. I was left with the clear impression that these staffs are dedicated; that they want to understand how agents work, how they get around the rules; and that the more they know, the better they can do their jobs. Many of the compliance people don't agree with all of the NCAA rules but realize they're charged with enforcing them until such time as they change. These compliance departments are understaffed and underfunded, but well-intentioned. Again, the truth was a great weapon.

Before the second Rules Meeting, in Tampa, I was having nightmares. I imagined talking about my experiences with Maurice Clarett in front of a very intimidating guy in a sweater vest in the front row, Ohio State coach Jim Tressel. Under NCAA rules, it was mandatory he be there and he would have been . . . until he found himself the target of another onslaught of accusations, this time about players trading memorabilia for tattoos, gifts, and possible kickbacks, all on his watch as head coach (see Tressel story, page 222). Lucky for me, but not for him, he had more pressing matters to deal with. Part of me was relieved. But another part wondered what it would have been like; maybe interesting fireworks.

Then, just before my appearance, the NCAA asked me to alter my presentation by removing a slide that showed a montage of recent sports investigation headlines and photos of Coach Tressel and players such as OSU's Terrelle Pryor or Marvin Austin of UNC (see their sordid stories on pages 223 and 217). The slide was composed of information from newspapers, magazines, and the Web, nothing that isn't available to everyone, but the NCAA felt it would be too sensitive and wanted it out. I agreed but replaced the offending slide with a blank one, and during my presentation I unsubtly said, "What I used to have here was a slide crammed full of headlines on recent alleged perpetrators, but I was 'encouraged' to remove it, and I did." I'd been invited to tell the truth . . . as long as it didn't hurt certain people's feelings. In any case, my section of the discussion elicited very good feedback, though the Q&A was short. One compliance officer from Ohio State claimed to have never read my *Sports Illustrated* article. I find that hard to believe, not because I think my personal story is so fascinating but because it's critical information for anyone whose job is compliance with NCAA, NFLPA, university, or state regulations. Besides, Ohio State had publicly responded to the Santonio Holmes mention in the article, saying they'd investigated the matter and were satisfied with the explanation Holmes had provided. I am beginning to learn that's largely because compliance people don't want to ask or answer a lot of specific questions in front of their peers, or bosses, or, most importantly, NCAA staff.

Not all the problems were due to lack of effort, though. At the National Association of Athletic Compliance (NAAC) convention in Orlando, I was on a panel, moderated by Jon Fagg, Senior Associate Athletic Director at the University of Arkansas, that addressed all aspects of regulation, conduct, and enforcement.

NCAA Vice President for Enforcement Julie Roe Latch— and a former college basketball player—was the keynote speaker on the topic of integrity. Given my history, she was a tough act to follow. It was if I were the counterpoint to what she'd been preaching. *If you liked Julie Latch on integrity, you'll love Josh Luchs on deceit, fraud, and corruption.*

And I was first up on a panel comprising besides me: NCAA Director of Agent, Gambling, and Amateurism Activities Rachel Newman Baker and Associate Athletic Director for Compliance at the University of Alabama, Mike Ward. Rachel talked about the NCAA broadening the definition of the term "agent" to include more participants in the process, a good intention but not particularly current or well defined. She also touched on trends in college sports, but they were hardly new to me: draft parties, which we'd been conducting since the 1990s. Third parties calling themselves brand managers, advisors, strategic coaches, or any other label that allows outsiders to make a buck on the backs of college stars. An alternative to high school football called 7 on 7 that serves as a college recruiting process—essentially a marketplace where young talent can be reviewed and auctioned off like on a commodities floor—and makes the people behind it very rich, bringing agenting, even if it's not called that, down to the high school level. This is what I suspected the Bob Leinart–Chuck Price–Gary Wichard Air 7 collaboration was going to be all about.

After the panel I had a chance to speak privately with Mike Ward about the conflict of interest inherent in coaches' agents also representing players from the same school. He agreed that it was a conflict and said that Alabama coach Nick Saban's agent, Jimmy Sexton won't represent 'Bama players for that reason. I replied that Sexton may not, but his partners do. In fact, this year's ESPN NFL draft-day Green Room coverage featured Saban with his players alongside—guess who? Saban's agent, Jimmy Sexton.

I'm scheduled for more law school panels and more NCAA meetings. I'm doing as many as I can possibly fit into my schedule . . . while trying to make a living at my career in real estate. I've found something that turns me on as much as recruiting players: telling the truth about recruiting players.

The More Things Change, the More They Stay the Same

Though I may not like the comparison, in more than one appearance or article I've been referred to as "the agent industry's Jose Canseco." I've blown the whistle loud and clear about the illegal procedure in big-time sports. Has the bad behavior stopped or at least slowed? Or was I exaggerating, making too much of nothing? Or was I an exception, a bad guy in a good business? Here's a partial list of recent investigations and infractions. You decide.

CASE: REGGIE BUSH, PETE CARROLL, USC,
AND THE HEISMAN TROPHY

June 2010: After an examination spanning four years, the NCAA announced sanctions against the University of Southern California for its lack of oversight in the behavior of star running back and Heisman Trophy winner Reggie Bush. Dating to 2004, Bush received gifts from sports marketing agent Lloyd Lake and his partner, Michael Michaels, that, according to Lake, totaled over $290,000. When Bush chose Mike Ornstein as his marketing agent, Lake, the agent spurned, wanted to be repaid. Bush refused, so Lake sued. The matter begged for investigation.

Revealed: Over the years, Bush and his family received lavish gifts, favors, and money, trips, living expenses, credit cards—from both Lake and Ornstein—in a battle of graft to win him as a client. In the view of the NCAA, responsibility for oversight of such relations rests with the school. NCAA Infractions Committee Chair Paul Dee said, "High-profile players merit high-profile enforcement."

Punishment: USC received four years of probation and had to forfeit its last two wins of the 2004 season, including the 2005 Orange Bowl, plus all wins of the 2005 season. The school was banned from bowl games in 2010 and 2011 and loses thirty scholarships over the next three years. Running backs coach Todd McNair was banned by the NCAA from off-campus player recruiting for a year because he'd been aware of Bush's arrangement with the agents, and his contract at USC was not renewed. (He has since sued the NCAA.)

July 2010—New USC President Max Nikias announced USC would take down all jerseys and displays that hon-

ored Reggie Bush and would return their copy of his Heisman Trophy.
September 2010—The Heisman Committee explored revok-
ing the trophy from Bush, but Bush voluntarily agreed to
return it. As of this writing, it has not been returned.

A slew of sanctions, harsh punishments, and justice done.
Or did the real culprits escape? If USC is responsible for
oversight of high-profile players, who oversees the oversight?
The head coach and the school's compliance department.
Pete Carroll was head coach and under his direction, the compliance department had a staff of exactly one person to keep
track of the activities of all the school's athletes. And the
compliance department is paid by the school, so their incentive to blow the whistle on their employer is less than compelling. What was the head coach's punishment in this sordid
affair? A five-year, $33-million contract with the Seattle
Seahawks, negotiated by his agent, Gary Uberstine. Before
USC decided what to do, if anything, to their head coach, he
slipped out the back door of his Trojan office and into the front
office of an NFL team. Hardly a fall from grace. And his former assistant coach took the fall, receiving an NCAA ban and
not having his contract renewed.

If there is any "punishment" it would be Gary Uberstine
losing his easy access to Trojan players as Pete Carroll's agent.
While other agents weren't allowed on campus, if Pete Carroll happened to introduce his own agent to players like
Saints left tackle Charles Brown, Browns tight end Jordan
Cameron, Panthers wide receiver Keary Colbert, and others,
and they happened to sign with his agent, that was no doubt,

just coincidence. Now, it seems, Gary Uberstine will have to recruit USC players without a high-placed conduit. Let's see if he does as well.

Hmm . . . a case of agents paying players or their families prior to the players' eligibility. Protests of innocence and ignorance. Last-minute confessions. Selective punishment. Rewards for the perpetrators. Sounds familiar. The more things change, the more they stay the same. The only difference is the amount of money. It's gotten a lot more expensive to do what I used to do.

CASE: CECIL NEWTON SHOPPING HIS SON CAM, FUTURE HEISMAN TROPHY WINNER, TO THE HIGHEST BIDDER

November 2010: Mississippi State University charged Cecil Newton, father of star quarterback Cam Newton, with shopping his son's amateur services to various universities for the best monetary offer. It was also alleged that on some occasions, Cam was in the room with his father and potential interested parties/universities. The elder Newton was quoted as saying it would take "more than a scholarship" to get Cam to play at a given school. Later, in a Dallas radio interview, he added that it would take "$100,000 to $180,000" for his son to transfer to MSU.

December 2010: The NCAA issued a statement that Auburn University, where Cam Newton ultimately played, had declared him ineligible after determining his father had solicited schools for money. Finally, outrage and justice?

Not so fast. Auburn immediately filed for Newton's reinstatement. The NCAA reinstated Newton, saying there was insufficient evidence that Auburn had been aware of the activities of Newton's father. The NCAA action made Cam Newton eligible to play in the SEC Championship Game which, if Auburn won, would put the team in the BCS (Bowl Championship Series) National Championship Game, the most lucrative college sports event in America. Auburn agreed to restrict Cecil Newton from access to any Auburn athletic activities or games. The NCAA's action also cleared the way for Cam to be a candidate for the Heisman Trophy, which he ultimately won.

So, his father put him up for auction, with his son allegedly aware and present; they got caught; and the young quarterback was severely punished with . . . the National Championship, the Heisman Trophy, and a huge rookie contract in the NFL. And by the way, in defiance of the NCAA and Auburn agreement with Cecil Newton, he did attend the BCS Championship.

CASE: GARY WICHARD, CREDIT CARDS, UNC ASSISTANT COACH JOHN BLAKE, AND PLAYER MARVIN AUSTIN

September 2010: *Yahoo! Sports* reported on an alleged improper financial relationship between my former boss, Gary Wichard, and John Blake, at the time assistant football coach at the University of North Carolina. Yahoo's work led to investigations by the NCAA and NFLPA. Blake was accused of arranging trips for Marvin Austin, UNC defensive tackle, including visits to a California training facility a stone's throw from Wichard's office. Hotel receipts showed the travel was paid for by Pro Tect, Wichard's agency.

The State of North Carolina and the NCAA investigated based on evidence including: six or more wire transfers from Wichard's bank to Blake, a personal loan of $45,000 to Blake from the same bank, and a Pro Tect credit card in Blake's name. Despite past marketing brochures that listed Blake as an employee of Pro Tect, Wichard and Blake denied Blake ever worked for the firm. Both Wichard and Blake denied that Blake was steering players to Wichard's agency, which is to say, they denied that he was a runner.

The university looked into the matter and the potential impact on the school, its football coach, Butch Davis, and the program itself. The *Raleigh News & Observer* uncovered a "Termination by University for Cause" clause in Coach Davis's contract that says he can be dismissed if a violation is committed by one of his assistants and if Davis "had reason to know or should have known through the exercise of due diligence."

The NFLPA followed with their own investigation, accusing Gary Wichard of breaking their agent–college player regulations. Wichard was represented in the NFLPA review by none other than Howard Silber, the same attorney who had worked for Wichard in getting the NFLPA to suspend me.

John Blake was forced to resign from UNC. Gary Wichard was suspended by the NFLPA for nine months "for having impermissible communication with University of North Carolina player Marvin Austin at a time Austin was not eligible for the NFL draft under the NFL/NFLPA Collective Bargaining Agreement." Interestingly, Wichard was not suspended for paying for flights, hotels, and player training, but for this euphemism that sounds like a parking meter violation, "impermissible communication." Marvin Austin was suspended by the Tar Heels for the LSU–UNC Chick-Filet Kickoff Bowl, with an almost laughable explanation from Coach Davis. "This decision is not a result of the ongoing NCAA review. Marvin has violated team rules and has neglected his responsibilities to the team."

Coincidence or Pattern?

I had first-hand knowledge of Gary arranging to pay for the training of players when we'd done it for Travis Johnson, a defensive end from Florida State. The details came out in our lawsuit. At first Johnson's trainer, Joseph Masiello, admitted to having been hired by Wichard, but he later "recanted" that he'd been paid. See the excerpts below from the *Sports Business Journal* and my note of clarification at the bottom.

PRIVATE TRAINER ACCUSES NFL AGENT

By Liz Mullen, Staff Writer—May 29, 2006

NFL player agent Gary Wichard paid a private trainer to work with Houston Texans defensive tackle Travis Johnson while Johnson was a student athlete at Florida State University, according to a sworn declaration by the trainer. Joseph Masiello, a Malibu, Calif.-based trainer who has worked for Wichard for more than a decade, said that he provided the training while Johnson was a junior in college.

"From April [to] May of 2004, I provided training services to Travis Johnson, a student athlete, at the specific request of Gary Wichard," Masiello states in the declaration.

In addition to the declaration, the court file contains a bill from Masiello to Wichard's company, Pro Tect Management, for $1,200. It contains the notation "Travis."

TRAINER RECANTS STATEMENT ABOUT AGENT

By Liz Mullen, Staff Writer—June 12, 2006

A private athletic trainer has recanted a sworn statement he made last year claiming that NFL player agent Gary Wichard paid him to train a student athlete at Florida State University. Joseph Masiello of Malibu, Calif., states in his new sworn statement that his original statement "contains a number of errors," and that he "did not have adequate time to review the declaration before executing it."

. . . Masiello said in his first statement in August 2005 that Wichard paid him to train defensive tackle Travis Johnson, who now plays for the Houston Texans.

Both of his declarations are part of a lawsuit filed against Wichard's company, Pro Tect Management, by Joshua Luchs, an NFL player agent and former employee of Wichard who claims he is owed money.

In the original declaration, Masiello stated, "From April [to] May of 2004, I provided training services to

Travis Johnson, a student athlete, at the specific request of Gary Wichard."

... In his new declaration, Masiello states "that the invoice attached to my previous declaration was created in error, and that the invoice was never paid by Gary Wichard or Pro Tect Management."

Note: Under whatever pressure Wichard's attorneys may have brought to bear, the trainer contradicted his original claim of having been paid by Pro Tect, and the *Sports Business Journal* ran the retraction story, but Masiello never denied that he had trained Johnson for Pro Tect (and that, even if not paid, is a violation).

October 2010: As a result of the NCAA investigation, Marvin Austin and two other Tar Heels players, Greg Little and Robert Quinn, were declared permanently ineligible for the team. UNC Athletic Director Dick Baddour referred to it as "a sad day when three young men are no longer able to represent their school based on actions they have taken and decisions they have made contrary to NCAA rules."

Butch Davis was ultimately fired, Baddour resigned, and the football program sustained a major setback. As for Marvin Austin, despite getting booted from the Tar Heels team, he played in the East-West Shrine Game in January 2011, wearing a UNC helmet. And despite questions about his character, he was drafted in the second round by the Giants.

Gary Wichard died of pancreatic cancer during the period of his suspension by the NFLPA. He likely won't be remembered for the great players or the good contracts he negotiated but as the first agent who died while serving an NFLPA suspension, facing potential jail time in the state of North Carolina. Unlike me, sadly he would never have the opportunity to rewrite the ending of his story.

CASE: JIM TRESSEL, OHIO STATE MEMORABILIA, AND THE TATTOO PARLOR

April 2010: Ohio State University head coach Jim Tressel (the same Jim Tressel accused by Maurice Clarett in a 2004 *ESPN* story of flagrant violations) was informed by an e-mail from a former Buckeye player that a local tattoo parlor owned by Eddie Rife had been raided by the FBI and valuable OSU football memorabilia had been found, including championship rings, jerseys, and awards. If such memorabilia is sold or traded for value by players, it is strictly forbidden by NCAA rules. Tressel responded that he'd "get on it ASAP." He did not inform the head of the athletic department or the president of the university or the school's compliance department. He forwarded the e-mail to a local businessman with ties to the team.

September 2010: The coach signed the routine compliance form that asks if he has knowledge of any NCAA violations, his signature indicating he had no such knowledge.

December 2010: The U.S. Attorney's Office notified the university that it had found the memorabilia evidence, which led to an internal inquiry by OSU Athletic Director Gene Smith. That review did not find the e-mails but did uncover the players involved. After conferring with the NCAA and Big Ten officials, Ohio State quarterback Terrelle Pryor and four other players—offensive lineman Mike Adams, running back Daniel "Boom" Herron, wide receiver DeVier Posey, and backup defensive lineman Solomon Thomas— were to be suspended for five games. Additionally, Pryor and the others had to repay money or benefits ranging from $1,000 to $2,500 by making contributions to a charity. But their suspension did not begin immediately with the next game on the schedule, which happened to be the prestigious and lucrative nationally televised Sugar Bowl. Instead, their suspension did not take effect until the first five games of the following season.

Tressel was given a two-game suspension and a fine of $250,000. Asked if Tressel's job was at risk, Ohio State University President Gordon Gee said, "No, are you kidding? Let me be very clear. I'm just hoping the coach doesn't dismiss me."

Meantime, the NCAA continued to look into the matter.

April, 2011: The NCAA, in a "notice of allegations," maintained that Tressel had "permitted football student-athletes to participate in intercollegiate athletics while ineligible," that he had "failed to deport himself . . . [with] honesty and integrity" and that he had lied when filling out a compliance form saying he had no knowledge of violations by his players. From that moment on, the athletic department and the university began distancing themselves from Tressel.

Then two significant things occurred in the media: ESPN columnist Pat Forde said enough was enough, that it was time for Tressel to be canned. Forde maintained that if Ohio State had had the guts to fire the winningest coach in their history, Woody Hayes, the day after he punched an opposing player (on national television), then the school should have the backbone to ax Jim Tressel. And *Sports Illustrated* determined the whole tale hadn't been told and sent George Dohrmann, the Pulitzer Prize–winning writer who had written the magazine's piece on me, to Columbus to dig up the rest of the sordid story.

George uncovered a lot of dirt. He not only found evidence of wrong-doing; he seemed to find a pattern. Way back in Tressel's first tour of duty at Ohio State, as an assistant to Earle Bruce in 1983–85, his image was as a man of integrity and Christian ethics. And contradictions. One of his jobs was to run the Buckeyes' summer camp, attended by a combination of prospects Ohio State was interested in as well as a bunch of enthusiastic but less talented players. The camp culminated with a raffle in which all the kids bought chances to win cleats and jerseys (team memorabilia, though not as valuable as the kind OSU players would get caught selling). An anonymous associate at the camp said Tressel fixed the raffle so the Buckeye prospects always won the prizes, which was a violation of NCAA rules—not to mention just a lousy thing to do to innocent kids. He said, "In the morning he would read the Bible with another coach. Then, in the afternoon he would go out and cheat kids who had probably saved up money from mowing lawns to buy those raffle tickets."

Tressel later left Ohio State for Youngstown University, where he engineered a remarkable football turnaround, winning the division championship. Again, he was a man of values, looking out for his players . . . perhaps too much so. He eventually left Youngstown University under a cloud of accusations that involved a star quarterback getting big sums of money and favors from a rich school trustee. The university and the NCAA insisted they'd looked into the matter and found no knowing misdeeds by Coach Tressel. As he would later with the tattoo-parlor incident, Tressel relied on the "ignorance defense" and his superiors bought it.

He returned to Columbus as head coach in 2001 and over the next decade led the Buckeyes to the third best record in the history of the school, winning Big Ten championships, trips to bowl games, and, most importantly, consistent victories over archrival Michigan. He became an icon who could do no wrong. And even if he did wrong, he seemed to handle it right. When the NCAA and OSU suspended his players for five games and him only two, he asked to have his punishment match the players'. Five-game suspension, fine paid, investigation over, case closed.

But Dohrmann found the investigation was hardly complete, and the punishment hardly up to the crime. He pieced together evidence that showed the memorabilia-market-cum-tattoo-parlor scandal hadn't just happened in the past year but went back to 2002, OSU's national championship year, and touched not five, but some twenty-eight players. And the trading of goods for services was hardly on a petty scale. Players had traded rings, trophies, signatures—including at least one item with Tressel's autograph—not just for garden-variety hundred-dollar tattoos but for "sleeves," top-to-bottom arm-murals that cost thousands of dollars.

Hours before the *Sports Illustrated* story would break, with rumors of its explosive content all over the sports blog-o-sphere, the athletic department and the university president had a talk with their coach. On Memorial Day, Jim Tressel "decided" to resign.

What will be the ultimate punishment for Ohio State? For Jim Tressel? For stars like Terrelle Pryor? Will the school be stripped of its 2010 Big Ten Championship? Will the university's athletic director be sacrificed, or the president? Or . . . will Ohio State, home of the Buckeyes, one of the iconic teams in college football, a stalwart of the NCAA, be given a slap on the wrist? Will it all be swept under the rug as were the allegations of Maurice Clarett?

As of this writing, the answers are: 1) In what may be the first step on the road back to coaching, Jim Tressel was hired by the Indianapolis Colts as, what ESPN.com writer Tim Keown called, "the most over-qualified replay-reviewer in the history of professional football," and given a self-imposed suspension of not five games like his former players, but one for good measure, six games. 2) Terrelle Pryor elected to forfeit his senior year, enter the NFL Supplemental Draft, and was selected by the Raiders in the third round. NFL Commissioner Roger Goodell said Pryor would not be able to play the first five games of the pro season. Goodell wouldn't acknowledge they were mirroring the NCAA punishment but said the decision was to prevent circumventing the rules of the pro draft. (Since when did the NCAA rules become the NFL rules? It's a dangerous road to travel.) 3) OSU preemptively offered self-imposed penalties: Jim Tressel's exit, "vacating" the entire 2010 season including the Big Ten Championship and Sugar Bowl win, and serving a two-year NCAA probation. 4) In August of 2011, the NCAA held hearings during which OSU officials testified on the entire case, enumerated their self-imposed penalties, and added another—donation of the school's share of the Sugar Bowl revenue of $338,000 to charity. The NCAA will now deliberate for up to twelve weeks before reaching their final conclusion on whether those sacrifices are enough or more should be added. They could ban Ohio State from one more bowl game or limit their recruiting or worse. They could hit them with "lack of institutional control," for which they can lose scholarships, wins, and most painfully, sports revenues, (second only to the "death penalty" or being banned from playing a sport). But the NCAA has said that charge is off the table. It was on the table for USC and UNC. Why not for OSU? Good question.

The scandals just keep coming. In July 2010, Alabama defensive tackle Marcell Dareus was investigated by the school along with the NCAA about his attending a party in Miami hosted by a sports agent, a clear violation. In September, he was suspended by the NCAA and required to repay almost $2,000 in impermissible benefits as a contribution to charity.

Georgia receiver A. J. Green was suspended for the first four games of the 2010 season by the NCAA for selling his 2009 Independence Bowl jersey for $1,000 to former UNC defensive back Chris Hawkins, who the NCAA determined to be an agent or person who markets amateur athletes.

After a report revealed the Fiesta Bowl CEO had engaged in extravagant spending and inappropriate use of funds, he was fired and the Bowl Championship Series threatened to end ties with the game. Ultimately, they opted to fine the Fiesta Bowl $1 million and maintain the relationship.

Four former Auburn players went on HBO's *Real Sports with Bryant Gumbel* and admitted they'd received thousands of dollars from boosters, in $100 handshakes and specially filled book bags, while being recruited by or playing for the Tigers. The show's producer had sent me an e-mail that this special was, in part, fueled by my appearance with Bernard Goldberg, which had spurred their interest to dig further.

Willie Lyles, the football trainer-scout, came under NCAA investigation for receiving $25,000 from University of Oregon coach Chip Kelly for player information and for allegedly telling Texas A&M to "beat" $80,000 to sign Patrick Peterson in 2007. Willie went public with his version of the story, also inspired, he says, by my confessions.

And rest assured, right now, as you read this, the next scandal is already happening. In fact, just before going to press with this book, just when some thought it couldn't get worse, it did. College sports reached a new low . . . again.

NEVIN SHAPIRO: PONZI SCHEME PERPETRATOR, UNIVERSITY OF MIAMI BOOSTER, AND THE MOST BRAZEN RULE VIOLATOR IN THE HISTORY OF THE NCAA

August 2011: *Yahoo! Sports* reporter Charles Robinson broke the story of Nevin Shapiro, jailed for conducting a $930 million Ponzi scheme and also guilty, by his own account, of using millions of his ill-gotten wealth to illegally recruit Miami Hurricane prospects, lavishly entertain star players, and later lure them to his sports agency.

The scope of Shapiro's actions is staggering: showering improper benefits—money, gifts, trips, parties, prostitutes, and bounties or rewards for injuring opposing teams—on as many as seventy-two players, with the knowledge and even participation of various university officials, coaches, and trainers, from 2002 to 2010.

Shapiro's involvement with the Hurricanes began with Willis McGahee in the NCAA-approved "living scholar" program, in which a booster pays the scholarship for a player and develops a one-on-one relationship. Shapiro came to know other players and soon inherited the paternalistic role once held by entertainer Luther Campbell, notorious for supplying cash to Miami players in the 1980s and '90s. "His role was diminished by the NCAA and the school, and someone needed to pick up that mantle . . . He was 'Uncle Luke,' and I became 'Little Luke,'" said Shapiro.

Among the marquee players in his flock were defensive tackle Vince Wilfork, linebacker Jon Beason, wide receivers Andre Johnson and Devin Hester, tight end Kellen Winslow Jr., safety Antrel Rolle, and defensive end Andrew Williams. "Everything started when I gave some Miami Heat basketball tickets to Andrew Williams," Shapiro said. Williams denied receiving the tickets but Shapiro says he later bought a big-screen TV for Williams and subsequently met Williams's roommates, defensive ends Cornelius Green and Jerome McDougle, on whom he also bestowed material benefits. Eight former Miami players or recruits confirmed they'd gotten such benefits, including running back Tyrone Moss, who Shapiro says he entertained on his $1.6-million yacht and gave $1,000 in cash. Moss said, "Yeah . . . It was me and a few more of the guys in my incoming class that he kind of showed some love to."

Along the way, Shapiro paid $1.5 million for a 30 percent interest in a sports agency, Axcess Sports & Entertainment, with a partner, then-NFL agent Michael Huyghue. Axcess signed two first-round picks, Wilfork and Beason. Huyghue wooed the players with money and other goodies, notably $50,000 in one chunk to Wilfork. Huyghue's pedigree, so to speak, was GM of the Birmingham Fire of the now-defunct World League of American Football, Vice President with the Detroit Lions, Senior Vice President with the Jacksonville Jaguars, associate of David Dunn at his Athletes First agency, and later Commissioner of the UFL.

Shapiro's activities could flaunt four key NCAA rules—bylaw 11, impermissible compensation to coaches; bylaw 12, dealing with amateurism; bylaw 13, improper recruiting; and bylaw 16, extra benefits to athletes—and could even go beyond the statute of limitations, allowable when there is "a pattern of willful violations" over a period longer than four years.

When asked about the allegations, the school, via Associate Athletic Director Chris Freet, gave the stock university-under-suspicion response: "We are fully cooperating with the NCAA and are conducting a joint investigation. We take these matters very seriously."

The specific incidents *Yahoo! Sports* uncovered read like a how-to manual on corrupting college sports. At least seventy-two players involved, seven coaches, and three support staff are accused of receiving improper benefits or of witnessing or playing a part in the improper actions.

- Violating NCAA rules with the knowledge or help of six coaches. In football, Clint Hurtt, Jeff Stoutland, and Aubrey Hill escorted top recruits to Shapiro's home or box to pitch them. Some signed with Miami (Ray-Ray Armstrong, Dyron Dye, and Olivier Vernon) and some did not (Andre Debose, Matt Patchan, Orson Charles, and Jeffrey Godfrey). The coaches and/or their current schools refused to comment. In basketball, Shapiro made similar accusations about coaches Frank Haith, Jake Morton, and Jorge Fernandez and they too either denied the charges or did not respond.

- Shapiro claims to have provided prostitutes for thirty-nine Miami players or prospects, though the names have not been revealed. So far, two players have confirmed Shapiro paid for sexual favors for themselves and others when they played for the Hurricanes, often at luxurious parties at South Beach's Mercury Hotel. Shapiro said he paid cash for the rooms and registered under his alias, Teddy Dupay (the actual name of a smallish basketball player Shapiro thought he ressembled). *Yahoo! Sports* found debit-card expenditures at the Mercury Hotel between major Miami games. Shapiro said, "In 2002 and 2003 we were really rocking it for a while and it was just out of control. But I decided to get away from the regular Mercury Hotel situations. I was getting too old for that kind of thing, and I had the boat for prostitution situations."

- Shapiro said he never had a player "payroll" but often gave cash to players at his house in Miami Beach. This was corroborated by the former CFO in the Ponzi-scheme company, Capitol Investments. Shapiro also held tournaments in which players could win money for fishing, bowling, and playing pool. And in 2002, as Luther Campbell had done, Shapiro set up a bounty program, rewarding players for the "hit of the game" or "big plays" against major rival teams and star players. Bounty targets included Florida Gators quarterback Tim Tebow and Seminoles quarterback Chris Rix: $5,000 if you could knock them out of the game. Three former players recall the bounty system. "We pounded the [expletive] out of that kid," Shapiro said of Rix. "Watch the tape of those games . . . [Jon] Vilma tried to kill him—just crushed him . . . trying to get that $5,000."

- All kinds of gifts—jewelry, watches, engagement rings, diamond-studded dog tags, clothing, SUV rims, plane tickets, televisions—were lavished on players to celebrate wins or as recruiting inducements for Axcess Sports.

- Shapiro had two Miami Beach residences—a large $2.7-million home with a pool and a $6.1-million coastal Mediterranean estate—both open to the players to hang out, watch sports, eat, drink, and bring their friends. Plus, Shapiro's $1.6-million yacht was available for fishing, leisure trips, and prostitution. And several times a week, Shapiro would take large groups of players to strip clubs and night clubs—Solid Gold, the Cheetah, Pink Pony, Tootsie's Cabaret, Mansion—and Shapiro's entourage always went into the VIP section. "We rocked Mansion so many times, I couldn't even count them," Shapiro said. "And I never went in there once without players . . ." Shapiro also picked up the tab for players' meals at Prime 112, Grazie, Prime Italian, Benihana, and other restaurants.

- Shapiro provided players housing on his yacht, in his homes, or in his rental properties—players including Devin Hester, running back Graig Cooper, tight end Kevin Everett, Vince Wilfork, and linebacker Tavares Gooden.

- Once, Shapiro paid for a player to go to the Pink Pony strip club and paid a dancer to have sex with the player. Later, when the dancer claimed to be pregnant, Shapiro gave her $500 for an abortion. "I was doing him a favor," said Shapiro. "That idiot might have wanted to keep [the baby]."

- Axcess Sports, his agency with Huyghue, was a funnel for players. Shapiro would introduce players to Huyghue and then leave it to his partner to close—a classic runner-agent operation. From that point on, according to Shapiro, Huyghue provided whatever financial benefits it took to make the deal. Huyghue denies the claims but some key players support it.

- Shapiro's stake in Axcess almost did him in. Drunk at halftime, with Miami losing 31-0 to Virginia, Shapiro spotted the university's head of compliance, David Reed, and ripped into him, blaming him for scrutinizing the program too much and causing the school's sports decline. Reed, in turn, instigated a background check on booster Shapiro's connection to a professional sports agency.

All the while, Shapiro was a big supporter of the school and its sports programs, a major donor; despite his improper behavior with players, he was cultivated and treated like royalty by the highest officials at the university. He was allowed to run with the team out of the tunnel and was honored on the field by former Miami Athletic Director Paul Dee. (Dee, now the chairman of the NCAA Committee on Infractions, was known for his scolding of USC on the Reggie Bush scandal, saying, ". . . high-profile players demand high-profile compliance." And in 2007, he chastised Long Beach College President Leonard Alexander for basketball infractions, saying, "You have to put in place the kind of institutional control we have at Miami." No comment.) In 2008, Shapiro made a $250,000 pledge for an athlete lounge named in his honor and donated $50,000 to the basketball program. In a photo that captures the whole ugly scenario, Shapiro is at the microphone next to Coach Haith, for whom Shapiro says he bought a recruit, and in the background is President Donna Shalala (former Secretary of Health and Human Services under President Clinton), smiling at the check he had just written with money made in his Ponzi scheme. Shapiro says, "If they had hired a private investigator for a day . . . it would have been over in five minutes. You would have had all the information you needed. Follow me to a nightclub or a strip club. Lunches. Dinners. The boat. Hotels for parties . . . These guys were at my house. There was all kinds of [expletive] going on in. Gambling. Pool tournaments. Prostitution. Drinking."

Why wasn't anyone suspicious? Why weren't his actions questioned? Why did David Reed's background check go nowhere? Shapiro says it's simply because the University of Miami didn't want to know. The same reason schools always look the other way. The booster is . . . boosting, supporting the school, being a big promoter, donating, saying good things about Miami. There's nothing wrong with recruiting good kids. Unless, of course, you break rules to do it. And if that happens, they don't want to know.

Nevin Shapiro's story is a lot like all the rest. But this time it's bigger, uglier, and more flagrant. The dollars have more ze-roes; the behavior has almost no limits; and the rules haven't been broken—they've been shattered. The University of Miami will see people punished—some players, coaches, ad-ministrators, maybe even the president. But, I predict, once again, nothing will be done to change the long-term outcome for amateur sports.

CHAPTER 10

Can This Sport Be Saved?

But what comes of all of this attention, all the hand-wringing, head-shaking, woe-is-sports? What do we do about it? I certainly do not claim to have magic answers. But I have some ideas. And I have some opinions on some of the ideas I've heard from other experts. I am, above all, a skeptic. I put every potential solution to two tests: First, can agents and other people with an agenda find a way around it? Can guys like me beat the system? Does it really improve anything or just put a little cosmetic cover on the acne? And second, is it fair? Does the fix give an unfair edge to one school, or type of school, over another?

I want to preface my discussion of solutions by reiterating that my experiences are limited to football, the only sport I was involved in. From what I understand the world of basketball is littered with behavior that may make football players and football agents look like Boy Scouts. Unlike baseball players, who have the option to pass on college and immediately start their professional careers in the minor leagues, or bas-ketball players, who can be "one and done" (one year of col-lege or at least nineteen years old), using college or overseas ball as a brief stopover on the way to the NBA, football play-ers are in a different, much more restrictive environment. Currently, after high school, it's either play college football (essentially, the unpaid minor league system of the NFL), or nothing. Athletes can't declare themselves eligible for the NFL until they are at least three years removed from high school. If they did nothing in that time period, they would lose their skills. No international or minor-league alternative exists. It's play for a college team or what . . . play semi-pro? Other than Eric Swann, the defensive tackle drafted by the Arizona Cardinals in 1991, and the occasional former soccer player turned place-kicker, the number of noncollege or semi-pro players in the NFL is as close to zero percent as you can get.

And the system is hard, if not impossible, to challenge. Mau-rice Clarett, who was arguably the rare talent ready to play in the NFL after his freshman year, fought the rule in court, won, then lost on appeal. No surprise that the billion-dollar enter-prise prevailed in the courts, maintaining what I believe to be an oppressive, monopolistic system. Maurice, deprived by that ruling of utilizing his best talents, was left in the cold to survive while sitting out and waiting, He never had good judgment, but he might have succeeded anyway if not for the restrictive draft rules. The undeniable fact is, football players have no al-ternative available. It's the NCAA or nothing.

The fixes for college football fall into two basic categories: 1) better policing of the system as it stands and 2) changing the system. Actually, there's a third category: Ignoring the problem. That's the route that has been taken to date, with an occasional dash of number one to keep the media and outraged citizens at bay.

Better Policing

Right now, the various regulatory bodies—NCAA, NFLPA, and the individual states—provide rules, and some laws, that are meant to govern behavior. In my opinion, if they were all enforced, we'd still have a huge problem: injustice. Screwing the geese who lay the golden eggs, the so-called student-athletes, aka indentured servants. Players make college football a success. The schools get all the money. The players get nothing. That's injustice. According to Richard Karcher, professor of sports law at Florida Coastal School of Law, it's an ideal, if cynical, economic model. An institution gets to make a fortune and doesn't have to pay its workforce. Zero labor costs (other than scholarships, which the institutions also hand out for academics, need, diversity, and other reasons). How ecstatic would General Motors be with a no-labor-cost model? Or Apple? Or Walmart?

Nonetheless, enforcement today is token at best, and at worst, a total joke. It could be better, much better, and that would decrease the flagrant corruption of supposed amateur athletics. To understand what can be done, you have to look at the issues from the top down, each one interlocking with the next; find the real points of vulnerability; and apply pressure where it matters. Not surprisingly, it's all about money.

The Uniform Athlete Agent Act

Passed in 2000, the Act requires agents to register in each state that ratifies the law and it allows for criminal and civil penalties to be sought at the state level *but* enforcement is on a state-by-state basis, with no overarching governing body. Some states are aggressive, some are not. Some prosecutors are zealous, some are not. Registration of agents doesn't take place in every state. And there is a growing trend to expand the definition of an "agent." The intention is to restrict more people's behavior but in fact it confuses the issue of who is and who isn't an agent. (For further discussion, see page 247, "Runners.") Each state adopts the act with its own twists and modifications. As of 2010, half of the forty-two states that had enacted Uniform Athlete Agent acts had never issued a single penalty. Oversight and regulation must be federal—federally funded, federally overseen, federally enforced. If it's a problem worthy of legislation—arguable in itself—then it's a national problem, not a local or regional one.

SPARTA: Sports Agent Responsibility and Trust Act

SPARTA is a federal law that bars giving false information to a college athlete and providing anything of value to a player or person associated with the player prior to entering into a contract. SPARTA permits states and/or colleges to investigate, *but* the states are limited in funds and time, and the colleges are not quick to encourage investigations into activities that generate substantial revenue. Federal enforcement would require cooperation from states and colleges. Colleges have no drive to find bad news that results in punishment contrary to their own economic self-interest. To have meaningful enforcement, you have to have economic lever-age. Follow the money. Apply pressure to those who stand to gain or lose.

The NCAA

The NCAA has oversight responsibility for college sports *but* it is composed of, and funded by, the member schools that collectively make the very rules the association is supposed to enforce. It shows favoritism toward some schools over others and it does not encourage schools to look into and correct problems.

Currently, if a school suspects a problem, and under SPARTA, pursues its rights to civil litigation against an of-fending party (i.e., agent), and during the discovery process uncovers more transgressions than the original, it puts itself in even greater potential jeopardy. The NCAA needs to grant some form of immunity—defining the scope of the issues or the time frame—similar to the way government prosecutors do, that limits the harm the school can do to itself while try-ing to uncover bad behavior.

If the NCAA wants to be effective in policing behavior (and that's a big "if"), it should employ its economic leverage with the NFL. The NCAA, via college football, is the de facto minor league of pro football. The NFL depends on a steady flow of outstanding players and therefore stands to gain or lose the most from assuring or interrupting that flow. The threat of turning off the spigot will work. When a handful of college coaches stood up recently and said no to NFL access to practice fields, players, and games, the NFL paid attention, if only briefly. Roger Goodell condemned "bad behavior" that violates NCAA rules and exerted pressure on the NFLPA to, in turn, pressure their members not to break the rules.

And on the rare occasions when the NCAA actually does take action, the punishments must be consistent, not arbitrary, and not favoring one school over another. Why were the Ohio State players suspended for five games but allowed to play in the prestigious Sugar Bowl? Why, in the Reggie Bush incident, was USC deemed to have had a lack of institutional control—a harsh verdict—when UNC, having had coaches aware of and part of violations, was not found to have had the same lack of institutional control?

The NFLPA

The NFLPA licenses, reviews, oversees, and monitors agent behavior *but* as the players' union, the NFLPA has no incentive to be more aggressive since its purpose is to bring the best players possible into the professional game and to get them paid as well as possible once they get there.

Again, if the NCAA wants to clean up conduct, they have to apply leverage where they have it: through economic influence on the NFL. If they restrict the NFL's access to talented marquee players, the league can then put pressure on the NFLPA to police its agents more vigilantly, more evenly— and not just punish a few sacrificial lambs from time to time. The NFL and NFLPA's combined economic leverage is far more compelling than any moral pressure, and far more efficient than any legal processes.

University Compliance Departments

Universities maintain compliance departments to self-monitor student-athlete conduct, including scholarships, academics, eligibility, personal issues, and other activities. But what they most focus on is educating players about the rules, chapter and verse on the specific regulations, what they can and cannot do. The plain fact is, most if not all the players *know* the central rule: You cannot accept anything of value. Period. It's not that complicated. They get it.

But if we delude ourselves into thinking compliance departments can police athlete-agent-booster activity, we've already had a case of short-term amnesia on the Nevin Shapiro–University of Miami debauchery—the mansions, yachts, meals, liquor, strippers, parties, plane tickets, jewelry, car rims, hookers, yachts, and lots and lots of cash made available right under the noses of coaches, trainers, and compliance officers.

Between the shortfalls of scholarships, the adulation of fans and the media, the less–than–Boy Scout backgrounds of too many players (see below), and simply the temptation, players break the rules. If the compliance department drums those rules into the players, they can rationalize that they have done their jobs. And even if they want to be vigilant in monitoring and enforcing the rules, the departments are typically small and underfunded and, amazingly, they report to the athletic director and/or the coaches. In other words, they are supposed to police their own bosses.

Sports Illustrated and CBS News jointly investigated 2,837 players on the *Sports Illustrated* 2010 preseason rosters of the top twenty-five teams. Results: 204 players had criminal records. A total of 277 different offenses ranging from 105 for drugs and alcohol, 75 nuisance crimes, 56 violent crimes, and 41 property crimes. Digging further they found, among a 318-player sample from Florida plus 300 from other areas, 58 of the total arrests were for crimes committed while juveniles. In other words, 7 percent of the best players had criminal records and 21 percent of those were juvenile offenders. Is it a surprise they get in trouble when they get to college? Or that their behavior rubs off on other players? Is it a shock to find the compliance departments aren't effective?

In cases like Miami, there's a natural reaction to place the blame squarely on the shoulders of the university's compliance staff, in this instance, Compliance Director David Reed. Before we make him responsible, though, ask who pays him, who he reports to, who he owes allegiance to—or, put another way, who decides if he has a job or not. It's the university's athletic department. And in a big sports school like Miami, the most powerful people in the athletic department are the head coaches of the football and basketball teams. Compliance works for the coaches. Conflict? Uh, yeah.

It's against the self-interest of the compliance department to find wrongdoing. (If that sounds similar to the criticism of Wall Street compliance departments being paid by Wall Street firms, during the financial meltdown, it's no coincidence.)

In my nearly twenty-year career, half of which was spent providing illegal benefits, I never once met or saw any compliance personnel. That is, until I was asked to participate in panel discussions at law schools around the country and speak at the NCAA regional rules seminars in front of hundreds of the Division I compliance staffers. They're invisible . . . by design. Why didn't I see them? They're often housed in the bowels of the athletic department's building, deep in the interior, with no windows to the practice fields or anywhere near the entrances to weight rooms or locker rooms. They literally don't see the players or who the players come in contact with. Hear no evil, see no evil, speak no evil.

Miami's David Reed is a member, and maybe a victim, of the same unrealistic structure as are all compliance personnel in college sports. One compliance officer I met at the NCAA Tampa Regional Rules Meeting told me when she was interviewed for her job, the head coach asked her, "Do you see your job more as firefighter or policeman?" Clearly the right answer to get and keep the job was "firefighter." Contain the flames, stop the damage from spreading. But don't be a cop; cops investigate. Compliance departments, in my cynical view, exist so the university can 1) say they have one, 2) claim to do their job, and 3) have someone to blame when the school is caught doing wrong.

Want a real solution—real change—instead of the next exposé? Don't blame the compliance departments; change the system. Make them like Eliot Ness's "Untouchables," who busted the bootleggers—not local cops on the take, but G-men. Take compliance departments off the local—or school—payroll that can be easily corrupted and put them on an autonomous payroll of the NCAA. And by the way, they should give the compliance departments offices with windows to the practice field. NCAA oversight just might produce more vigilant compliance staffs and an atmosphere more conducive to rules enforcement as opposed to self-preservation.

Then the NCAA should drastically increase the severity of

punishment, penalizing from the top down, not just the bottom up. That means the university president. If a school, team, players, or coaches are found to have violated NCAA regulations or state statutes, do not restrict the punishment to the players or coaches or compliance departments. Penalize the university president. Fine him or her on the first infraction. Fire him or her on the second infraction, along with the coach. Period.

One more thing: Offer rewards for whistle-blowers for bringing infractions to light.

Athletic departments will hate this recommendation— it's a loss of power and an admission of failure—but it's time that the NCAA member institutions acknowledge that the NCAA enforcement model reliant on self-monitoring by athletic departments has failed. Just ask Nevin Shapiro after his free-rein rampage at Miami. Like me, he never got caught. (If it weren't for his Ponzi scheme, he might still be flaunting the rules.)

Agent Day

A lot of schools' compliance departments set up Agent Day at the college. They invite any agent who wants to meet and talk to players, and any players who want to meet agents, to a room full of tables, chairs, notepads, and Gatorade. Each player-agent meeting is for a few minutes, then a buzzer goes off and the player moves to the next agent's table. It's speed-dating for agents and players. It's fair, open, and totally worthless. First, it's impossible to decide if you click with an agent in five minutes and vice versa. But more importantly, the agents who come aren't the ones to worry about. It's the ones who don't come, who have already made contact with the players, or who will make it on their own, or through a well-placed runner. Agent Day is another way to look like they're doing the right things—*Hey, we invite the agents to meet the players under our supervision, totally transparently*—a CYA for the college. My attitude was always, Agent Day is whatever day I can meet with a player.

The Junior Rule

The NCAA has no rules regarding contact between agents and players, only that the players, family, and friends can't accept anything of value or enter into an agreement without risking their college eligibility.

The Junior Rule, as it's known, came into being in 2007 at the urging of USC coach Pete Carroll with support from Executive Director of the NFLPA Gene Upshaw. Carroll was incensed over agents and runners pursuing his players in the aftermath of the stories of Reggie Bush receiving improper benefits. The rule prohibited agents from contacting players until January 18, or three days following the deadline to declare for the NFL draft. An unintended consequence was that a player therefore couldn't get professional input on one of the most important decisions of his career. The rule was changed in 2009 to bar agents or their reps from player contact until the last regular season or conference championship game, or December 1, whichever date is later—not much of an improvement for the players. And instead of curbing the practices of agents, it has fueled the influence of uncertified agents, financial advisors, marketing reps, and runners, for their own benefit and as conduits to certified agents. It gave power to people the NFLPA can't control. The Junior Rule is still broken. Until authorized agents are allowed contact with players, the rule will be flaunted. Agents will get to players one way or the other. Fix the rule or get rid of it.

Runners

Runners connect agents to players. But runners can no longer be defined in the casual street terms of the past—a friend of a player, teammate, roommate, cousin. Today anyone and everyone may be a runner—mother, father, girlfriend, college booster, financial advisor, minister, personal trainer, reps of high-profile training facilities, high school coach, junior college coach, and big-time college coach—anyone who stands to gain by making the connection. You can't get most coaches to talk about the problem because they're in the game. They're there to win. But once they're out, it's a different story. In an ESPNLosAngels.com online feature, former coaches John Robinson of USC and Terry Donahue of UCLA talked about the problem candidly.

By Ramona Shelburne ESPNLosAngeles.com

OCTOBER 14, 2010

ROBINSON AND DONAHUE ADDRESS AGENTS

... Robinson and Donahue wanted to talk. Out loud, openly and honestly. About what has gone on, why it has gone on, and whether there is a solution or compromise.

"I don't think there's a coach in the country, unless he's a liar, that's going to say, 'It never happened at my school, my kids wouldn't do that,'" Robinson said. "There's no way."

... Robinson said he and his coaching staff were constantly on the lookout for agents' "runners," who would approach players after games and practices and offer them money. "Agents would give runners $100 [to give to players] so they could take their girl out for dinner that night," he said. "They'd shake hands with them, and there'd be a $100 bill folded up. We used to try to identify who the runners are and then threaten 'em."

It was, of course, a losing battle. All the warnings could go only so far, Robinson said.

Donahue said UCLA coaches and administrators spoke to players often about agents and what benefits they could not accept under NCAA rules. "We talked about it all the time," Donahue said. "There wasn't anybody that did anything out of ignorance. Everybody understood what was permitted, what wasn't permitted. No one acted out of ignorance. I can guarantee you that."

... Some of the meetings with players were heartbreaking. "That was one of the toughest things for me as a head coach, was the kid who was stressed for whatever reason," Robinson said. "His girlfriend was pregnant, his parents were this or that, he had a car and couldn't make the payment. He'd come to me and say, 'What do I do, Coach?' You were stuck. The only thing you could do is try to get him a job on the weekends or in the off-season. But then they made it so you couldn't do that.

"Every coach who has ever coached has had a kid in his office that says, 'Coach, I'm dying here,' and you wind up giving him 100 bucks or letting him use your phone. I used to have a kid that would come into my office and he was so homesick that he'd start crying. I would dial his mom on the phone and he talked to her for 10 minutes and he'd say, 'Oh, I'm OK now.'

"Well, that was a violation. But hell, I didn't have any other solution."

Ironically, maybe the most influential of all of the "runners" is the college coach.

In the midst of another round of investigations into agent violations in the SEC, Nick Saban, the Alabama head coach, said, "The agents that do this—and I hate to say this, but how are they any better than a pimp?" But Saban, like other big-time college coaches, has his own agent and that agent will have unique access to his players. That agent can be in the coach's office, in the locker room, on the field. The players see him, meet him, and see that the coach, often the most important authority figure in their lives, has given that agent his tacit stamp of approval.

Nick Saban's agent is Jimmy Sexton, who also happens to represent high-profile college coaches Steve Spurrier (University of South Carolina), Houston Nutt (Ole Miss), and Tommy Tuberville (Texas Tech). According to an online article from *Birmingham News* writer Kevin Scarbinsky, "Sexton said he avoids talking to their players when he stops by practice to talk to Tuberville or Saban. And although he says representing a coach gives him "a good entrée to the player," he balks at the notion that a coach "can hand-deliver you players." Tuberville commented on Sexton pursuing players, "I tell him, 'You can go after any guys we have. (But) you're on your own unless they ask me.'" Oh, unless they ask him? Well, thank goodness, no problems there.

Players ask their coaches everything. How to run pass patterns, which workouts to do, if they can get more playing time, what it takes to get into the NFL, what to eat, how much to sleep, whether they can go home for the weekend, what time the team plane leaves. So, when it comes to a life decision like picking an agent, you think the player and coach won't talk? And that coach decides if and when the player plays, determines how much national exposure he'll get, and even comments to the media about his play after the game. Do you think the player wants to go against what his coach thinks is best? Let me answer all those questions with another question: Is it a coincidence that so many players at a given school happen to sign with the same agent or other agents at the same agency as their coach? At the Arizona NCAA meeting, I asked compliance people if they knew who their coach's agent was. Most had never thought to find out.

If, as Nick Saban says, agents are no better than pimps, let's play out the analogy. What does that make the players and the coaches? Who are the johns and the hookers? Who's getting screwed and who's doing the screwing? I see a lot of hypocrisy and finger-pointing.

The obvious solution is that agents who represent coaches

should not be allowed to represent players currently on the same team.

There is another twist to the attempts to crack down on runners of all types. Many state governments, as well as athletic governing bodies, are broadening the definition of "agent" to include runners, recruiters, financial advisors, brand managers, family, friends, and anyone who makes contact with a player for potential gain. The intention of this change is basically good. But the execution is flawed. Plenty of players who are supposedly taught the rules by their compliance departments will have trouble accepting the counterintuitive notion that a college booster is an agent, a roommate is an agent, a street runner is an agent, or a friend from the old neighborhood is an agent. *Hey, I'm not an agent. I'm a fan. Class of eighty-nine!* Players may understand they can't take money from an agent, but why can't they take something from an alum, or their cousin? The real solution would be to have two clear-cut legal definitions: 1) Agent: A person who has been certified by the NFLPA, credentialed, vetted, and approved. 2) Runners/Recruiters: Anyone who approaches a player for the purpose of establishing a relationship for gain or connecting a player to someone for gain. Without that clear definition and explanation, players have the excuse of not understanding, the excuse to give in to temptation, and there is the possibility of unintended consequences.

Go back to the case of Willie Lyles, the former scout accused of taking $25,000 in exchange for information. Willie and I had an interesting conversation about the possible injustices that could result from a broadened definition of agent status. Remember, it was Willie who went public with his story, not someone else. Under a definition broadened to include runners, trainers, scouts, advisors, et alia, Willie's actions could be construed as the actions of an "agent," making him vulnerable to criminal prosecution. But he's not an agent, and he shouldn't be prosecuted like one. Not wanting to incriminate himself, he may not provide that information, thereby inadvertently letting University of Oregon, its coach Chip Kelly, and other athletic department personnel off the hook.

Define agents and define runners and enforce the rules on both.

Getting to Players

So how do agents get to players with the Uniform Athlete Agent Act, SPARTA, compliance departments, and coaches trying to limit access? Easily.

First of all, this supposedly protective body—the team itself—brands its players like cattle. You don't have to know what the star running back looks like. You just have to know his jersey number. And since he's a star, constantly on TV, you know. Number 22. Then you hang out near the athletic facilities or the practice field. Pretty soon a guy will walk up carrying a school-issued backpack with "22" stenciled on it. If you miss the backpack, he may be wearing sweats or shorts with the same "22" on them. As responsible parents today, we're told not to send our kids to school with their names on their clothes or book bags because it makes it easier for predators to act like they know them. Predators around schoolkids are scary but, fortunately, uncommon. The type of predators who go after college athletes might not be quite as frightening but they're everywhere—anyone and everyone who wants a piece of the athlete. Yet colleges label the players they're trying to protect so agents can find them, talk to them, buy them lunch, and even give them cash. It doesn't take a genius to fix that problem.

Then there's social networking—almost universal access— notably on Facebook and Twitter. That access is a lot harder to control. And thanks to "ghosting," even people who don't exist can get to almost anyone they want. Ghosting is a form of identity theft, or identity invention, whereby someone creates a name, background, and seemingly real person and uses that new personality to contact other people. Scam artists use it to try to get credit card and other financial information, for sexual contact, or just for harassment. For sports agents, it's like a key to a player's front door. If you want to learn all about a player, just create an identity for a sexy-looking girl, paste in some hot photos you can easily find on the Internet, and then "friend" the player. Chances are he'll accept your friend request, and then you can go to his Face-book page and see his profile, photos, friend list, info, and start exchanging messages, pokes, even texts. The "you" that's been created doesn't even exist. But by the time that agent gets to campus, he knows everything there is to know about the player: where he hangs out, where he parties, who his friends are, his girlfriends, what kind of car he drives, the movies and music he likes, and lots of pictures so you know exactly what he looks like, with or without his jersey number. Social networking is like a GPS for an agent. It's the modern version of "find the fat chick."

The NCAA, through officers like, Director of Agent,

Gambling and Amateurism Activities Rachel Newman Baker, recognizes the problem but faces issues of free speech in efforts to control it. However, it would be possible for all players to agree that their college's or university's compliance department would have access as a "friend" to their Facebook page so that all communications were at least visible.

This is a nice little list of fixes: federal enforcement of agent laws, NCAA pressure on the NFL and NFLPA, independent compliance departments not employed by colleges, restrictions on agents from representing both coaches and players at the same school, changing the Junior Rule, not issuing paraphernalia with player numbers, and monitoring social networking. Each may be effective at reducing certain types of infractions. But they are Band-Aids, not treatments for the disease. At best, they will modify behavior but not change it. There's an old expression that the definition of insanity is when you do the same thing over and over but expect different results. That's what we've done with college sports. If we want different results, we have to change the system.

Changing the System

To turn the old phrase around, if it's broke, fix it. Stop patching it, face reality, and make real changes. Emancipate the athlete. Recognize the real value of the players in the economic model—the business—of college football; recognize that there would be no college football without star quarterbacks and wide receivers and blitzing linebackers, and reward the stars. Pay the players. The question is how.

Realistic Scholarships

The 2009 study by Ithaca College and the National College Players Association found that a typical "full-ride" scholarship for a Division I athlete actually left a shortfall. On average, student-athlete expenses, meaning tuition plus room and board, exceed the amount of the average scholarship by $2,951. With the schedule they keep in order to perform at the highest level in sports, how are the players supposed to get that money? Many cannot turn to their families. They're restricted from working during the school year, and, in any case, they wouldn't have time between workouts, games, and classes to hold down even a part-time job. So, they either live at a subsistence level or they find other ways, such as taking money from agents. I typically loaned guys $300 to $1,500 per month. Most of the loans we made would have filled the shortfall of the Ithaca study (not that that was my motivation; I just wanted to sign the players). There was simply a need and we conveniently filled it. If an athlete is getting a "full scholarship," it should be full, not partial. Pell Grants and other programs that players could be taking advantage of are often not explained in easily understood terms and anyone who's ever tried to fill out an application for a grant or student loan knows it's not easy to navigate. There are some who argue that the amounts players receive is enough. But the player's perception is reality. If he perceives that the need exists, it exists and he will try to fill it. There is no question that if the shortfall were removed, some of the violations would be eliminated.

Of course, plenty of players who take money from agents or boosters aren't doing it just to cover expenses. Some do it out of greed, or just because it's there for the taking. Increasing to true full scholarships will not be a deterrent. The greedy will always be willing to take the risk of being caught regardless of the consequences. Harsher penalties may slow them down, but they won't stop them.

South Carolina coach Steve Spurrier even got a group of other top coaches to propose they pay players $300 a game, out of their own pockets, to supplement players' finances. But frankly, it's a headline-making but impractical gesture. How many coaches could do it? How many would? Would the coach really pay, or would the school? Is it fair from coach to coach and school to school? And aren't coaches being paid way too much if they can offer to pay every player on their team?

What About the Value of Education?

So, if you give true full rides, the athlete covers his expenses and gets a college education, right? Oh sure. The college football purists' argument that the players are getting paid in the form of an education is almost laughable. The concept may be logical but it simply is not realistic. I didn't need the experience of preparing players for the Wonderlic test to show that they may have received a degree (though more than 50 percent of the players don't graduate), but clearly they did not get the education promised them. I could see it and hear it in every conversation. Too many players came into college uneducated and left the same way. Between player-friendly professors and "rogue tutors" (as in the UNC case), these institutions of higher learning too often fail to live up to their end of the bargain. The player's academic schedule is usually built around the team schedule, a clear signal of priorities. Classes and study are to be fit in between practices, film study, workouts, team meetings, and anything else that affects on-the-field performance. School doesn't come first. Or even second. For most players, it's way down the list, if it's on the list at all.

Share the Wealth

Big-time college sports programs make a lot of money from the sale of jerseys, shorts, hats, you name it, with the school name and the number of star players emblazoned on them. Reggie Bush made the number 5 jersey a top seller for USC. Cam Newton's number 2 moved a lot of memorabilia for Auburn. Ohio State, Notre Dame, Texas, Michigan, Penn State, Miami, LSU, Oklahoma, Alabama, and others make a small fortune every year literally off the backs of their players. And the players who make those numbers famous get nothing. Why not give those star players a piece of every sale? You can argue that the support players, the linemen who protect Cam Newton or make a hole for Reggie Bush, are unsung heroes. But it's the same way in the NFL, and anyway, that's no reason to cut star players out of the revenue for their own accomplishments. The real problem is, only a handful of players are stars whose numbers sell. And the others still need to be treated fairly ... or they remain vulnerable to money from other sources.

How About Total Revenue?

According to CNNMoney.com in 2010, the total take of the richest college football programs was over $1 billion, including all sources of income from tickets to jerseys to television broadcast rights. (The chart below highlights some of those programs.)

MOST PROFITABLE COLLEGE FOOTBALL TEAMS

SCHOOL	REVENUE	PROFIT
Texas	$95,749,684	$71,242,332
Georgia	$74,888,175	$52,851,837
Penn State	$72,747,734	$53,728,446
Michigan	$70,300,676	$46,748,443
Florida	$72,807,236	$46,543,697

RESULTS FOR 2010–2011 SCHOOL YEAR: SOURCE: DEPT. OF EDUCATION

Why not share the college's total revenue with the players? Give the team a predetermined percentage of all income, with bonuses for championships and bowl games and being named to All-America teams. Let the teams divide it up among the players based on playing time, stats, or reaching individual goals. Or let them pay everyone the same amount. But let the players who are bringing in the money share the money.

If college is the minor league of the NFL, then pay the minor league players just like baseball does. It would certainly be more fair than the current system. But it's flawed, highly flawed. First, it tilts in favor of those schools that can draw big audiences. Notre Dame gets viewers whether they win or lose. Plenty of very good teams don't. So, if they pay players based on what they take in, some schools will be able to pay more and get more good players. Sort of like the Yankees in baseball.

But the biggest reason it won't work is the colleges won't let it work. They consider this money theirs. They're used to getting it. Why would they be willing to give up even a portion of it? Unless all the college prospects in America decide to go on strike, they're not getting a share of college football dollars.

An Idea That Just Might Work
Agent Loans

Agents advance money to players now. It's against the rules but it keeps happening, whether for need or greed or both. Why not do it aboveboard? With total transparency? Set up oversight and regulation. Establish interest rates, at or below market value. Provide standardized forms and loan agreements. Create a fair market system.

Here's how it could work:

1. Any certified agent who wishes to participate could register to lend money to athletes.
2. Interest rates would be set at or below market rates and published.
3. The agent and player would be allowed to meet openly and freely to discuss the amounts, terms, and details. The Junior Rule would be abolished to allow for this. (As an NCAA-sanctioned program, it would prevent underage or high school kids from participation, plus investing in very young players is at best a long shot considering how greatly abilities change during those years.) Once agent and player arrive at

an agreement, they would meet regularly, which would enable the agent to parcel out the funds on a piecemeal basis, rather than in a lump sum, and therefore simultaneously establish an ongoing relationship with the player.

4. The agent and the marketplace would determine how much it would make sense to lend. If agent X determines that player Y is worth $10,000 a year—that is, that the player will earn enough once signed to a pro contract to repay that amount—then the agent can lend $10,000. If agent Z determines the player is worth more, say $15,000, then he can take the risk, like any lender, that the player will pay back more. It would truly be a free-market system.

5. Notices of agent-player agreements would be posted in locker rooms to end or minimize locker-room runners from wooing players for agents. Everyone would know who each player was working with.

6. The transaction would be a true business deal, a loan. The player would owe the money to the agent. If and when the player signed a pro deal, he would begin to repay the money on pre-agreed terms. It would protect all of the parties in the transaction.

7. If the player's career did not pan out, if he were not drafted or signed, then the agent would have made a bad investment without recourse.

8. A player could openly switch agents if or when he determined that another agent offered him a better deal, or would simply be a better fit. Again, it would be the agent's choice, based on his assessment of market

value, whether to lend more or less. And the new agent would assume the liability for the loans from the previous agent. Postings would be made of the switch.

9. The NCAA would retain paperwork on all transactions. And the NCAA would have access to agent phone and bank records, which they do not currently have, in order to track activities, movement of money, etc. This would allow for the equivalent of subpoena power for any requested documents; otherwise an agent would be immediately removed from participation in the loan program.

10. This would remove the NFLPA from all agent oversight other than certification of agents.

11. This system would be totally consistent with Title IX, often a stumbling block for new college sports legislation. Rather than favoring only the top sports, it could fuel any or all sports. If an agent determined that a soccer player could earn substantial money in the marketplace, he would be free to lend money to the soccer player. Or the hockey player. Or swimmer. Male and female athletes alike.

Agent loans would be a totally transparent program with advantages over the current system, or nonsystem. The process would be out in the open, under the scrutiny of anyone who wanted to see it, instead of being done clandestinely, in dark bars, or at parties, or through street runners. It would provide for payback of the money. It would not be a gift or a pay-off, but a business deal. The player would agree to take the money, pay the money back, and work with that agent when he declared for the draft. The money could be given in varying amounts dependent upon the need and status of the individual players. Market value would determine what a player could borrow. Market value can change as the player's performance and his ability to pay back changes when he turns pro. The agent would be taking the risk. The model does not provide one school an advantage in recruiting over another. It rewards the players. And players don't have to take money from questionable people. In fact, under this system, why would they take money from unsavory characters? Everyone would know who is lending and who is borrowing.

Why would the colleges go for it? Well, for one thing, there is already precedent for it. Players can now borrow against future earnings to buy disability insurance while playing in college. But most importantly, this new system of loans wouldn't cost the colleges a dime. The money involved would be separate from the revenue the schools now take in from the sale of seats, jerseys, and bowl-game TV rights and adamantly do not want to give up or share. This would be the agents' money.

Will it happen? Doubtful in the short run. Some may view it as taking money from the bad guys. In fact, it's a dose of reality. It's already going on. But instead of doing it in the shadows, this would do it openly, legitimately, with a system, rules, and oversight. It could work. And what we have now does not work. That's one thing everyone can agree on.

POSTSCRIPT

There are no easy solutions when games become big business. I grew up loving sports. Today, my feelings are more complicated. But I would still like to see things get better. I don't regret being "on the outside." I like it here. In 2010, I admitted to paying players and other questionable actions. Now, in this book, I've said even more about what I did and what I saw others do. I wanted to feel cleaner, feel better about myself, and be a better role model for my daughters.

In late summer 2011, I was invited by U.S. Congressman Bobby Rush of Illinois to participate in a roundtable discussion entitled "Hypocrisy or Hype: The Impacts of Back-Room Deals, Payoffs, and Scandals in American Collegiate Student Athletics." The forum was held in Washington D.C., on November 1, and moderated by six-time Emmy Award–winner Jeremy Schaap of ESPN, with a panel comprised of Congressman Rush, Congressman John Conyers of Michigan, sports economist Andy Schwarz; Derek Samson, Assistant Managing Editor of Recruiting for Rivals.com (*Yahoo! Sports*); Shane Battier, former NCAA All-American and Memphis Grizzlies forward; Thaddeus Young, forward for the Philadelphia 76ers; Dr. Ellen Staurowsky, Professor of Sports Management at Drexel University; Warren K. Zola, Assistant Dean for Graduate Programs at Boston College;

Mrs. Valerie Hardrick, mother of Kyle Hardrick, a University of Oklahoma basketball scholarship player; Kyle Hardrick, who was injured and lost his scholarship; Joan Jolly, mother of Andrew Jolly, a Hampton University football player who was injured and lost his scholarship; Ramogi Huma, President of the National College Players Association . . . and me, Josh Luchs, former loophole-finder, rule-breaker, and Pied Piper to pro prospects turned sports reformer. In the audience were members of other congressional staffs, sports advocates, coaches, university officials, and members of the media (including HBO) that wanted to hear what could be done about the sad state of college athletics.

To say I've come a long way is an understatement . . . from hanging out on the University of Colorado campus, handing Kanavis McGhee some of my bar mitzvah money, to arriving at the U.S. Capitol, on First Street between Independence and Constitution Avenues, walking down the marble steps to the Congressional Auditorium to be greeted by Representative Rush, a former Black Panther and the only candidate to ever defeat Barack Obama. It was a profound honor to be selected to serve on this panel of all-stars, Emmy winners, journalists, and world-class academics. Who would've thought I'd have come this far? But there I was.

Jeremy Schaap welcomed everyone and Congressman Rush did the intros. To set the tone of the day, Mr. Rush described the NCAA as "one of the most vicious, most ruthless organizations ever created by mankind. I think you would compare the NCAA to Al Capone and to the Mafia." Reference was made to Pulitzer Prize–winner Taylor Branch's recent article, *The Shame of College Sports,* in which he called the NCAA a "cartel." No one on the panel disputed those characterizations. Andy Schwarz said that as a result of NCAA "collusion," 344 Division I schools (the six big conferences) control and "pervert the amateur market." He and other panel members said the solution is simple and obvious. Embrace free market economics—pay people what they're worth. With $1.3 billion in profits, the money goes to facilities, coaches, recruiters . . . everywhere but to those who provide the profits—the laborers, the players. Worse, they sign away all rights once they accept their scholarship. Their likenesses appear on video games, their numbered jerseys are sold, and all the money goes to the school, none to them.

The NCAA does not treat players as employees for one basic reason: to avoid antitrust laws. If they were employees, the employers would be guilty of monopolizing the market. If they were employees, the schools would be responsible for workers comp claims and have to compensate players for the injuries sustained while under their "employ." Instead, the schools maintain they are providing athletes with something of great value, an education. But in exchange for that education (for those who get it—only about half of players graduate), student-athletes put in sixty to eighty-hour weeks of practices, games, travel, and, oh yeah, school. Shane Battier acknowledged that his schedule as a professional basketball player is easier than what he had as a Duke player, and that he was a religion major because those classes were available when he wasn't practicing. Jeremy Schaap pointed out the obvious conflict between the supposed high-minded academic goals of these educational institutions and their unbridled commercial greed when it comes to athletics. And we as citizens, fans, and voters support, encourage, and pay for it. On game day, University of Nebraska stadium is the second largest city in the state.

As for the value of the education student-athletes receive, it's hardly a sure thing. Schools can revoke scholarships any time they want. Witness the cases cited by athlete moms Joan Jolly and Valerie Hardrick, whose sons, one a football player, one a basketball player, each had scholarships pulled once they sustained injuries. Both lost out in their efforts to win hardship appeals from the NCAA. Professor Staurowsky put it bluntly, saying that the way scholarships work is one college player is ushered out the door the moment there's a better prospect. She referred to a quote from Walter Byers, former Executive Director of the NCAA, "Amateurism is not a moral issue; it is an economic camouflage for monopoly practice." She said, "College sports' past is now catching up with it." The NCAA created the pay-for-play concept with the athletic scholarship and now should have to compensate the "full measure of the contribution of the athletes."

Thanks to a nonstop lobbying effort by the National College Players Association and President Ramogi Huma, athletic scholarships can now be "voluntarily" increased by $2,000, which is still between $1,000 and $3,000 per year short of the real cost of a college education, depending on your figures. Eighty-five percent of student athletes live below the poverty line. But inching up the cost of scholarships is hardly meaningful when the NCAA and its powerhouse schools are earning staggering record profits off the labor of their athletes.

Not only that, I pointed out, but as long as scholarships fall short, the door is open for "guys like me" who can provide the extra cash the players need. Increasing scholarships by $2,000 is "just like throwing a guy on a ten-story burning building a three-story ladder. It makes absolutely no sense."

Asked to weigh in on better enforcement of the rules as they stand, I focused on my four points:

1. Sports agents are a problem but only part of it. The nonagents, the financial advisors, marketing guys, and runners are as much or more of a threat. They aren't regulated. And they can be players, trainers, coaches, or family.
2. Coaches have agents and often use that relationship to circumvent the rules restricting agents' access to players.
3. Compliance staffs are handcuffed because they're paid by the schools they're supposed to be policing.
4. There needs to be more accountability all around. Not just from agents or outsiders but from insiders, coaches, athletic directors, and college presidents. But all the enforcement in the world won't solve the problem. The problem is the system is just plain unfair.

The panel took on the obvious question: Could a free market system be fair? Should schools pay more to a star quarterback than to a lineman, even though they're getting the same scholarship now? The answer I and others voiced is that, in one form or another, it's already the reality and stars get more. Once the athletic scholarship was allowed, amateurism was out the window. A scholarship is the equivalent of pay for services, provided in lieu of a salary. But the scholar-ships are hardly equal in value. A scholarship at a pricey school like Stanford or Duke is worth more than one at Penn State, and powerhouse sports schools like LSU and USC do more for you athletically than Portland State. Some guys get full scholarships while others only get partials. Some players are wooed by boosters; some aren't. Some are offered a lot of money from agents; some only a little or none. Some are sought after by financial advisors, marketing reps, or run-ners, and some are not. It's a free market system now but a bad one—unregulated, inadequate, underpaying, and under-ground. Almost everyone on the panel agreed that somehow players should be compensated for their contributions. Per-sonally, I favor the agent-loan system over paying players with revenue from a school's sports profits, especially recognizing NCAA members' track records of resistance to giving up a dime of "their money" or even acknowledging a problem. But either way, some way, the answer is pay the players.

Near the end of the session, an audience member asked when we could expect to see real solutions. Representative Conyers put it in perspective: Who knew when we'd have a one-payer health plan, when we'd stop entering bad wars, or when there would be a real jobs program? So he sure didn't know when college sports would be fixed. But Congressman Rush said a forum like this brings the situation to light, not to be discouraged, that there is growing support, and there will be change.

I believe there will be change. Maybe slow, maybe frustrat-ing, but it will happen. That's why when I was asked to be on this panel in Washington D.C., I made sure my wife and daughters were there. I wanted them to see their dad talk about how to offer fairer, more legitimate choices to young athletes in America. I like the person my daughters see and I now see in the mirror. I credit my wife Jennifer for saving my soul and never losing faith in me. If I can reform, so can sports.

ACKNOWLEDGMENTS

Josh Luchs: I have many people to "acknowledge," that is, "to recognize as having force or power; to express gratitude for." First, Jennifer, my wife, my teammate, with whom I share the journey. You opened our home to an odd array of humanity and embraced them all, you formed solid ground when the world was crumbling, never losing faith in me, always there as my compass. Daddy's little girls: Sophie, the little general, and Sydney, the little rock star—for your smiles and hugs, for hanging on through Daddy's roller coaster ride, for fueling my recovery with your love, and for making me aspire to be a better person. My in-laws, Ann Simons and Dr. Herbert Simons, who both encouraged me to continue to fight for what I believe in. I hope that I can provide the same support to my future sons-in-law, but pray it won't be necessary. Harold "Doc" Daniels—I've said you "taught me the right way to do the wrong thing," but it doesn't do justice to your unselfish compassion, your protection of and caring about those who needed help, your lifting up of those who needed lifting (including me), and your heart. Steve Feldman, who weathered a "shit storm" not of his creation, and suffered the collateral damage of my battles. I'm humbled by your loyalty, support, and friendship—a little guy with surprisingly broad shoulders. George Dohrmann, an unparalleled journalist, who stumbled upon me at my most vulnerable. I'm forever indebted to your helping me present the unpopular truth about the industry. James Dale, my collaborator, who, within days of reading my *Sports Illustrated* story, tracked me down to express his desire to expand upon it, to tell the whole truth. Jim was able sift through an eighteen-year career and make sense and a story of it. You were a pleasure to work with. David Larabell of the David Black Agency was one of many literary agents that tracked me down after the *Sports Illustrated* story. You distinguished yourself with persistence and passion and became an exceptional advocate. But for your efforts, I doubt this book would have been published. Benjamin Adams of Bloomsbury Publishing—your vision and conviction for this story were apparent from the beginning. Your input was critical to the flow, the structure, and the tone of the book. I feel fortunate to have had the opportunity to work with you. Former clients, all of you, from whom I learned brutal life lessons in our years together, whether I was hired, fired, appreciated, disrespected, rewarded, or stiffed (or sometimes all of the above from the same guy), I hope you recognize the greater good that may derive from the truth.

James Dale: Above all, Josh Luchs, the man with the story to tell, who chose me to tell it; the "Davids"—David Black, my agent, and David Larabell, Josh's agent, who happen to work across the hall from each other; Ben Adams, our editor, who wanted this story and made it happen; and my son, Andy, for teaching me about sports.

A NOTE ON THE AUTHORS

Josh Luchs was a sports agent from 1990 to 2008, before being suspended by the NFL Players Association. He now works in commercial real estate agent in Encino, California.

James Dale has collaborated on books with Hall of Fame pitcher Jim Palmer and renowned sports agent and negotiator Ron Shapiro. His book with Johns Hopkins cardiologist Dan Munoz is forthcoming in 2012. He is also the author of *The Obvious: All You Need to Know in Business. Period.*